KINGPIN

EARTH'S HEROES RECENTLY PREVENTED A CATACLYSMIC EVENT THANKS TO A NEW INHUMAN NAMED ULYSSES WHO SEEMS TO BE ABLE TO PREDICT THE FUTURE. THOUGH THE JURY'S STILL OUT ON THE MORALITY OF ULYSSES' POWERS, THE HEROES HAVE CRACKED DOWN ON CRIME — PICKING UP WOULD-BE CRIMINALS BEFORE THEY EVEN COMMIT THEIR HEINOUS ACTS.

THIS NEW "PREDICTIVE JUSTICE" HAS MADE IT NEARLY IMPOSSIBLE FOR EVEN THE MOST EXPERIENCED CRIMINAL MASTERMINDS TO CONDUCT THEIR BUSINESS. BUT FOR SOMEONE AS RESOURCEFUL AS WILSON FISK, A.K.A. THE KINGPIN, A CIVIL WAR BETWEEN HEROES MEANS OPPORTUNITY...

WRITER
MATTHEW ROSENBERG

ARTIST
RICARDO LÓPEZ ORTIZ WITH
HAYDEN SHERMAN (#3-4)

COLOR ARTISTS
MAT LOPES WITH
ANTONIO FABELA (#2)

LETTERER
VC's TRAVIS LANHAM

"THE DEATH & BIRTH OF JANUS JARDEESH"

PENCILER
DALIBOR TALAJIC

INKER
JOSE MARZAN JR.

COLORIST
MIROSLAV MRVA

COVER COLORISTS
ISRAEL SILVA (#1), MATTHEW WILSON (#2),
FRANK MARTIN (#3) & JASON KEITH (#4)

ASSISTANT EDITOR
CHARLES BEACHAM

EDITORS
WIL MOSS & MARK BASSO

SENIOR EDITOR
MARK PANICCIA

EXECUTIVE EDITOR
TOM BREVOORT

COLLECTION EDITOR
JENNIFER GRÜNWALD
ASSOCIATE MANAGING EDITOR
KATERI WOODY
ASSOCIATE EDITOR
SARAH BRUNSTAD
EDITOR, SPECIAL PROJECTS
MARK D. BEAZLEY

VP PRO̶... ...OJECTS

SV...

EDITOR IN CHIEF
AXEL ALONSO
CHIEF CREATIVE OFFICER
JOE QUESADA
PUBLISHER
DAN BUCKLEY
EXECUTIVE PRODUCER
ALAN FINE

CIVIL WAR II: KINGPIN. Contains material originally published in magazine form as CIVIL W... ...#51. First printing 2016. ISBN# 978-1-302-90253-7. Published by MARVEL WORLDWIDE, INC., a subsidiary of MARVEL ENTERTAINMENT, LLC. OFFICE OF PUBLICATION... ...New York, NY 10020. Copyright © 2016 MARVEL No similarity between any of the names, characters, persons, and/or institutions in this magazine with those of any living or dead person or institution is intended, and any such similarity which may exist is purely coincidental. Printed in Canada. ALAN FINE, President, Marvel Entertainment; DAN BUCKLEY, President, TV, Publishing & Brand Management; JOE QUESADA, Chief Creative Officer; TOM BREVOORT, SVP of Publishing; DAVID BOGART, SVP of Business Affairs & Operations, Publishing & Partnership; C.B. CEBULSKI, VP of Brand Management & Development, Asia; DAVID GABRIEL, SVP of Sales & Marketing, Publishing; JEFF YOUNGQUIST, VP of Production & Special Projects; DAN CARR, Executive Director of Publishing Technology; ALEX MORALES, Director of Publishing Operations; SUSAN CRESPI, Production Manager; STAN LEE, Chairman Emeritus. For information regarding advertising in Marvel Comics or on Marvel.com, please contact Vit DeBellis, Integrated Sales Manager, at vdebellis@marvel.com. For Marvel subscription inquiries, please call 888-511-5480. Manufactured between 9/23/2016 and 10/31/2016 by SOLISCO PRINTERS, SCOTT, QC, CANADA.

10 9 8 7 6 5 4 3 2 1

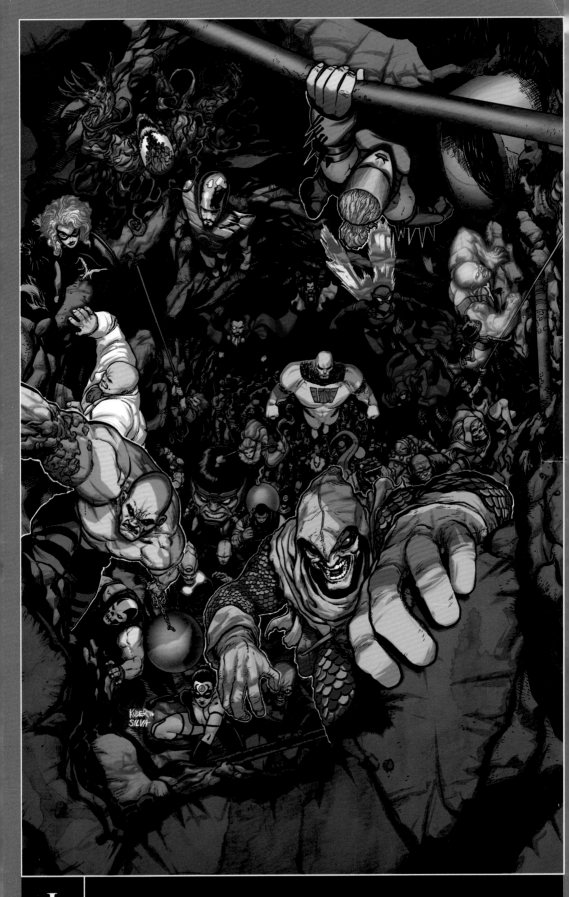

I SHOULDN'T HAVE COME BACK

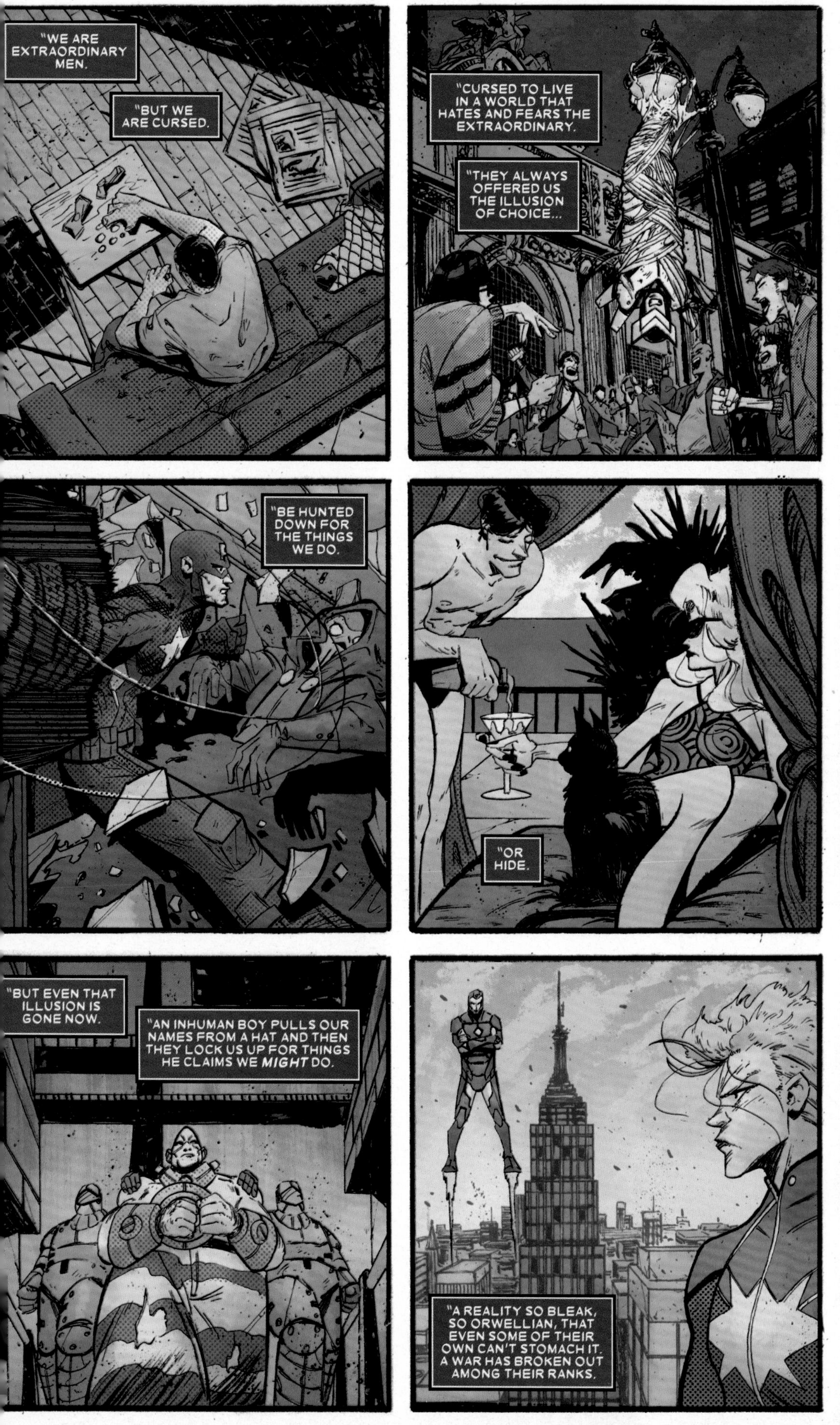
"WE ARE EXTRAORDINARY MEN.
"BUT WE ARE CURSED.
"CURSED TO LIVE IN A WORLD THAT HATES AND FEARS THE EXTRAORDINARY.
"THEY ALWAYS OFFERED US THE ILLUSION OF CHOICE...
"BE HUNTED DOWN FOR THE THINGS WE DO.
"OR HIDE.
"BUT EVEN THAT ILLUSION IS GONE NOW.
"AN INHUMAN BOY PULLS OUR NAMES FROM A HAT AND THEN THEY LOCK US UP FOR THINGS HE CLAIMS WE *MIGHT* DO.
"A REALITY SO BLEAK, SO ORWELLIAN, THAT EVEN SOME OF THEIR OWN CAN'T STOMACH IT. A WAR HAS BROKEN OUT AMONG THEIR RANKS.

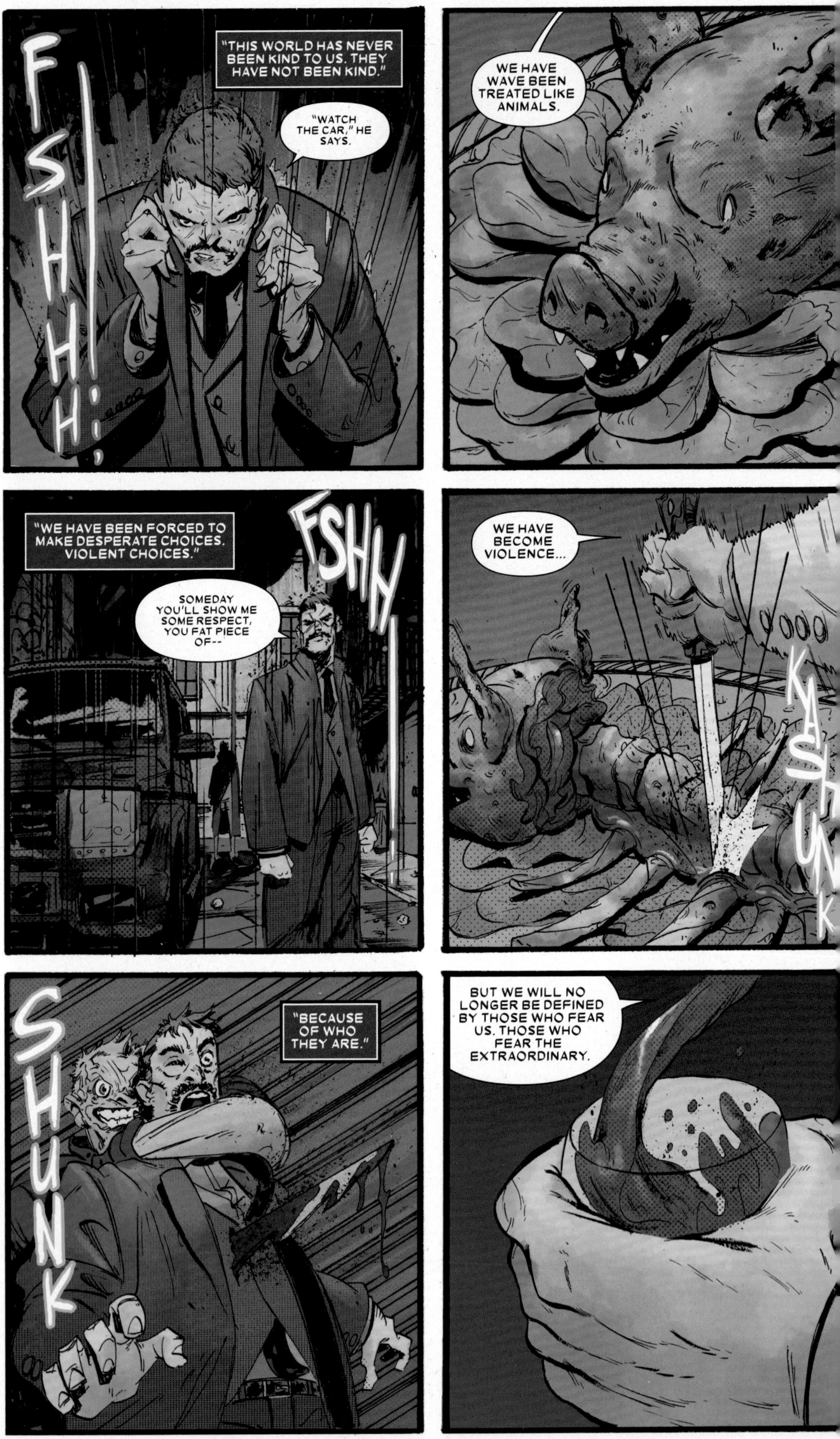
FSHHH!
"THIS WORLD HAS NEVER BEEN KIND TO US. THEY HAVE NOT BEEN KIND."
"WATCH THE CAR," HE SAYS.
WE HAVE WAVE BEEN TREATED LIKE ANIMALS.
"WE HAVE BEEN FORCED TO MAKE DESPERATE CHOICES. VIOLENT CHOICES."
FSHH
SOMEDAY YOU'LL SHOW ME SOME RESPECT, YOU FAT PIECE OF--
WE HAVE BECOME VIOLENCE...
KMASHUNK
SHUNK
"BECAUSE OF WHO THEY ARE."
BUT WE WILL NO LONGER BE DEFINED BY THOSE WHO FEAR US. THOSE WHO FEAR THE EXTRAORDINARY.

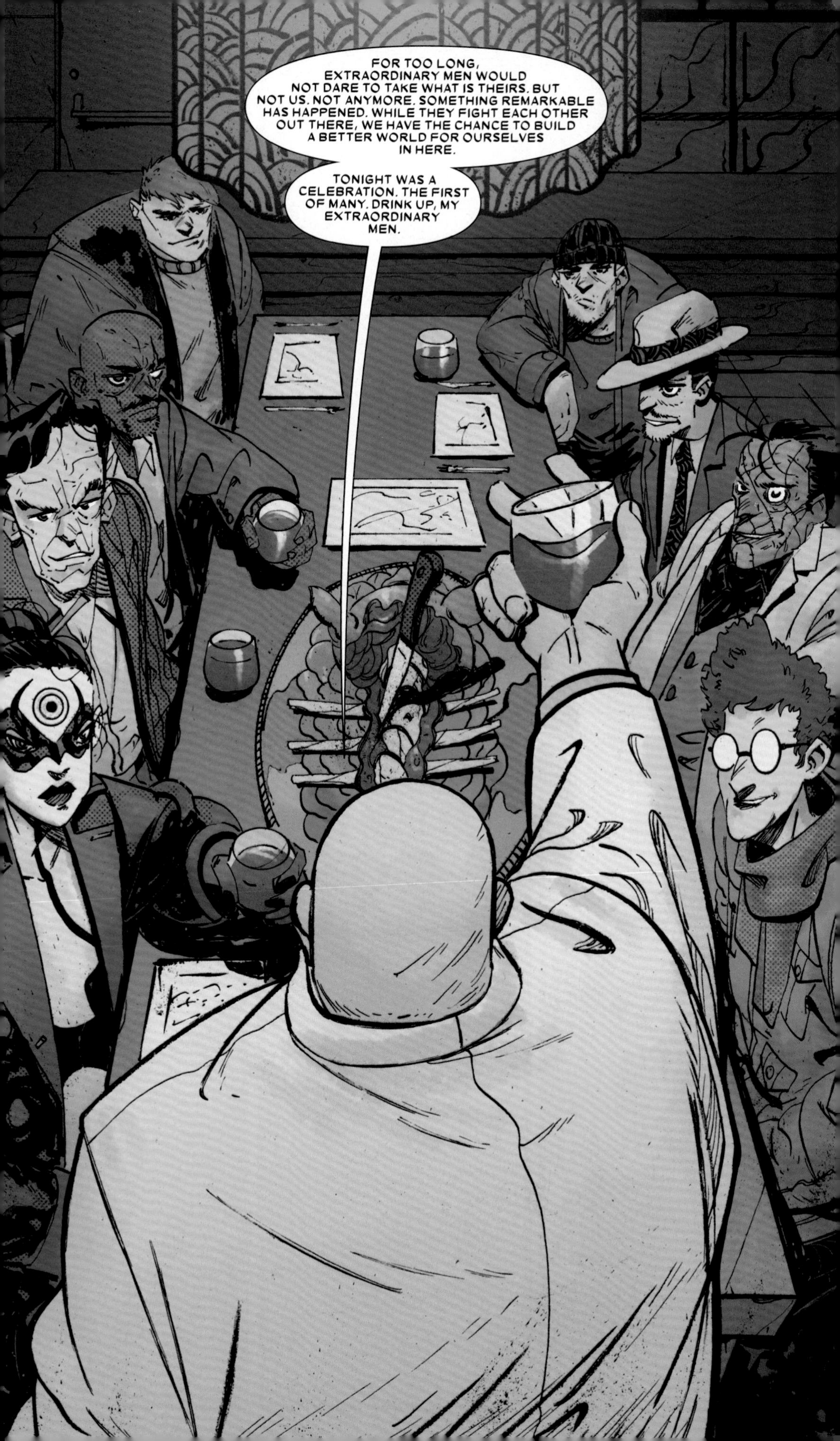
FOR TOO LONG, EXTRAORDINARY MEN WOULD NOT DARE TO TAKE WHAT IS THEIRS. BUT NOT US. NOT ANYMORE. SOMETHING REMARKABLE HAS HAPPENED. WHILE THEY FIGHT EACH OTHER OUT THERE, WE HAVE THE CHANCE TO BUILD A BETTER WORLD FOR OURSELVES IN HERE.
TONIGHT WAS A CELEBRATION. THE FIRST OF MANY. DRINK UP, MY EXTRAORDINARY MEN.

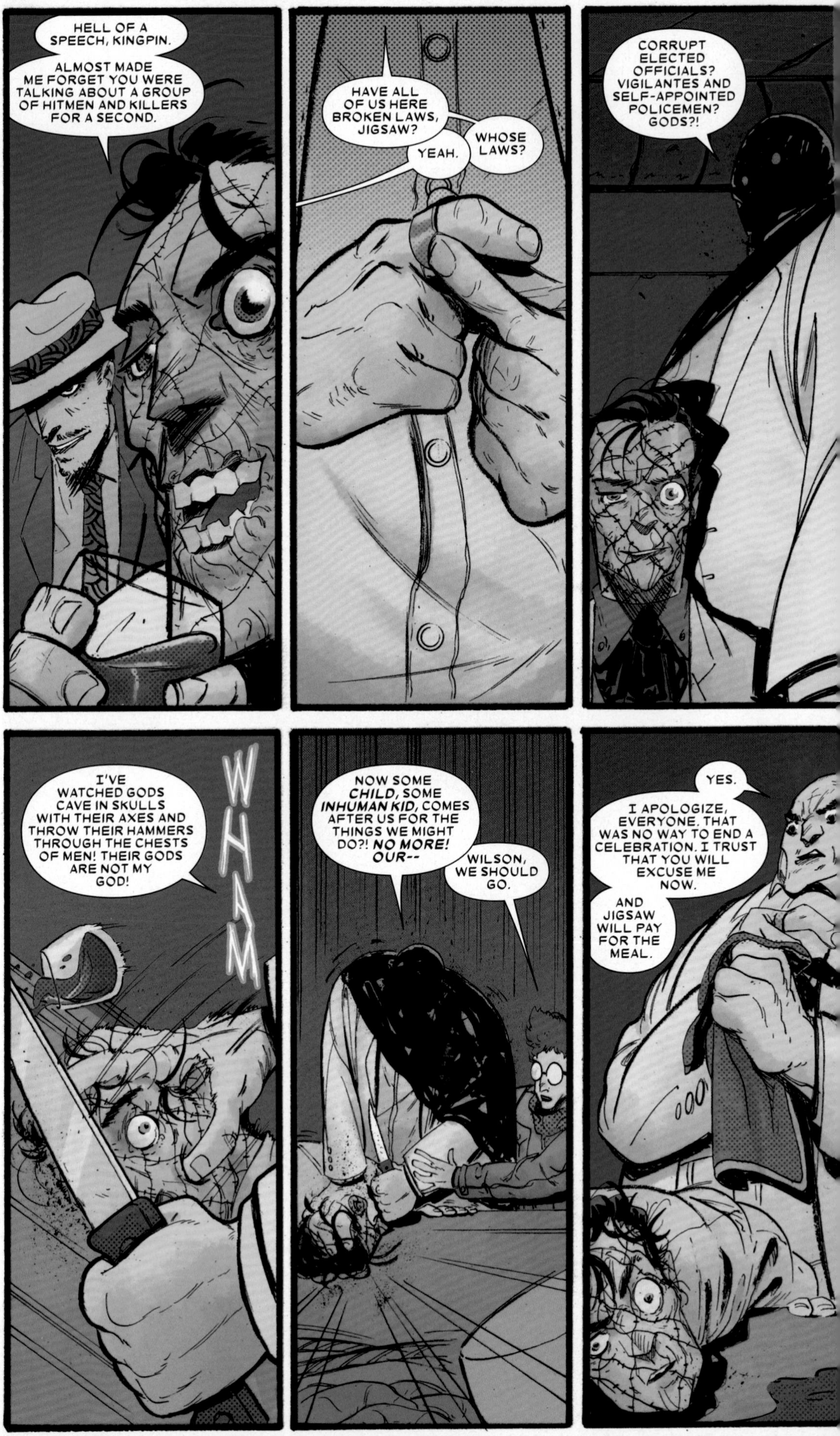
HELL OF A SPEECH, KINGPIN.
ALMOST MADE ME FORGET YOU WERE TALKING ABOUT A GROUP OF HITMEN AND KILLERS FOR A SECOND.
HAVE ALL OF US HERE BROKEN LAWS, JIGSAW?
YEAH.
WHOSE LAWS?
CORRUPT ELECTED OFFICIALS? VIGILANTES AND SELF-APPOINTED POLICEMEN? GODS?!
I'VE WATCHED GODS CAVE IN SKULLS WITH THEIR AXES AND THROW THEIR HAMMERS THROUGH THE CHESTS OF MEN! THEIR GODS ARE NOT MY GOD!
WHAM
NOW SOME *CHILD*, SOME *INHUMAN KID*, COMES AFTER US FOR THE THINGS WE MIGHT DO?! *NO MORE! OUR--*
WILSON, WE SHOULD GO.
YES.
I APOLOGIZE, EVERYONE. THAT WAS NO WAY TO END A CELEBRATION. I TRUST THAT YOU WILL EXCUSE ME NOW.
AND JIGSAW WILL PAY FOR THE MEAL.

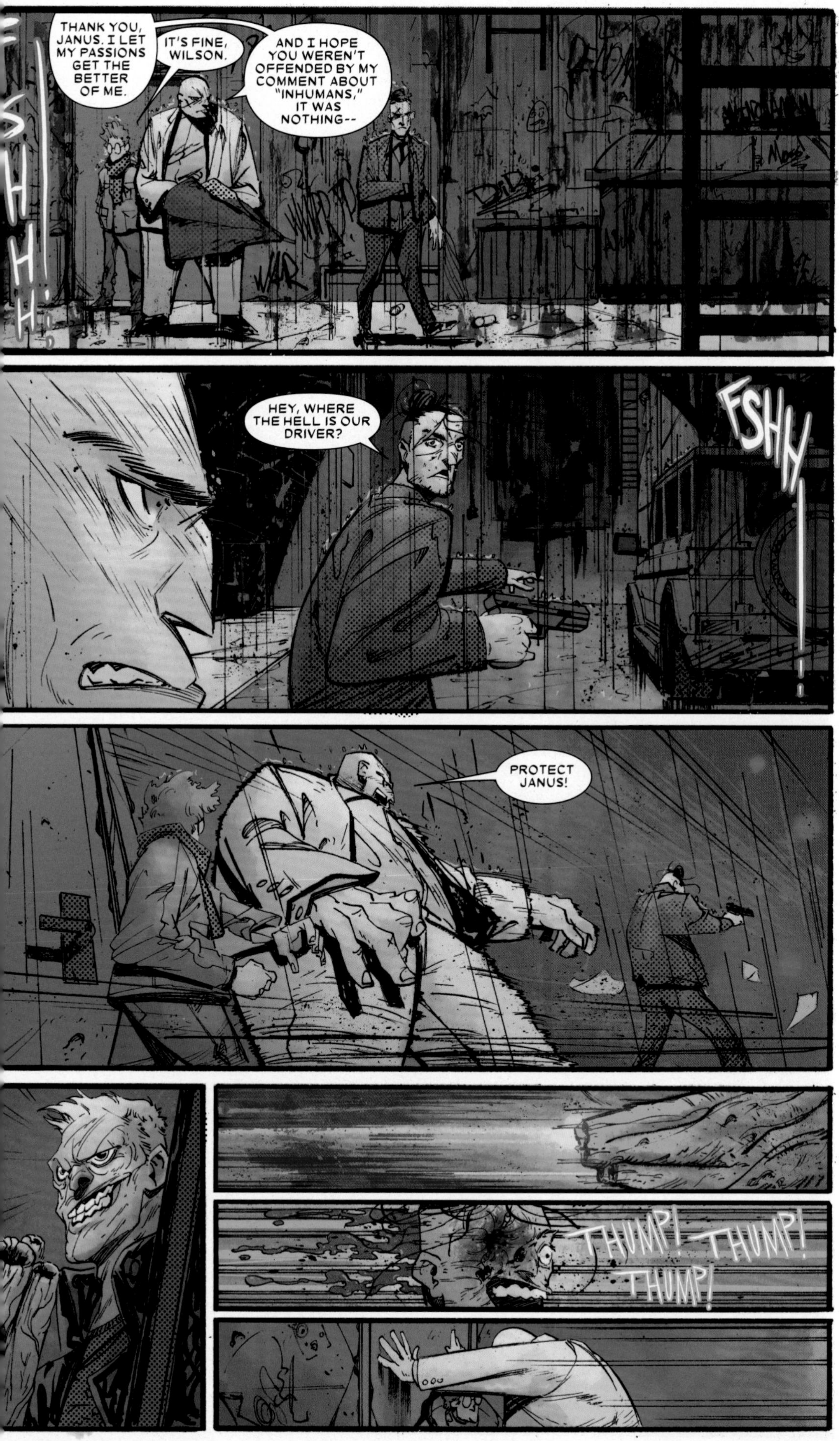
FSHHHH!!
THANK YOU, JANUS. I LET MY PASSIONS GET THE BETTER OF ME.
IT'S FINE, WILSON.
AND I HOPE YOU WEREN'T OFFENDED BY MY COMMENT ABOUT "INHUMANS," IT WAS NOTHING--
HEY, WHERE THE HELL IS OUR DRIVER?
FSHHH
PROTECT JANUS!
THUMP! THUMP! THUMP!

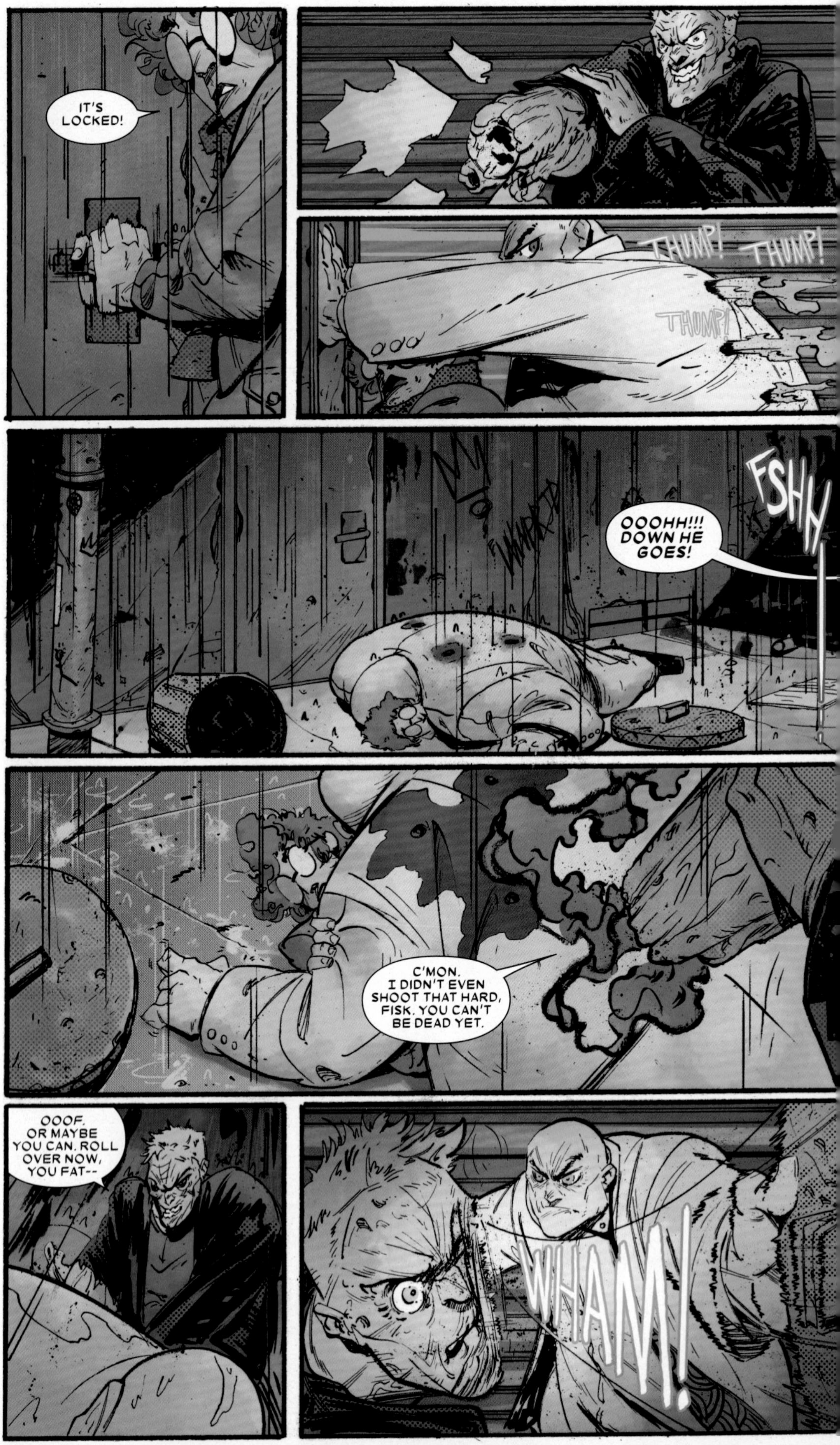
IT'S LOCKED!
THUMP! THUMP!
THUMP!
FSHH
OOOHH!!! DOWN HE GOES!
C'MON. I DIDN'T EVEN SHOOT THAT HARD, FISK. YOU CAN'T BE DEAD YET.
OOOF. OR MAYBE YOU CAN. ROLL OVER NOW, YOU FAT--
WHAM!

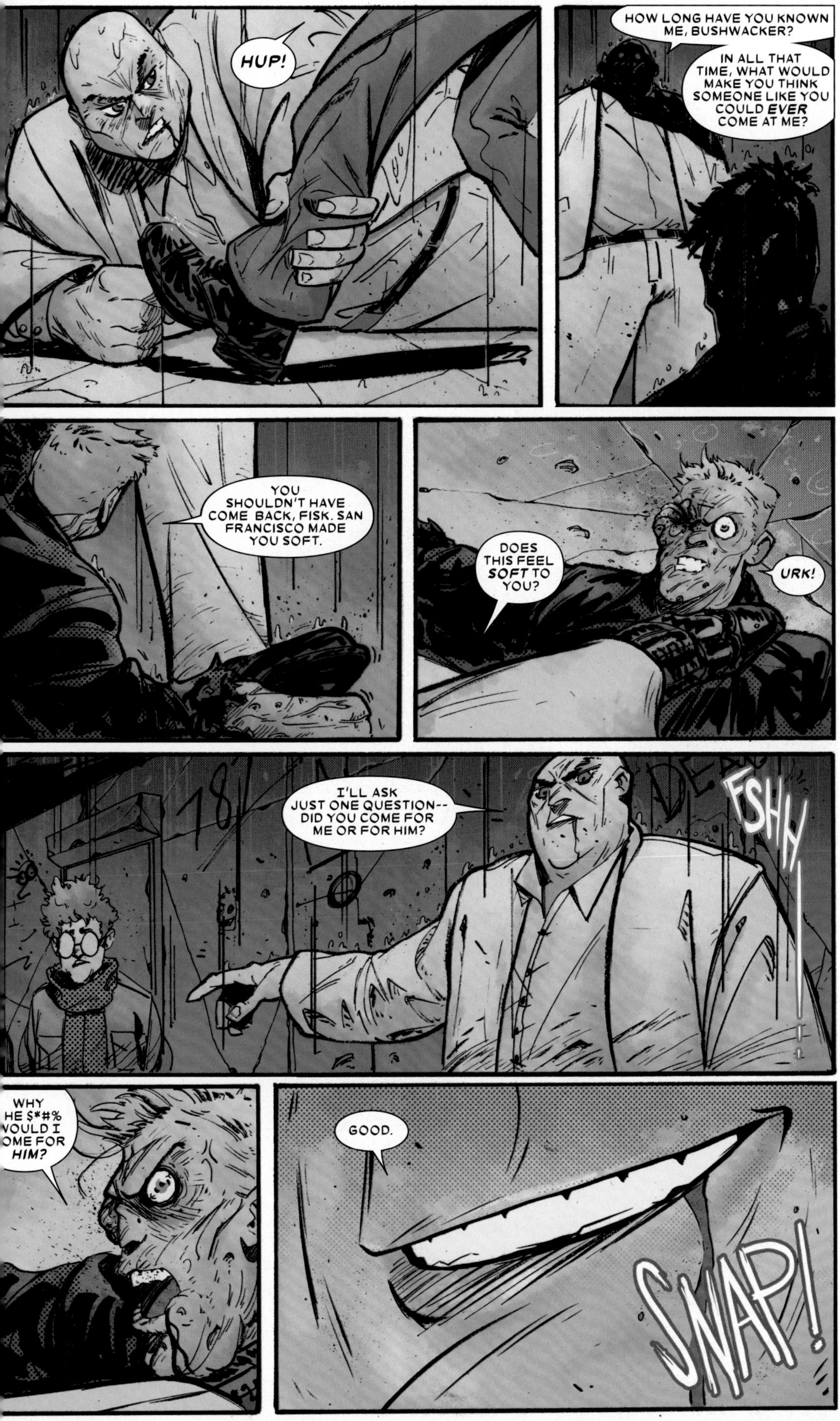
HUP!
HOW LONG HAVE YOU KNOWN ME, BUSHWACKER?
IN ALL THAT TIME, WHAT WOULD MAKE YOU THINK SOMEONE LIKE YOU COULD *EVER* COME AT ME?
YOU SHOULDN'T HAVE COME BACK, FISK. SAN FRANCISCO MADE YOU SOFT.
DOES THIS FEEL *SOFT* TO YOU?
URK!
I'LL ASK JUST ONE QUESTION-- DID YOU COME FOR ME OR FOR HIM?
FSHH
WHY HE $*#% WOULD I OME FOR *HIM?*
GOOD.
SNAP!

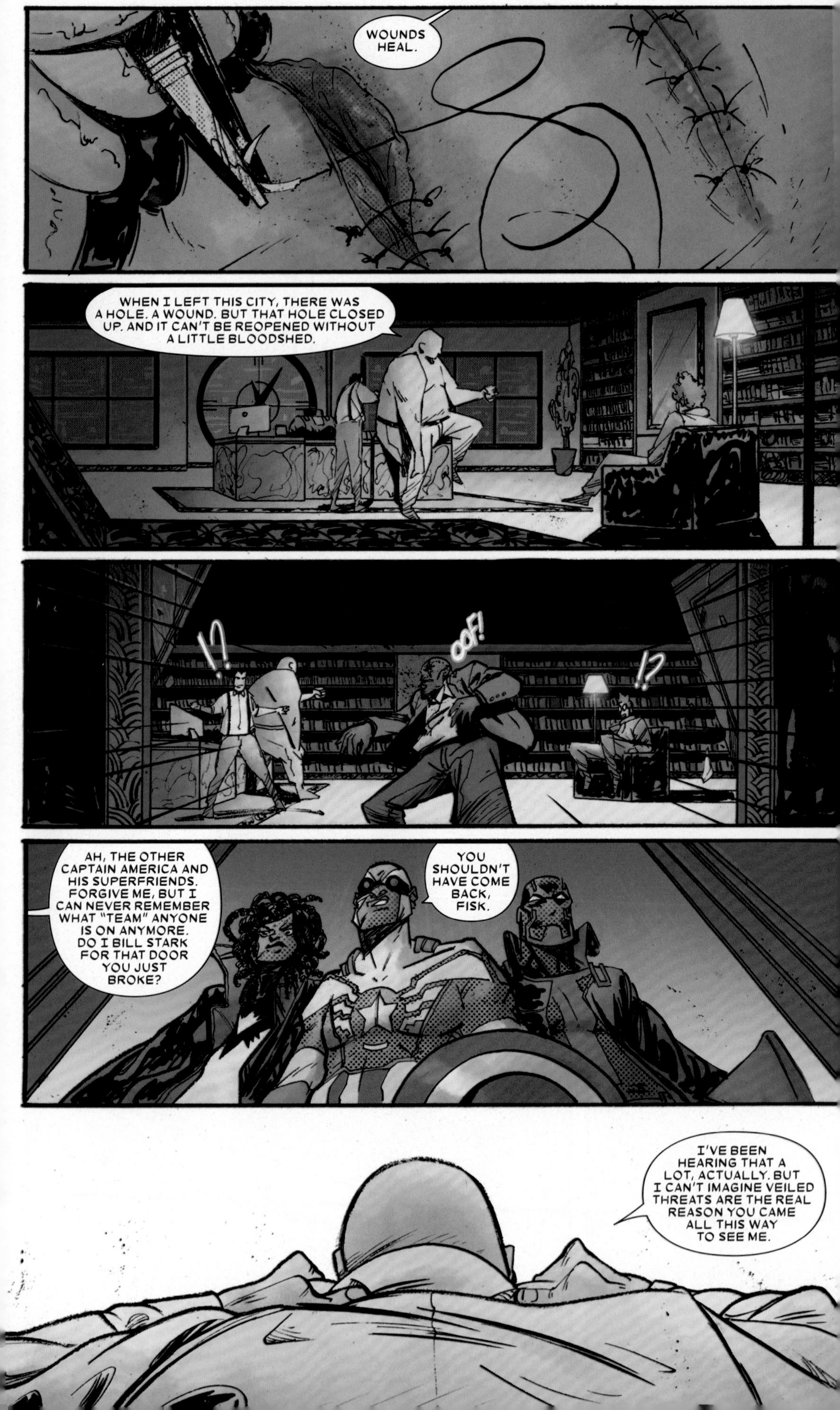
WOUNDS HEAL.
WHEN I LEFT THIS CITY, THERE WAS A HOLE. A WOUND. BUT THAT HOLE CLOSED UP. AND IT CAN'T BE REOPENED WITHOUT A LITTLE BLOODSHED.
!?
OOF!
!?
AH, THE OTHER CAPTAIN AMERICA AND HIS SUPERFRIENDS. FORGIVE ME, BUT I CAN NEVER REMEMBER WHAT "TEAM" ANYONE IS ON ANYMORE. DO I BILL STARK FOR THAT DOOR YOU JUST BROKE?
YOU SHOULDN'T HAVE COME BACK, FISK.
I'VE BEEN HEARING THAT A LOT, ACTUALLY. BUT I CAN'T IMAGINE VEILED THREATS ARE THE REAL REASON YOU CAME ALL THIS WAY TO SEE ME.

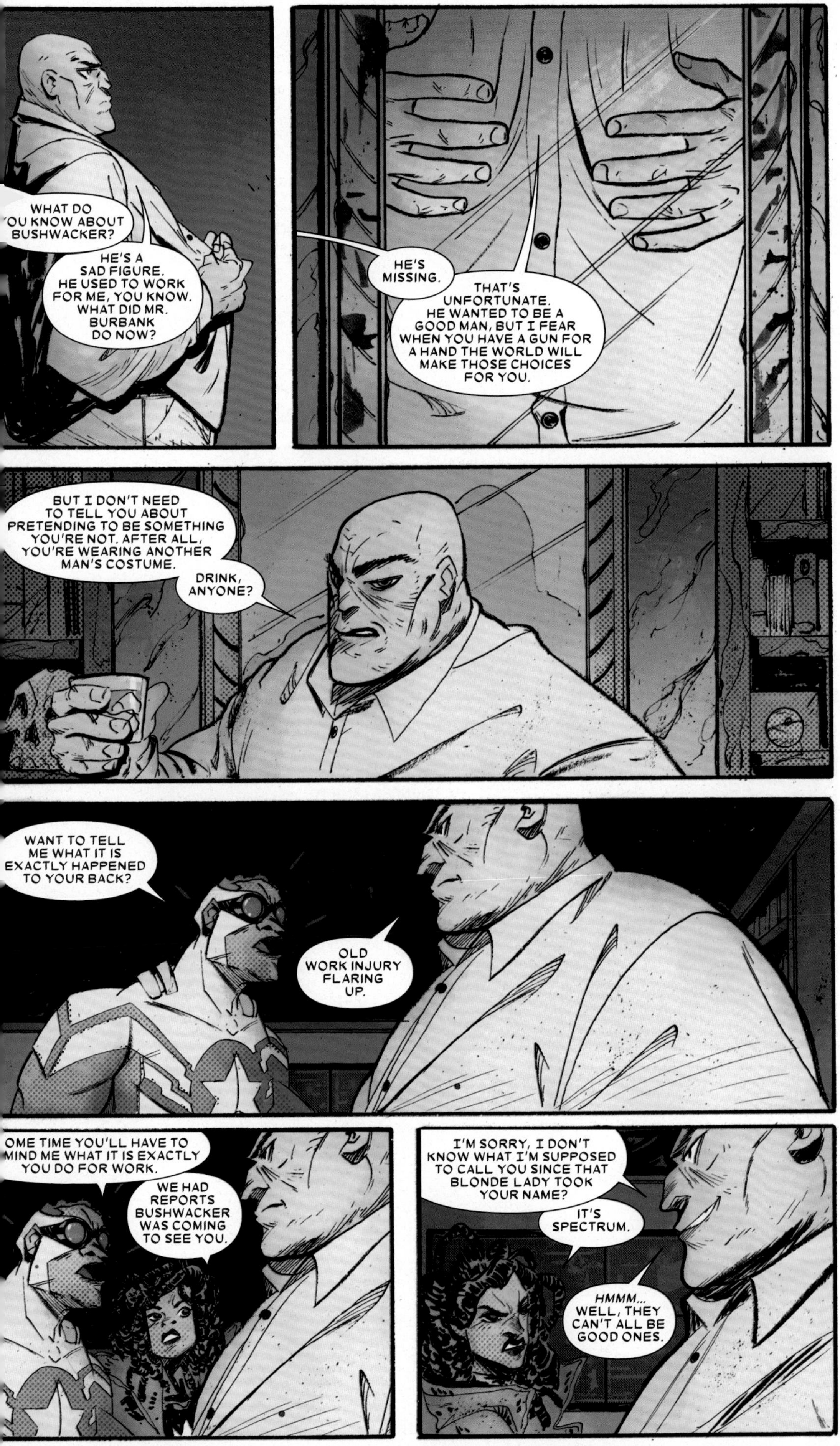
WHAT DO
'OU KNOW ABOUT
BUSHWACKER?
HE'S A
SAD FIGURE.
HE USED TO WORK
FOR ME, YOU KNOW.
WHAT DID MR.
BURBANK
DO NOW?
HE'S
MISSING.
THAT'S
UNFORTUNATE.
HE WANTED TO BE A
GOOD MAN, BUT I FEAR
WHEN YOU HAVE A GUN FOR
A HAND THE WORLD WILL
MAKE THOSE CHOICES
FOR YOU.
BUT I DON'T NEED
TO TELL YOU ABOUT
PRETENDING TO BE SOMETHING
YOU'RE NOT. AFTER ALL,
YOU'RE WEARING ANOTHER
MAN'S COSTUME.
DRINK,
ANYONE?
WANT TO TELL
ME WHAT IT IS
EXACTLY HAPPENED
TO YOUR BACK?
OLD
WORK INJURY
FLARING
UP.
OME TIME YOU'LL HAVE TO
MIND ME WHAT IT IS EXACTLY
YOU DO FOR WORK.
WE HAD
REPORTS
BUSHWACKER
WAS COMING
TO SEE YOU.
I'M SORRY, I DON'T
KNOW WHAT I'M SUPPOSED
TO CALL YOU SINCE THAT
BLONDE LADY TOOK
YOUR NAME?
IT'S
SPECTRUM.
HMMM...
WELL, THEY
CAN'T ALL BE
GOOD ONES.

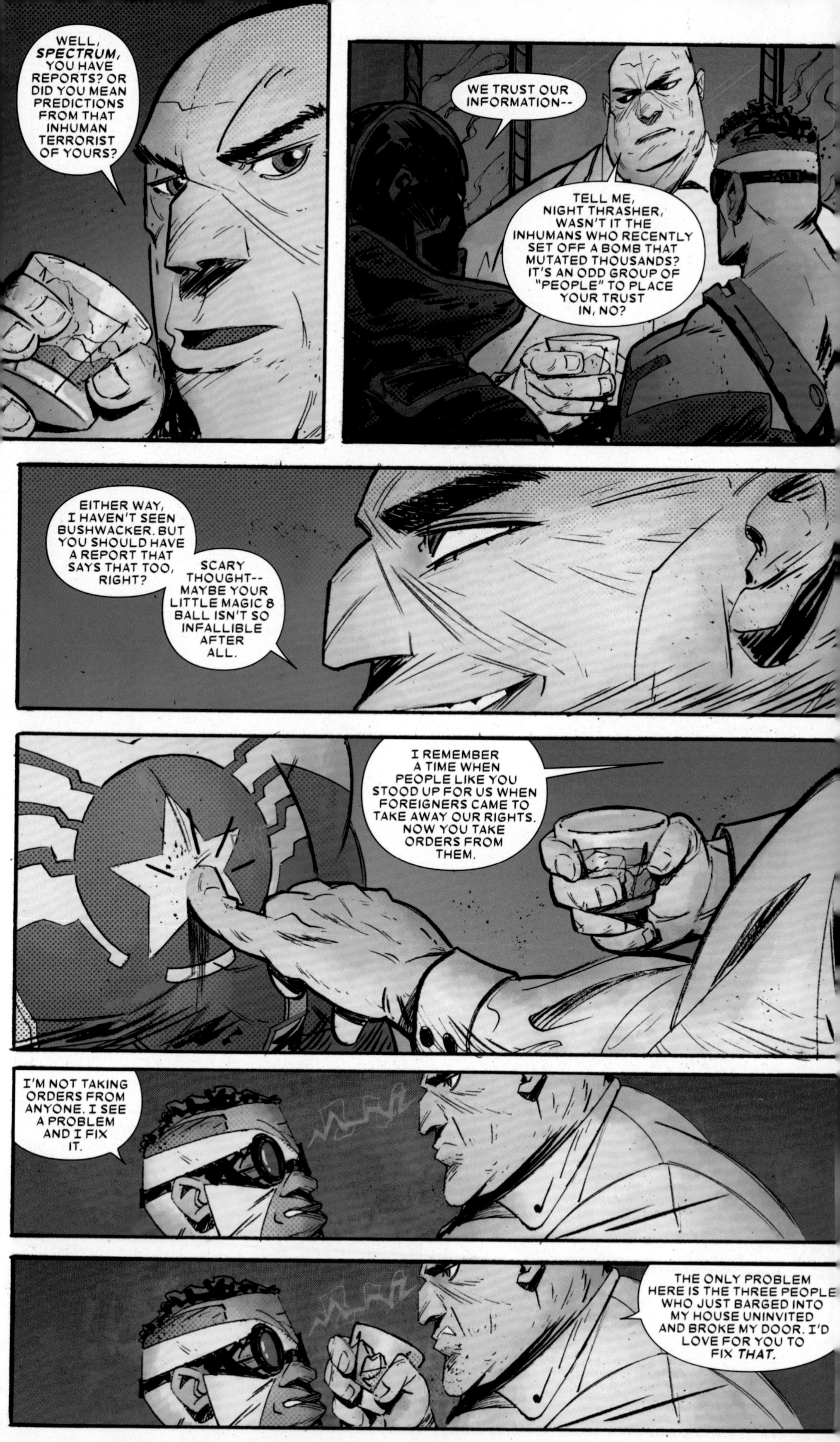
WELL, SPECTRUM, YOU HAVE REPORTS? OR DID YOU MEAN PREDICTIONS FROM THAT INHUMAN TERRORIST OF YOURS?
WE TRUST OUR INFORMATION--
TELL ME, NIGHT THRASHER, WASN'T IT THE INHUMANS WHO RECENTLY SET OFF A BOMB THAT MUTATED THOUSANDS? IT'S AN ODD GROUP OF "PEOPLE" TO PLACE YOUR TRUST IN, NO?
EITHER WAY, I HAVEN'T SEEN BUSHWACKER. BUT YOU SHOULD HAVE A REPORT THAT SAYS THAT TOO, RIGHT?
SCARY THOUGHT-- MAYBE YOUR LITTLE MAGIC 8 BALL ISN'T SO INFALLIBLE AFTER ALL.
I REMEMBER A TIME WHEN PEOPLE LIKE YOU STOOD UP FOR US WHEN FOREIGNERS CAME TO TAKE AWAY OUR RIGHTS. NOW YOU TAKE ORDERS FROM THEM.
I'M NOT TAKING ORDERS FROM ANYONE. I SEE A PROBLEM AND I FIX IT.
THE ONLY PROBLEM HERE IS THE THREE PEOPLE WHO JUST BARGED INTO MY HOUSE UNINVITED AND BROKE MY DOOR. I'D LOVE FOR YOU TO FIX THAT.

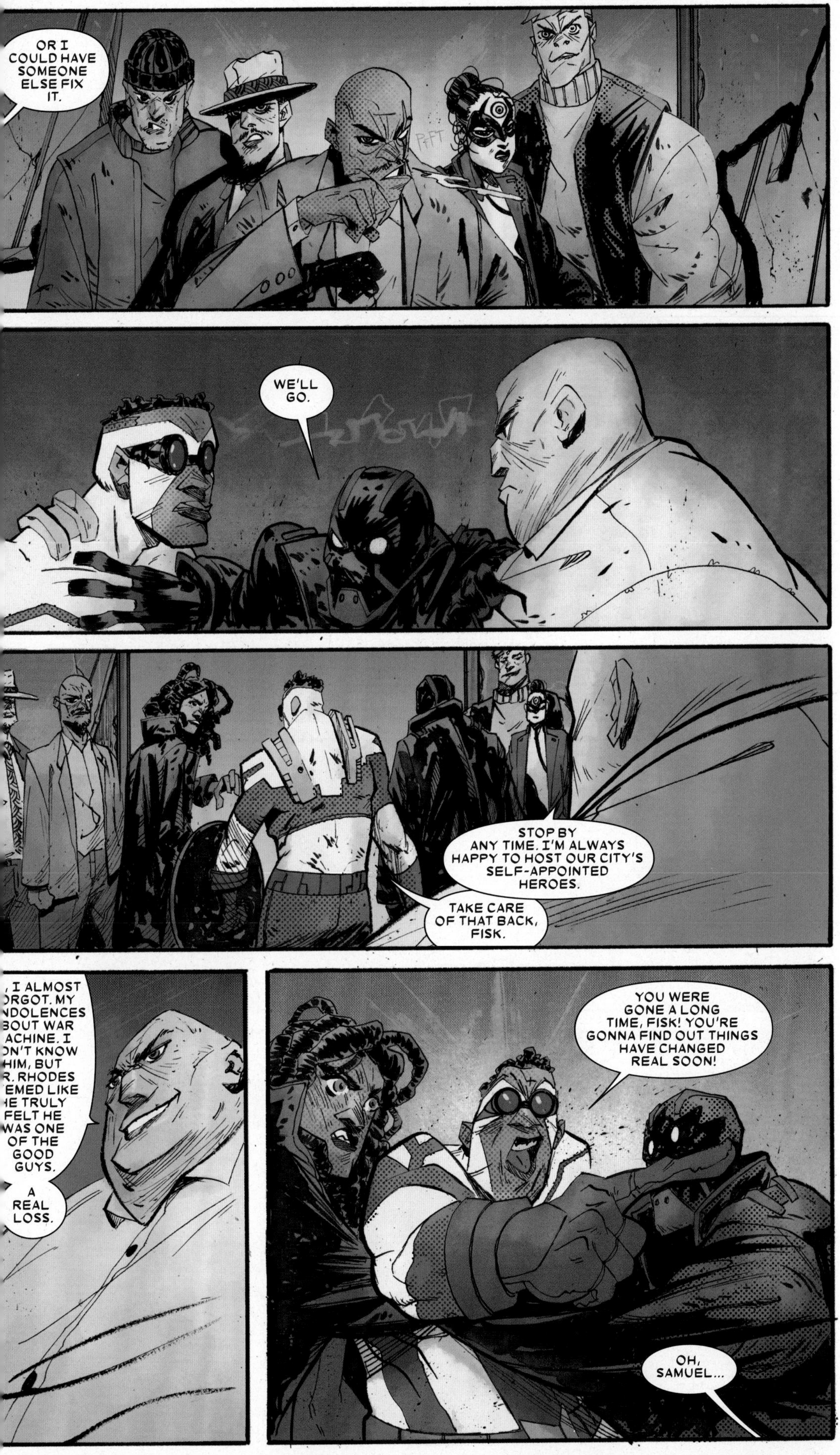
OR I COULD HAVE SOMEONE ELSE FIX IT.
PFFT
WE'LL GO.
STOP BY ANY TIME. I'M ALWAYS HAPPY TO HOST OUR CITY'S SELF-APPOINTED HEROES.
TAKE CARE OF THAT BACK, FISK.
, I ALMOST ORGOT. MY NDOLENCES BOUT WAR ACHINE. I ON'T KNOW HIM, BUT R. RHODES EEMED LIKE HE TRULY FELT HE WAS ONE OF THE GOOD GUYS.
A REAL LOSS.
YOU WERE GONE A LONG TIME, FISK! YOU'RE GONNA FIND OUT THINGS HAVE CHANGED REAL SOON!
OH, SAMUEL...

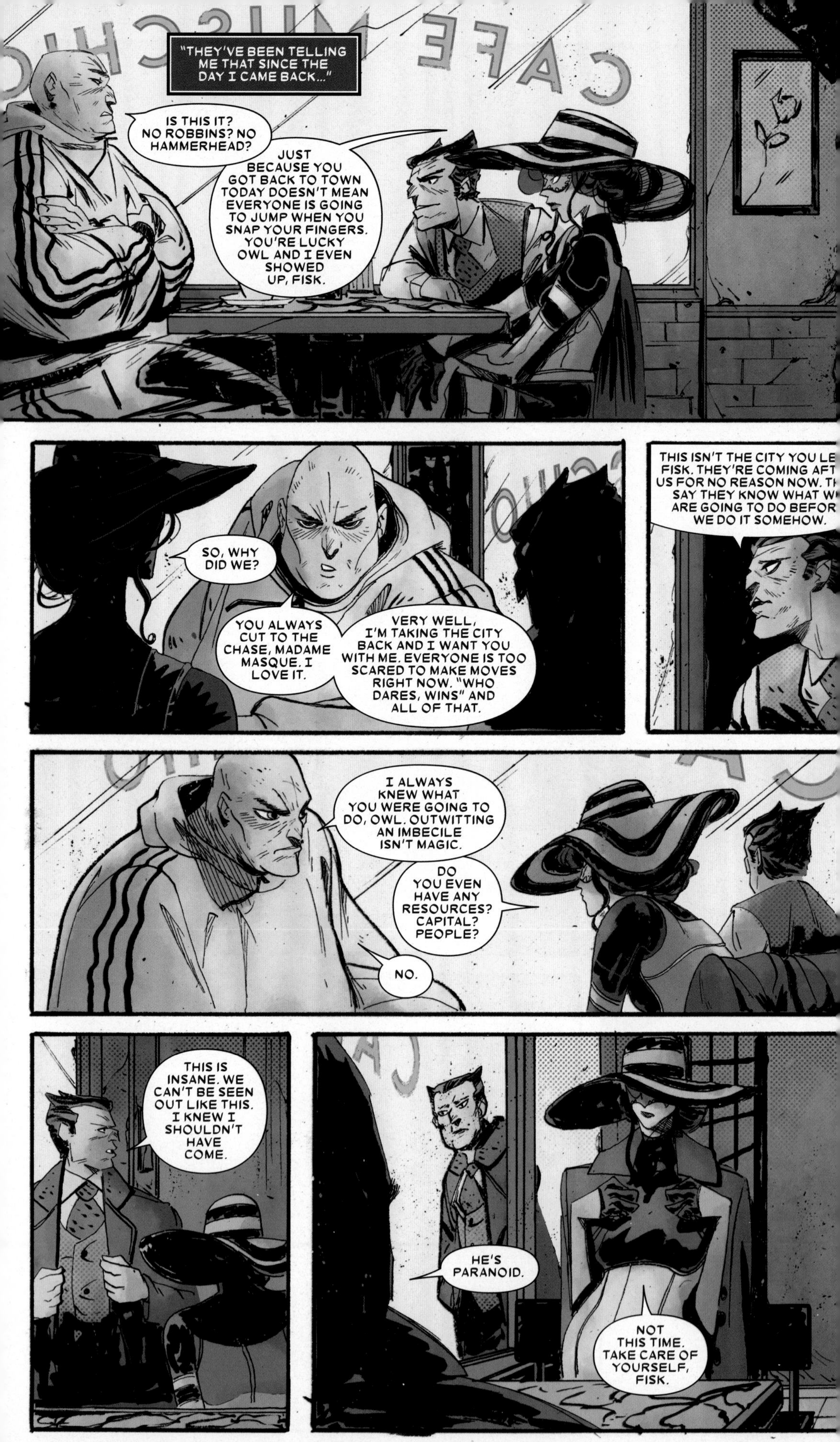
"THEY'VE BEEN TELLING ME THAT SINCE THE DAY I CAME BACK..."
IS THIS IT? NO ROBBINS? NO HAMMERHEAD?
JUST BECAUSE YOU GOT BACK TO TOWN TODAY DOESN'T MEAN EVERYONE IS GOING TO JUMP WHEN YOU SNAP YOUR FINGERS. YOU'RE LUCKY OWL AND I EVEN SHOWED UP, FISK.
SO, WHY DID WE?
YOU ALWAYS CUT TO THE CHASE, MADAME MASQUE. I LOVE IT.
VERY WELL, I'M TAKING THE CITY BACK AND I WANT YOU WITH ME. EVERYONE IS TOO SCARED TO MAKE MOVES RIGHT NOW. "WHO DARES, WINS" AND ALL OF THAT.
THIS ISN'T THE CITY YOU LE FISK. THEY'RE COMING AFT US FOR NO REASON NOW. T SAY THEY KNOW WHAT W ARE GOING TO DO BEFOR WE DO IT SOMEHOW.
I ALWAYS KNEW WHAT YOU WERE GOING TO DO, OWL. OUTWITTING AN IMBECILE ISN'T MAGIC.
DO YOU EVEN HAVE ANY RESOURCES? CAPITAL? PEOPLE?
NO.
THIS IS INSANE. WE CAN'T BE SEEN OUT LIKE THIS. I KNEW I SHOULDN'T HAVE COME.
HE'S PARANOID.
NOT THIS TIME. TAKE CARE OF YOURSELF, FISK.

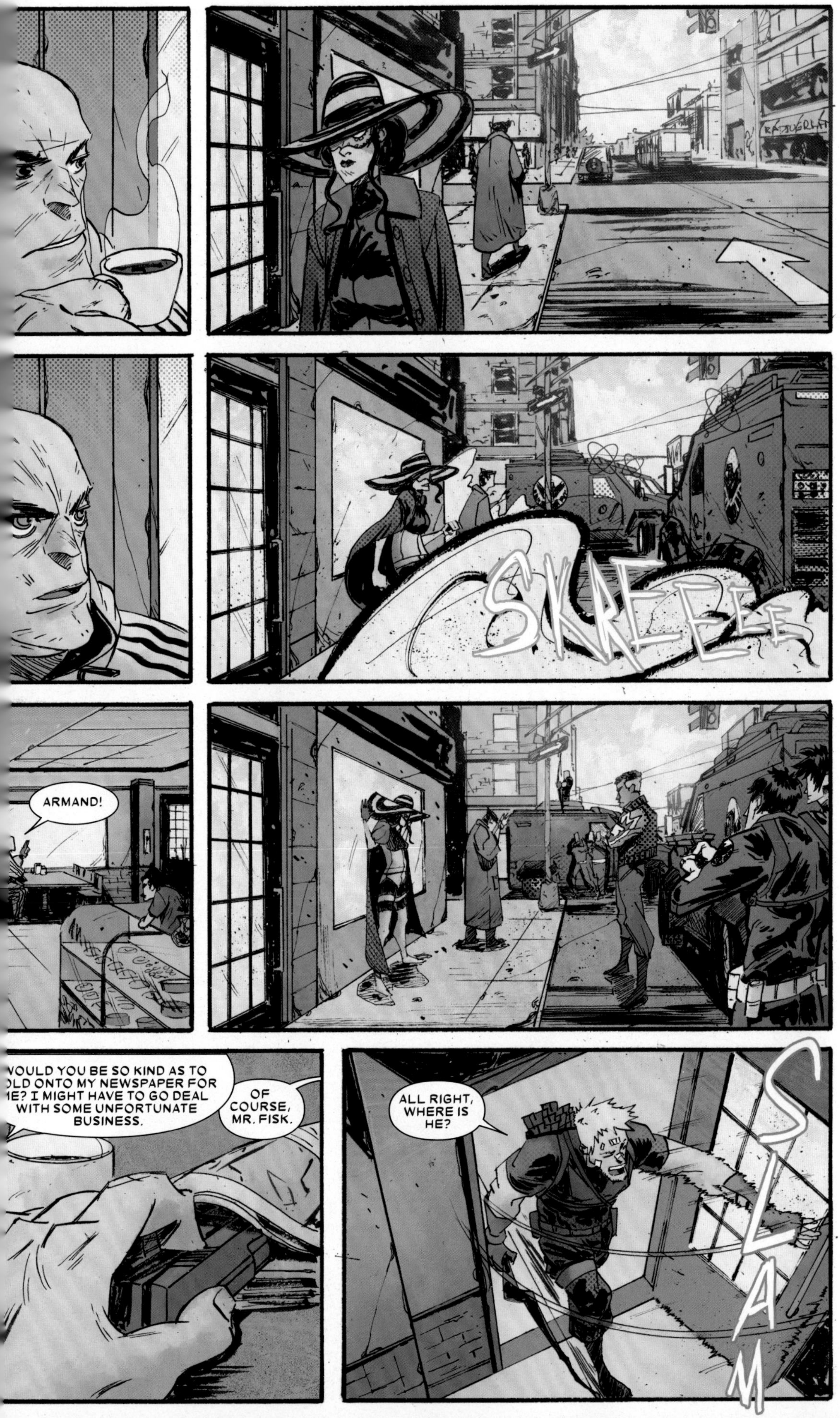

SKREEEEE
ARMAND!
WOULD YOU BE SO KIND AS TO HOLD ONTO MY NEWSPAPER FOR ME? I MIGHT HAVE TO GO DEAL WITH SOME UNFORTUNATE BUSINESS.
OF COURSE, MR. FISK.
SLLAM
ALL RIGHT, WHERE IS HE?

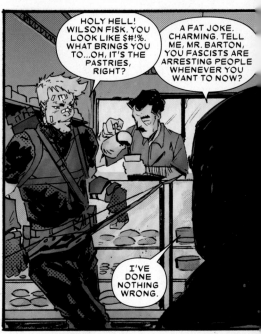

PLEASE, NO TROUBLE.

THERE HE IS! I NEED A *GRANDE* BLACK COFFEE. TO GO.

GRANDE?

IT MEANS LARGE.

HOLY HELL! WILSON FISK. YOU LOOK LIKE $#!%. WHAT BRINGS YOU TO...OH, IT'S THE PASTRIES, RIGHT?

A FAT JOKE. CHARMING. TELL ME, MR. BARTON, YOU FASCISTS ARE ARRESTING PEOPLE WHENEVER YOU WANT TO NOW?

I'VE DONE NOTHING WRONG.

ANYONE WHO'S EVER READ A FASHION MAGAZINE CAN SEE THAT'S NOT TRUE. BUT I CAN'T ARREST YOU FOR THAT.

SUGAR

WHY THEN?

SO PARANOID, MAN. YOU SHOULD WATCH THAT. IT MAKES YOU SEEM... PATHETIC.

SUGAR SUGAR SUGAR

I'M NOT HERE TO ARREST YOU.

YET.

SUGAR SUGAR SUGAR SUGAR SUGAR SUGAR SUGAR SUGAR SUGAR

BUT I'M GONNA BE CHECKING THOSE REPORTS EVERY DAY FOR YOUR NAME.

THANKS FOR BUYING MY COFFEE FOR ME. HAVE A SWELL DAY, WILLY.

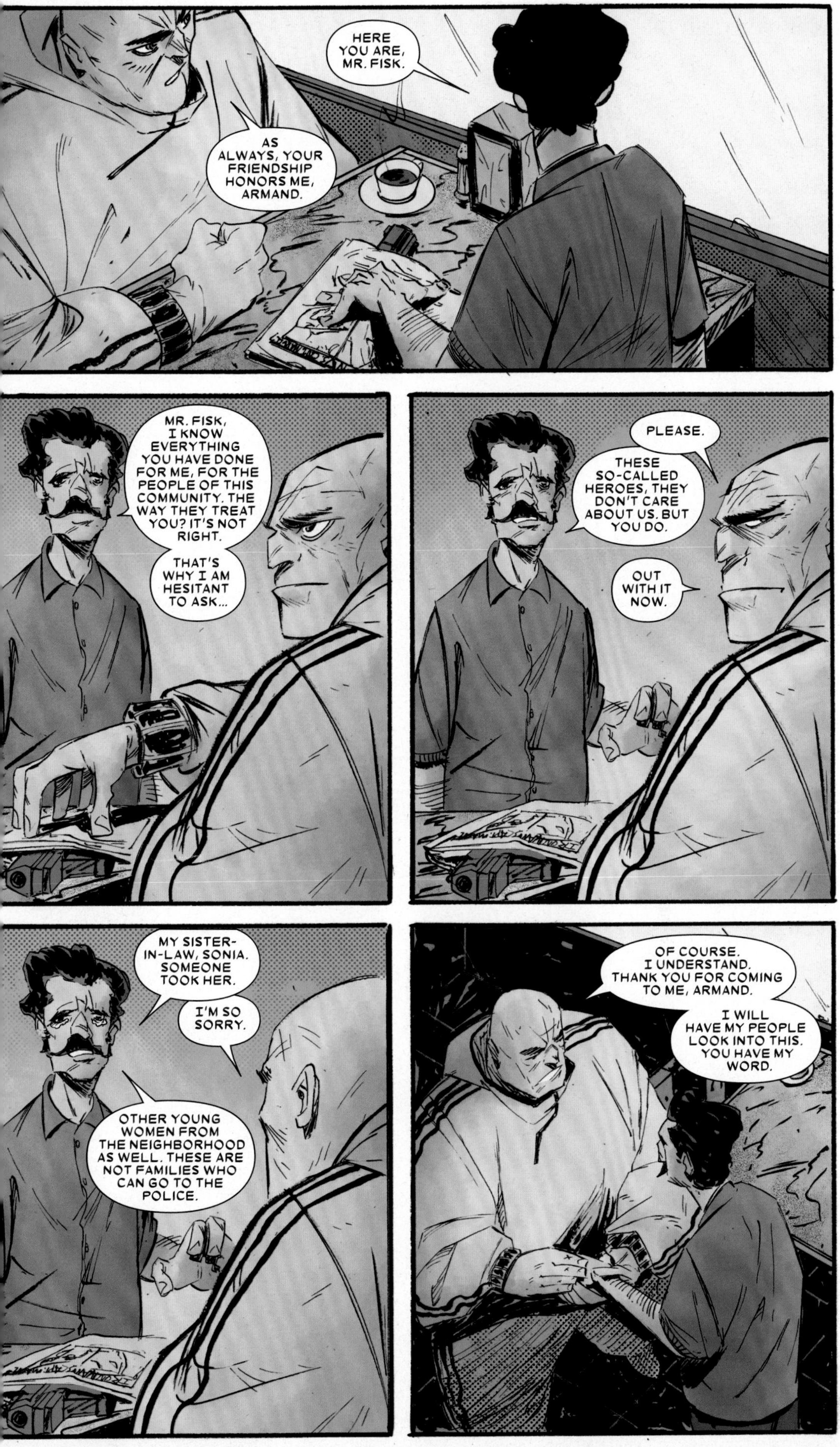
HERE YOU ARE, MR. FISK.
AS ALWAYS, YOUR FRIENDSHIP HONORS ME, ARMAND.
MR. FISK, I KNOW EVERYTHING YOU HAVE DONE FOR ME, FOR THE PEOPLE OF THIS COMMUNITY. THE WAY THEY TREAT YOU? IT'S NOT RIGHT.
THAT'S WHY I AM HESITANT TO ASK...
PLEASE.
THESE SO-CALLED HEROES, THEY DON'T CARE ABOUT US. BUT YOU DO.
OUT WITH IT NOW.
MY SISTER-IN-LAW, SONIA. SOMEONE TOOK HER.
I'M SO SORRY.
OTHER YOUNG WOMEN FROM THE NEIGHBORHOOD AS WELL. THESE ARE NOT FAMILIES WHO CAN GO TO THE POLICE.
OF COURSE. I UNDERSTAND. THANK YOU FOR COMING TO ME, ARMAND.
I WILL HAVE MY PEOPLE LOOK INTO THIS. YOU HAVE MY WORD.

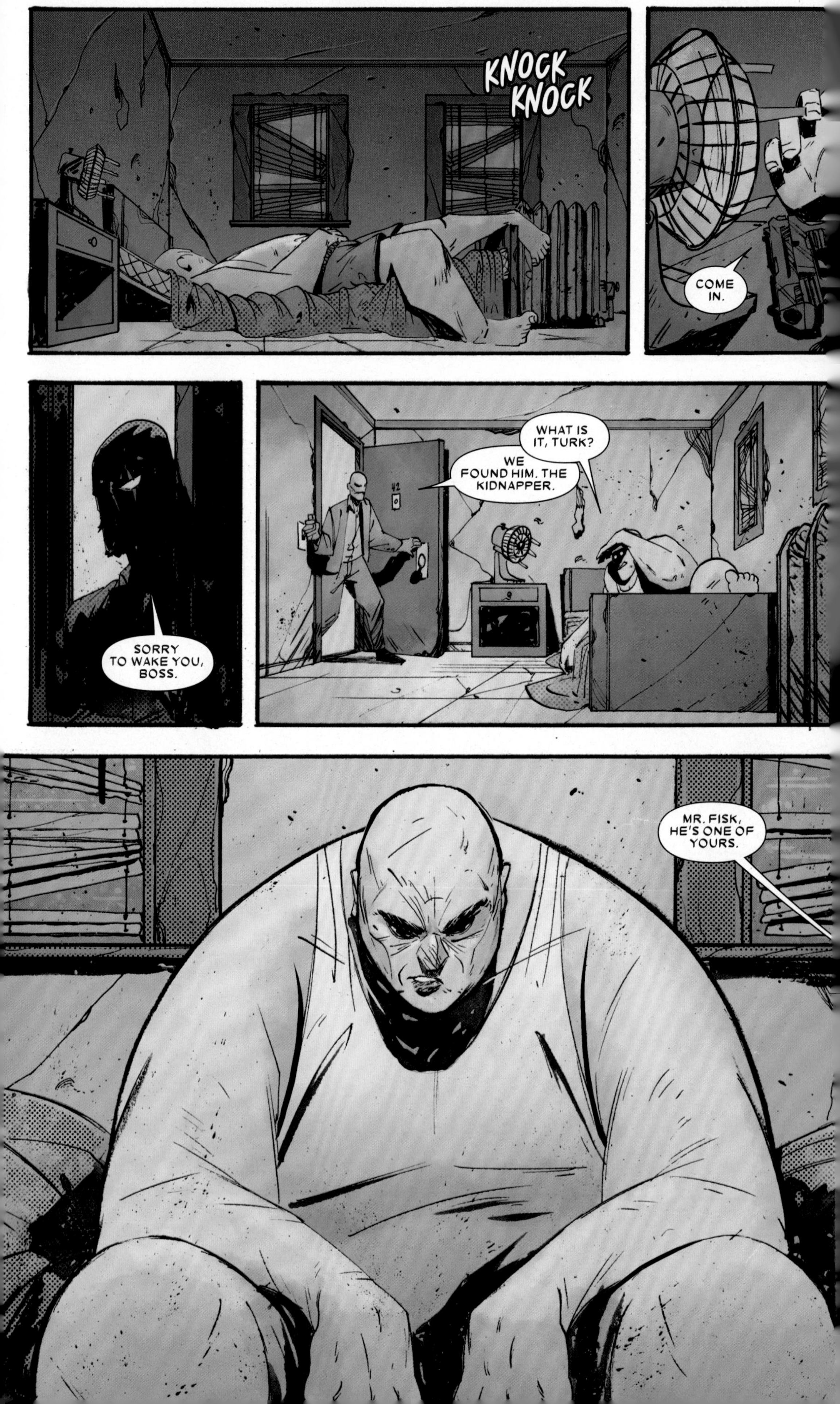
KNOCK KNOCK
COME IN.
SORRY TO WAKE YOU, BOSS.
WHAT IS IT, TURK?
WE FOUND HIM. THE KIDNAPPER.
MR. FISK, HE'S ONE OF YOURS.

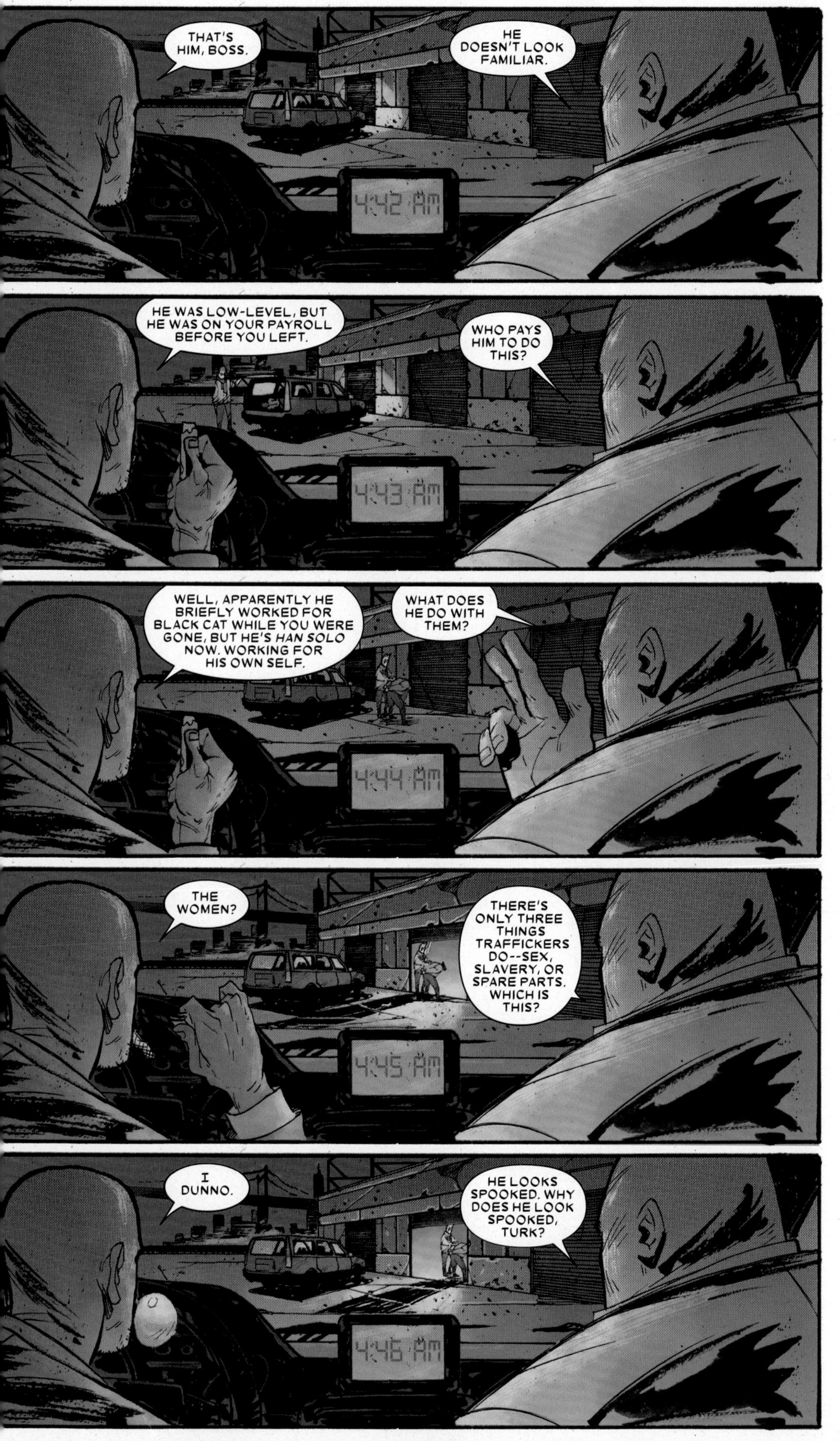

THAT'S HIM, BOSS.
HE DOESN'T LOOK FAMILIAR.
4:42 AM
HE WAS LOW-LEVEL, BUT HE WAS ON YOUR PAYROLL BEFORE YOU LEFT.
WHO PAYS HIM TO DO THIS?
4:43 AM
WELL, APPARENTLY HE BRIEFLY WORKED FOR BLACK CAT WHILE YOU WERE GONE, BUT HE'S *HAN SOLO* NOW. WORKING FOR HIS OWN SELF.
WHAT DOES HE DO WITH THEM?
4:44 AM
THE WOMEN?
THERE'S ONLY THREE THINGS TRAFFICKERS DO--SEX, SLAVERY, OR SPARE PARTS. WHICH IS THIS?
4:45 AM
I DUNNO.
HE LOOKS SPOOKED. WHY DOES HE LOOK SPOOKED, TURK?
4:46 AM

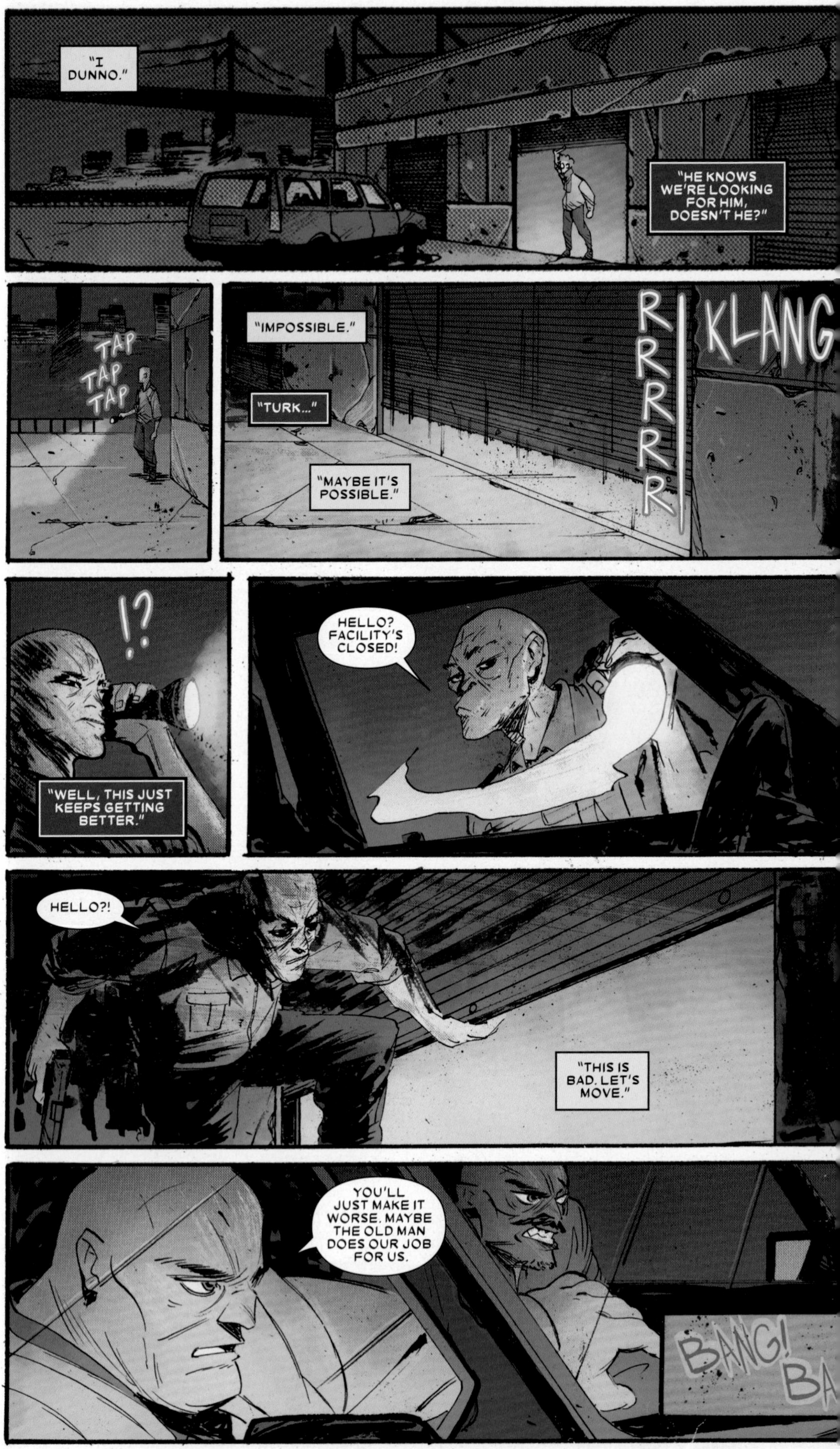
"I DUNNO."
"HE KNOWS WE'RE LOOKING FOR HIM, DOESN'T HE?"
TAP TAP TAP
"IMPOSSIBLE."
"TURK..."
"MAYBE IT'S POSSIBLE."
RRRRRR
KLANG
!?
"WELL, THIS JUST KEEPS GETTING BETTER."
HELLO? FACILITY'S CLOSED!
HELLO?!
"THIS IS BAD. LET'S MOVE."
YOU'LL JUST MAKE IT WORSE. MAYBE THE OLD MAN DOES OUR JOB FOR US.
BANG!

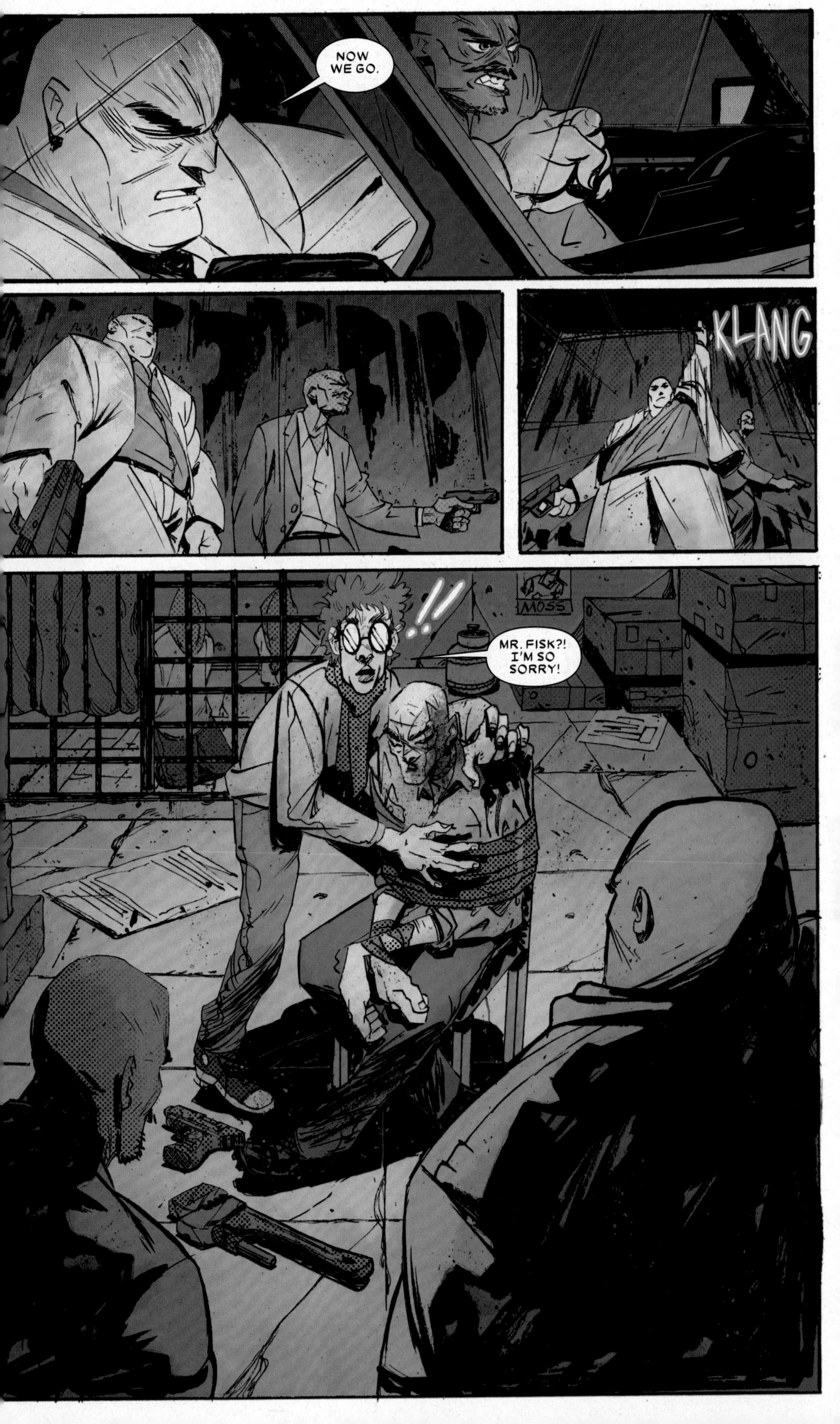
NOW WE GO.
KLANG
!!
MR. FISK?! I'M SO SORRY!
MOSS

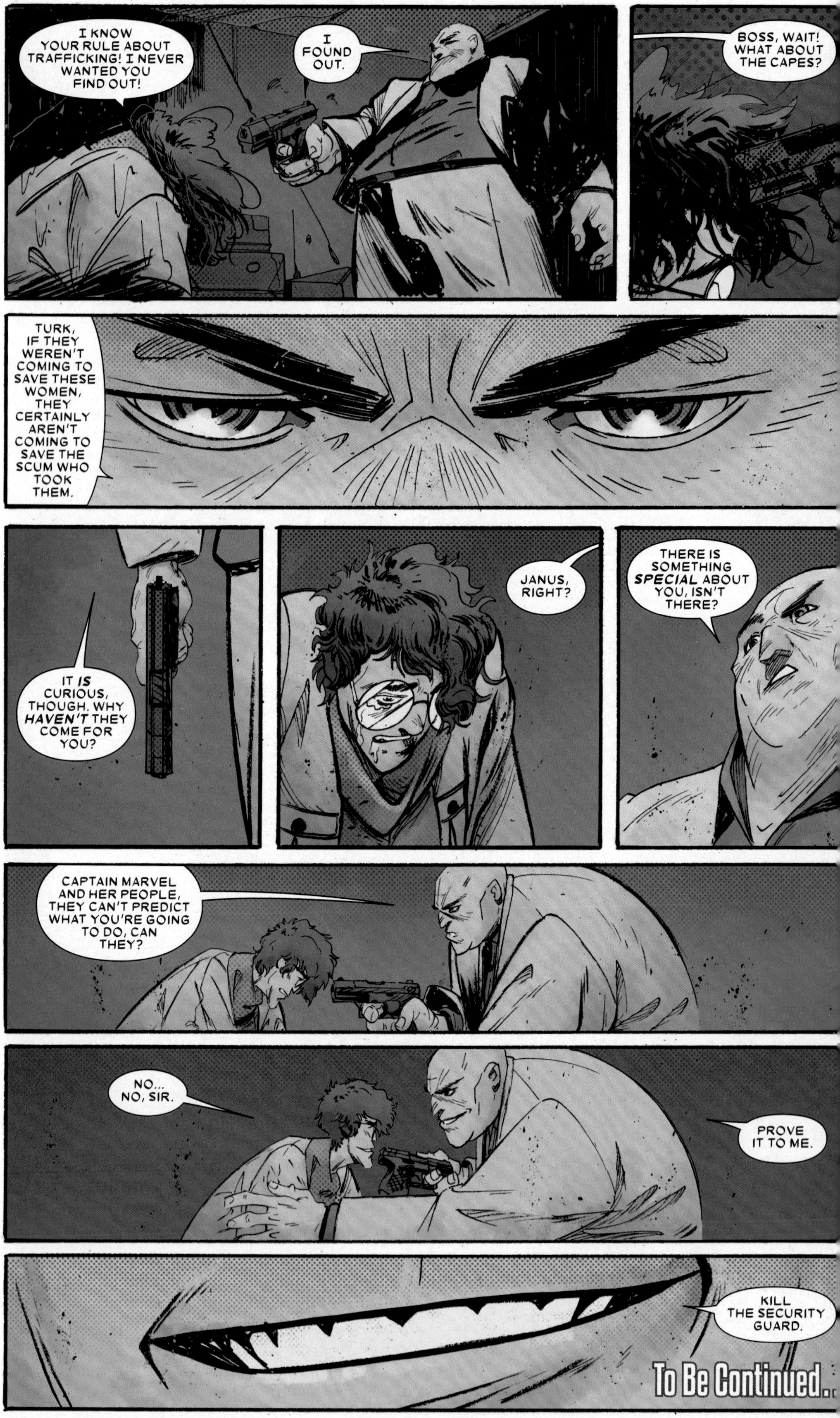
I KNOW YOUR RULE ABOUT TRAFFICKING! I NEVER WANTED YOU FIND OUT!
I FOUND OUT.
BOSS, WAIT! WHAT ABOUT THE CAPES?
TURK, IF THEY WEREN'T COMING TO SAVE THESE WOMEN, THEY CERTAINLY AREN'T COMING TO SAVE THE SCUM WHO TOOK THEM.
IT IS CURIOUS, THOUGH. WHY HAVEN'T THEY COME FOR YOU?
JANUS, RIGHT?
THERE IS SOMETHING SPECIAL ABOUT YOU, ISN'T THERE?
CAPTAIN MARVEL AND HER PEOPLE, THEY CAN'T PREDICT WHAT YOU'RE GOING TO DO, CAN THEY?
NO... NO, SIR.
PROVE IT TO ME.
KILL THE SECURITY GUARD.
To Be Continued...

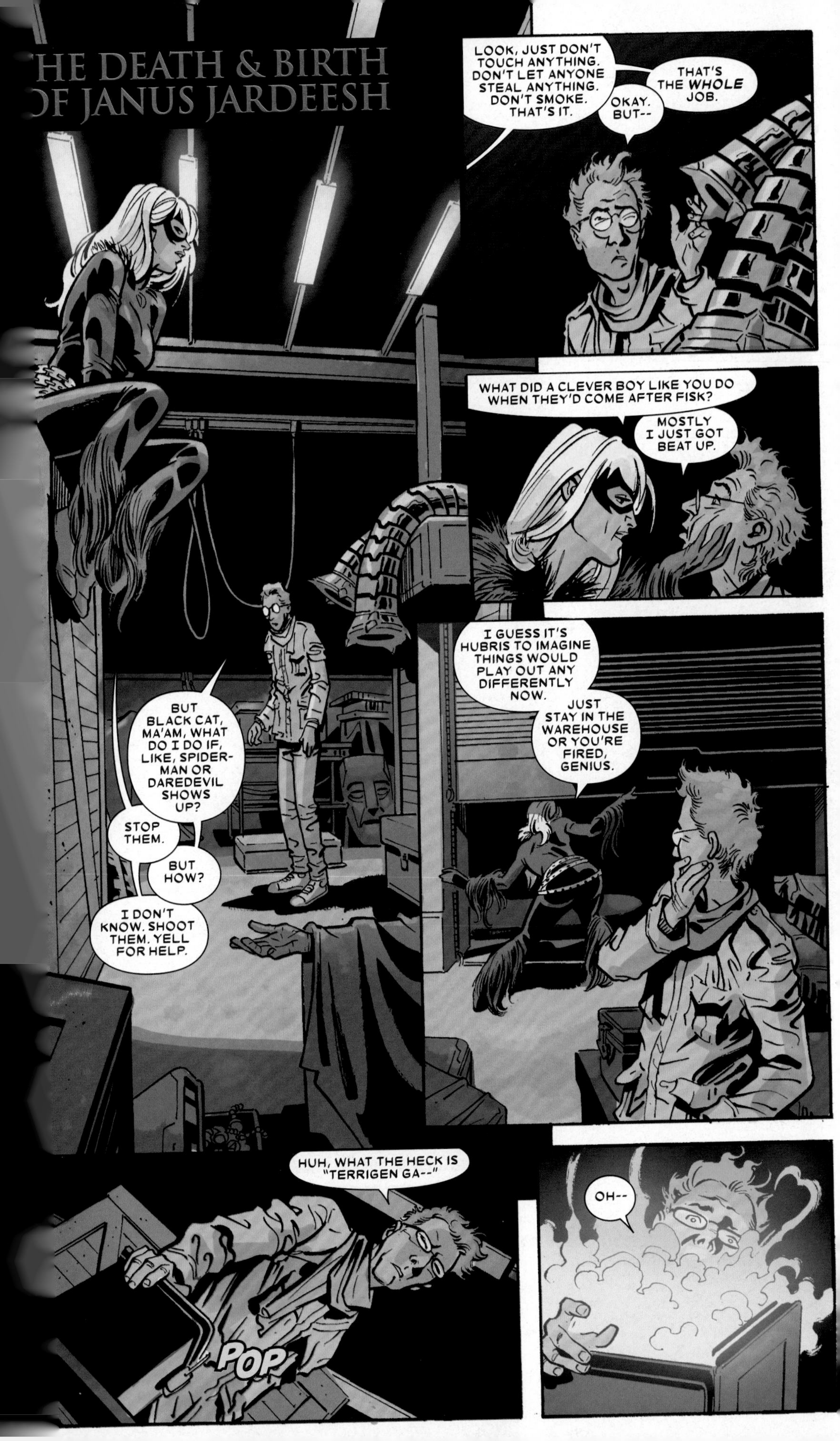
THE DEATH & BIRTH OF JANUS JARDEESH
LOOK, JUST DON'T TOUCH ANYTHING. DON'T LET ANYONE STEAL ANYTHING. DON'T SMOKE. THAT'S IT.
OKAY. BUT--
THAT'S THE WHOLE JOB.
BUT BLACK CAT, MA'AM, WHAT DO I DO IF, LIKE, SPIDER-MAN OR DAREDEVIL SHOWS UP?
STOP THEM.
BUT HOW?
I DON'T KNOW. SHOOT THEM. YELL FOR HELP.
WHAT DID A CLEVER BOY LIKE YOU DO WHEN THEY'D COME AFTER FISK?
MOSTLY I JUST GOT BEAT UP.
I GUESS IT'S HUBRIS TO IMAGINE THINGS WOULD PLAY OUT ANY DIFFERENTLY NOW.
JUST STAY IN THE WAREHOUSE OR YOU'RE FIRED, GENIUS.
HUH, WHAT THE HECK IS "TERRIGEN GA--"
POP
OH--

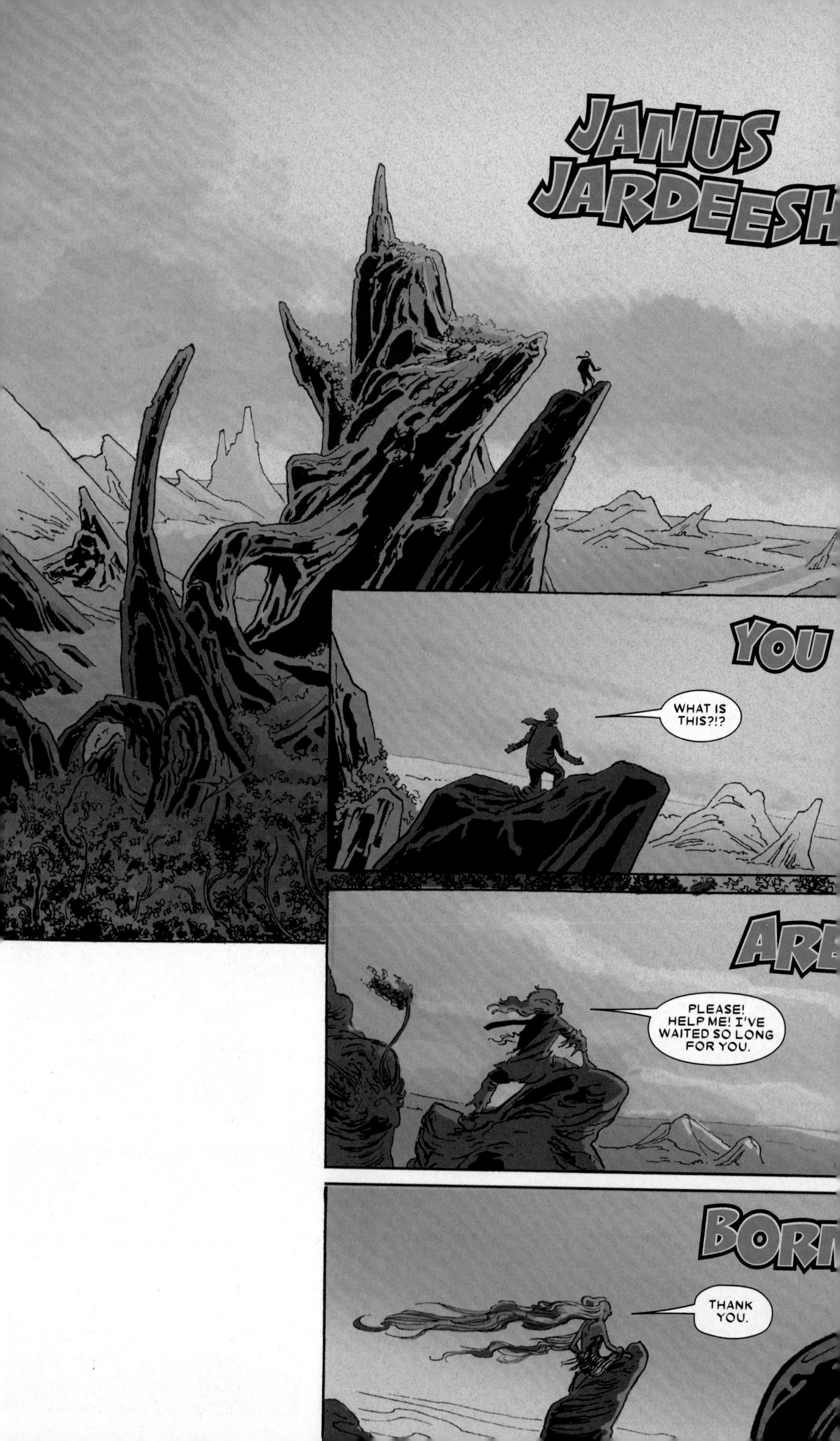
JANUS JARDEESH
YOU
WHAT IS THIS?!?
ARE
PLEASE! HELP ME! I'VE WAITED SO LONG FOR YOU.
BORN
THANK YOU.

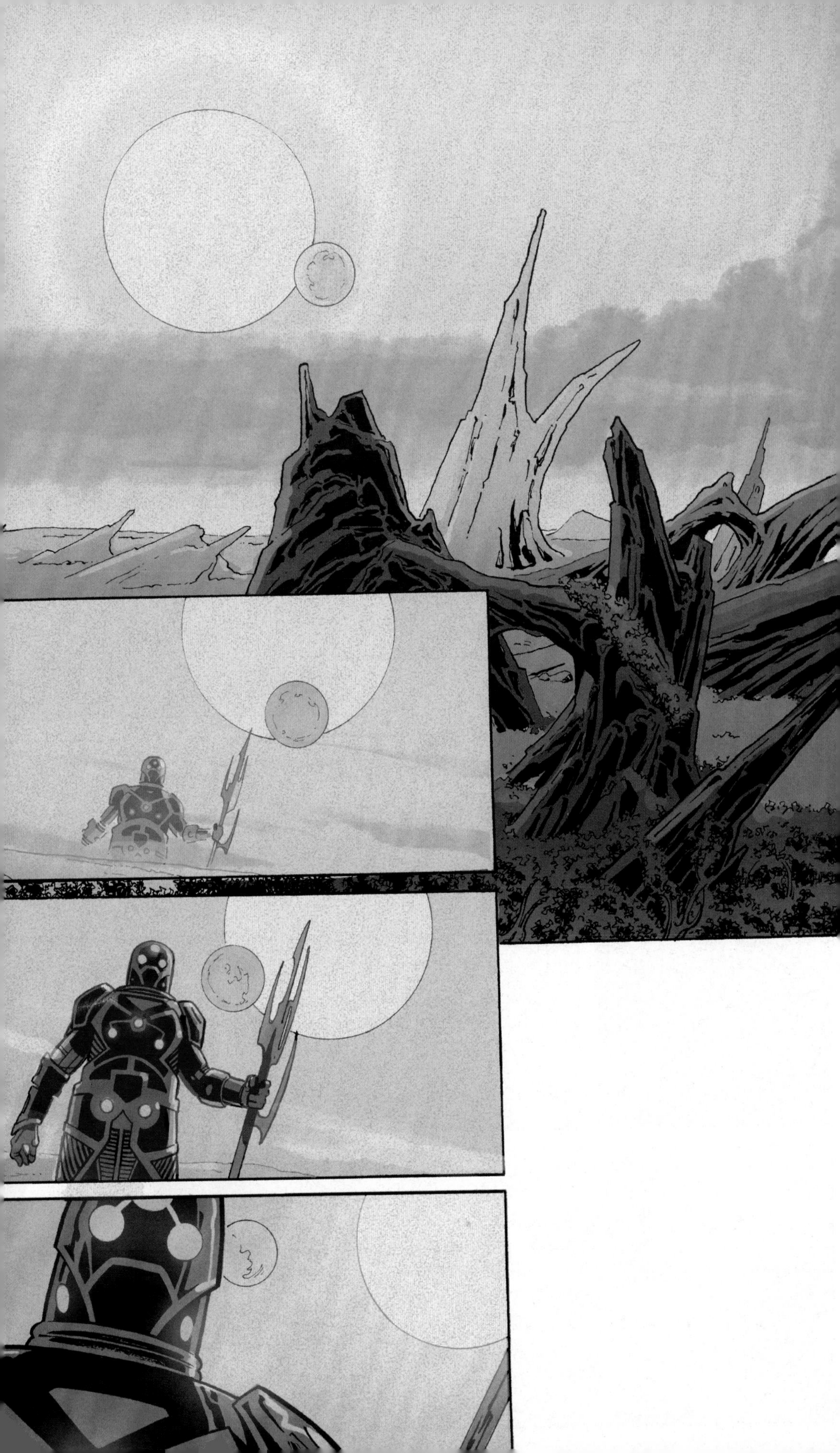

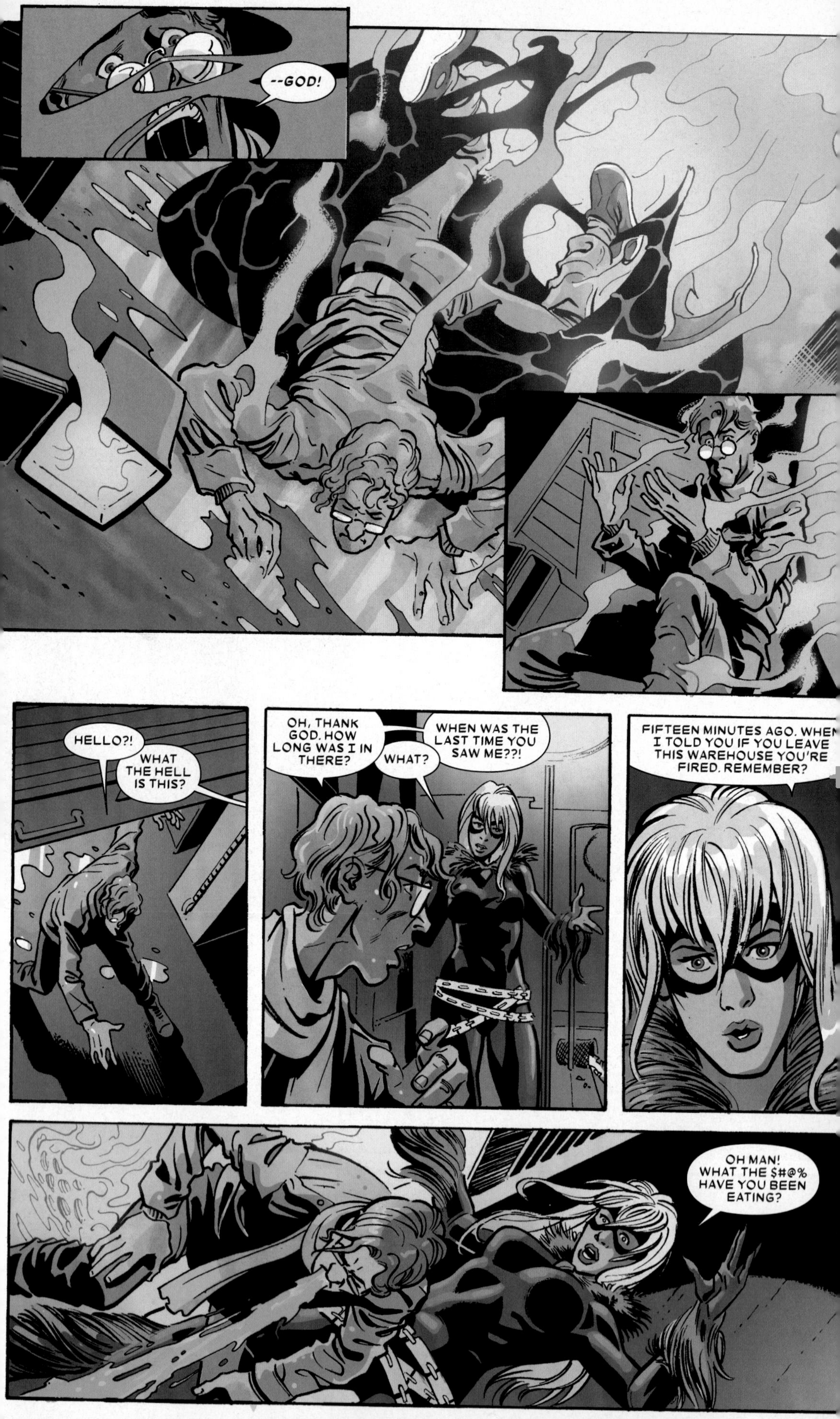
--GOD!
HELLO?!
WHAT THE HELL IS THIS?
OH, THANK GOD. HOW LONG WAS I IN THERE?
WHAT?
WHEN WAS THE LAST TIME YOU SAW ME??!
FIFTEEN MINUTES AGO. WHEN I TOLD YOU IF YOU LEAVE THIS WAREHOUSE YOU'RE FIRED. REMEMBER?
OH MAN! WHAT THE $#@% HAVE YOU BEEN EATING?

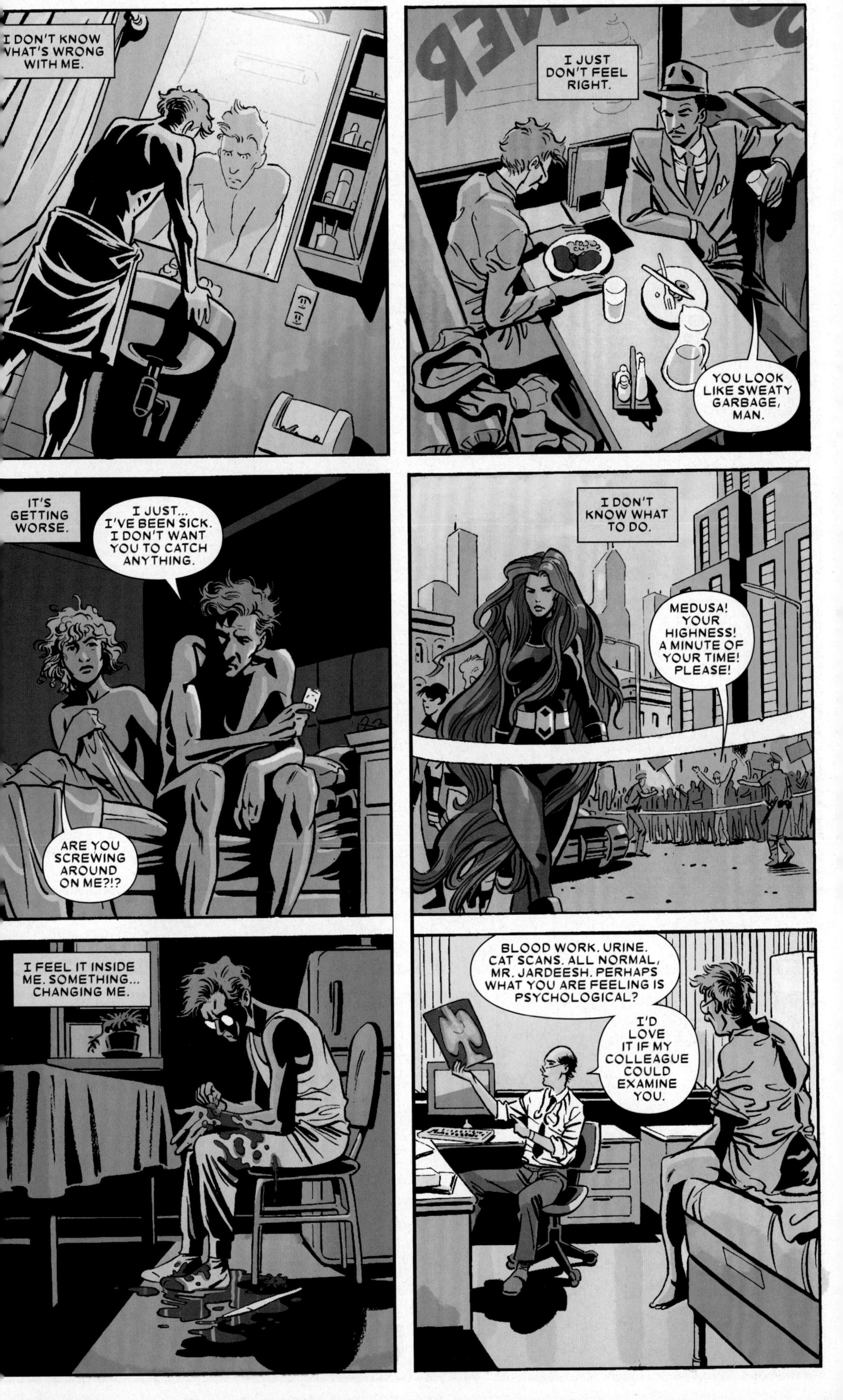

I DON'T KNOW WHAT'S WRONG WITH ME.
I JUST DON'T FEEL RIGHT.
YOU LOOK LIKE SWEATY GARBAGE, MAN.
IT'S GETTING WORSE.
I JUST... I'VE BEEN SICK. I DON'T WANT YOU TO CATCH ANYTHING.
ARE YOU SCREWING AROUND ON ME?!?
I DON'T KNOW WHAT TO DO.
MEDUSA! YOUR HIGHNESS! A MINUTE OF YOUR TIME! PLEASE!
I FEEL IT INSIDE ME. SOMETHING... CHANGING ME.
BLOOD WORK. URINE. CAT SCANS. ALL NORMAL, MR. JARDEESH. PERHAPS WHAT YOU ARE FEELING IS PSYCHOLOGICAL?
I'D LOVE IT IF MY COLLEAGUE COULD EXAMINE YOU.

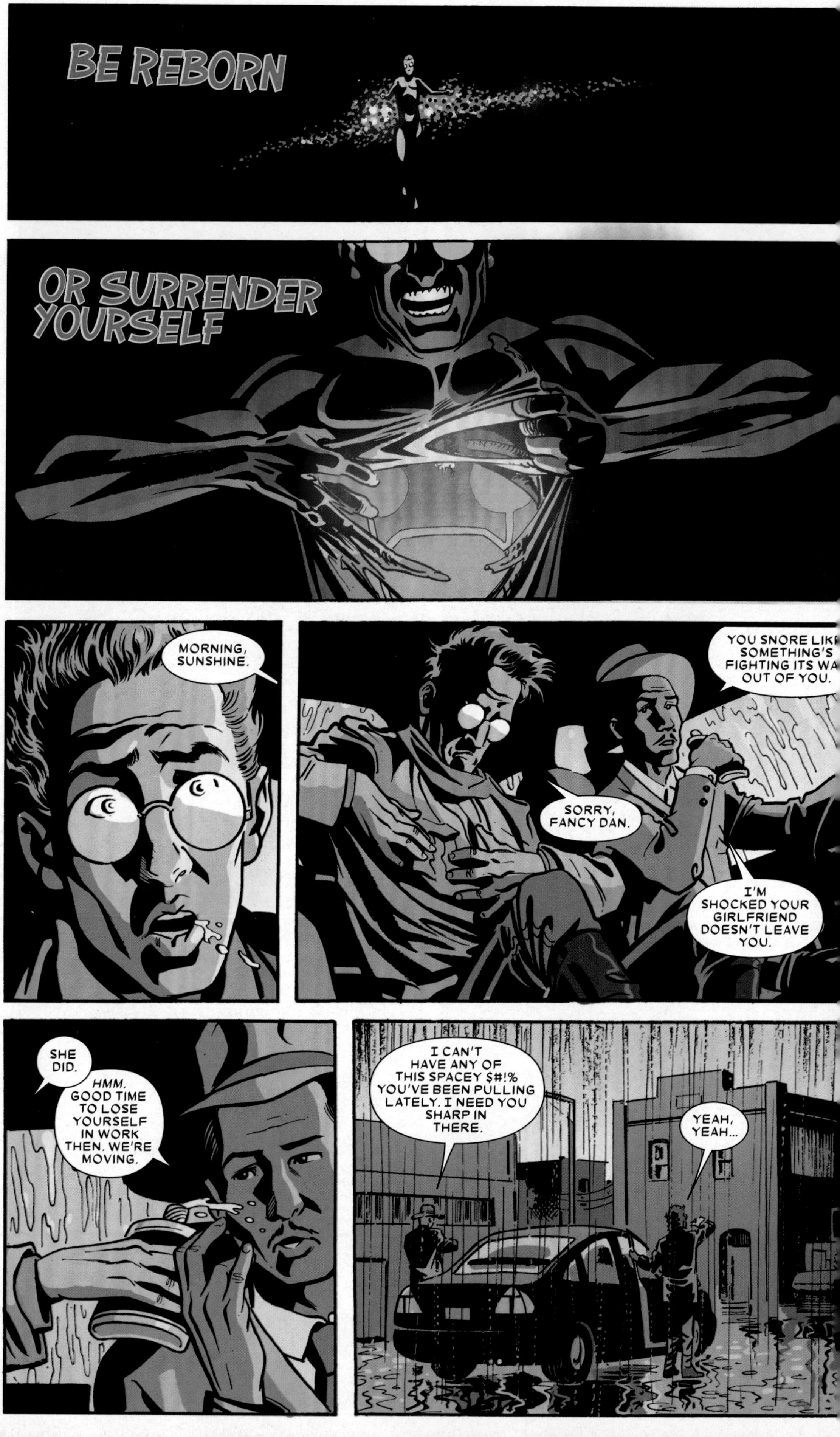
BE REBORN
OR SURRENDER YOURSELF
MORNING, SUNSHINE.
YOU SNORE LIKE SOMETHING'S FIGHTING ITS WA OUT OF YOU.
SORRY, FANCY DAN.
I'M SHOCKED YOUR GIRLFRIEND DOESN'T LEAVE YOU.
SHE DID.
HMM. GOOD TIME TO LOSE YOURSELF IN WORK THEN. WE'RE MOVING.
I CAN'T HAVE ANY OF THIS SPACEY $#!% YOU'VE BEEN PULLING LATELY. I NEED YOU SHARP IN THERE.
YEAH, YEAH...

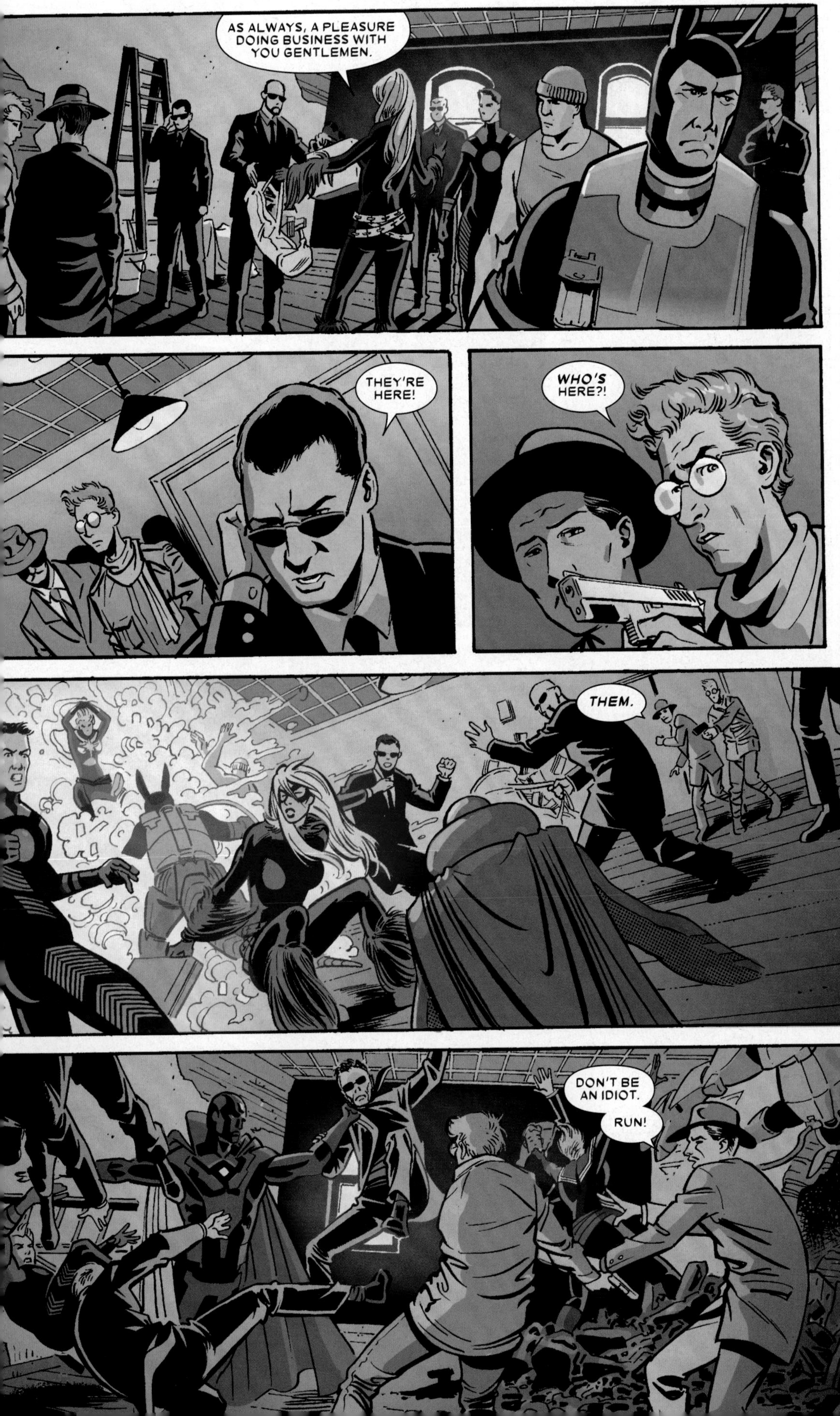
AS ALWAYS, A PLEASURE DOING BUSINESS WITH YOU GENTLEMEN.
THEY'RE HERE!
WHO'S HERE?!
THEM.
DON'T BE AN IDIOT.
RUN!

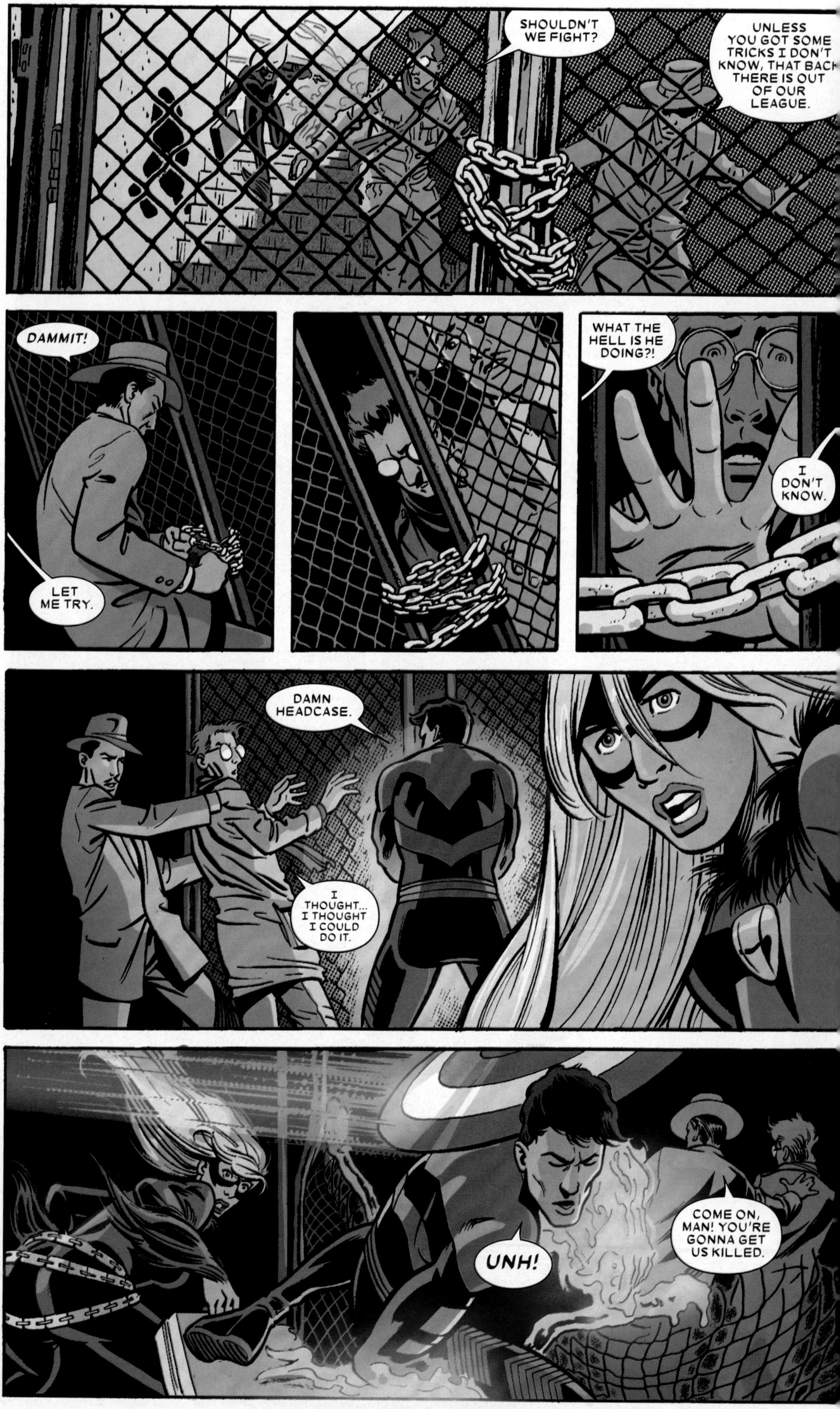
SHOULDN'T WE FIGHT?
UNLESS YOU GOT SOME TRICKS I DON'T KNOW, THAT BACK THERE IS OUT OF OUR LEAGUE.
DAMMIT!
LET ME TRY.
WHAT THE HELL IS HE DOING?!
I DON'T KNOW.
DAMN HEADCASE.
I THOUGHT... I THOUGHT I COULD DO IT.
UNH!
COME ON, MAN! YOU'RE GONNA GET US KILLED.

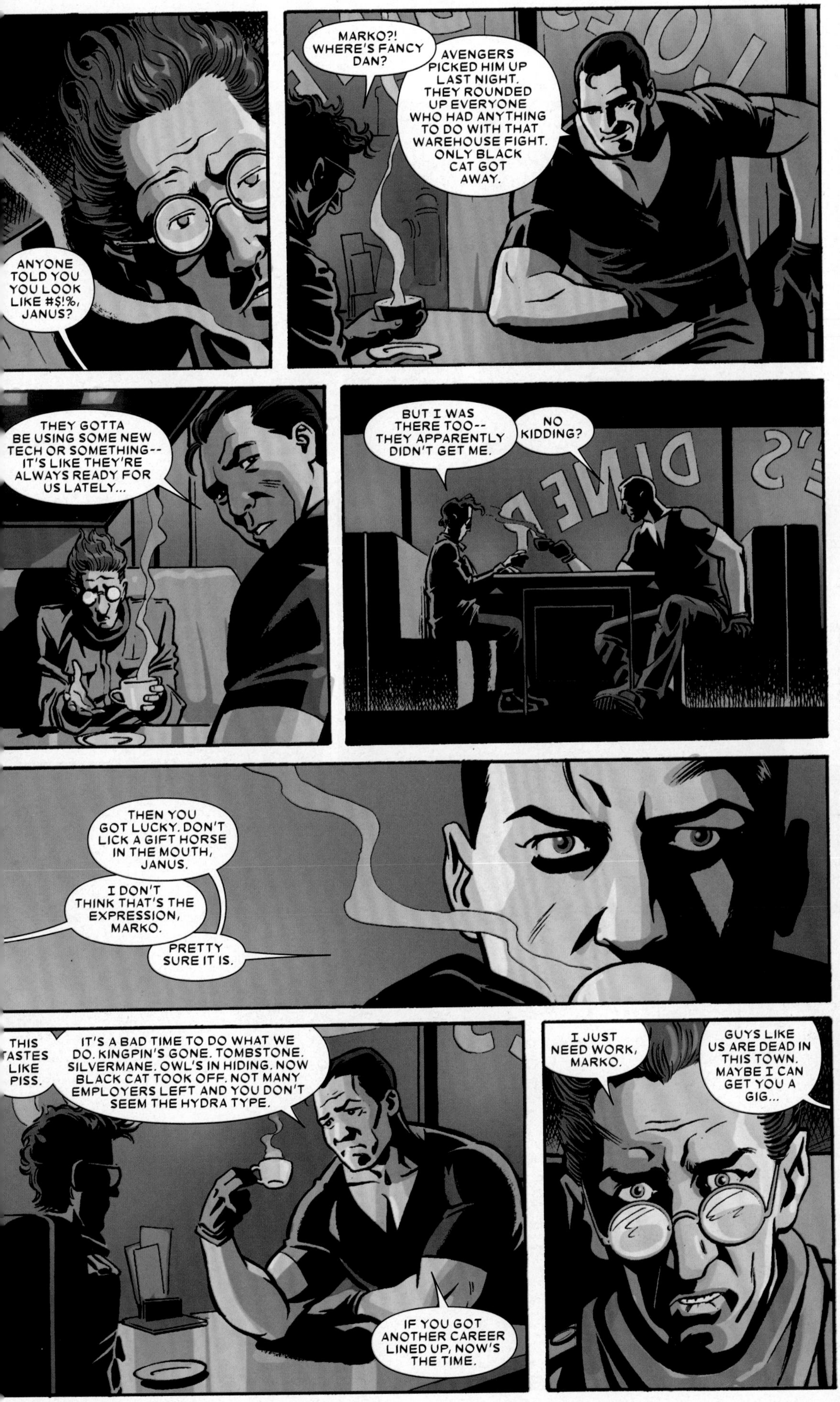
ANYONE TOLD YOU YOU LOOK LIKE #$!%, JANUS?
MARKO?! WHERE'S FANCY DAN?
AVENGERS PICKED HIM UP LAST NIGHT. THEY ROUNDED UP EVERYONE WHO HAD ANYTHING TO DO WITH THAT WAREHOUSE FIGHT. ONLY BLACK CAT GOT AWAY.
THEY GOTTA BE USING SOME NEW TECH OR SOMETHING-- IT'S LIKE THEY'RE ALWAYS READY FOR US LATELY...
BUT I WAS THERE TOO-- THEY APPARENTLY DIDN'T GET ME.
NO KIDDING?
THEN YOU GOT LUCKY. DON'T LICK A GIFT HORSE IN THE MOUTH, JANUS.
I DON'T THINK THAT'S THE EXPRESSION, MARKO.
PRETTY SURE IT IS.
THIS TASTES LIKE PISS.
IT'S A BAD TIME TO DO WHAT WE DO. KINGPIN'S GONE. TOMBSTONE. SILVERMANE. OWL'S IN HIDING. NOW BLACK CAT TOOK OFF. NOT MANY EMPLOYERS LEFT AND YOU DON'T SEEM THE HYDRA TYPE.
IF YOU GOT ANOTHER CAREER LINED UP, NOW'S THE TIME.
I JUST NEED WORK, MARKO.
GUYS LIKE US ARE DEAD IN THIS TOWN. MAYBE I CAN GET YOU A GIG...

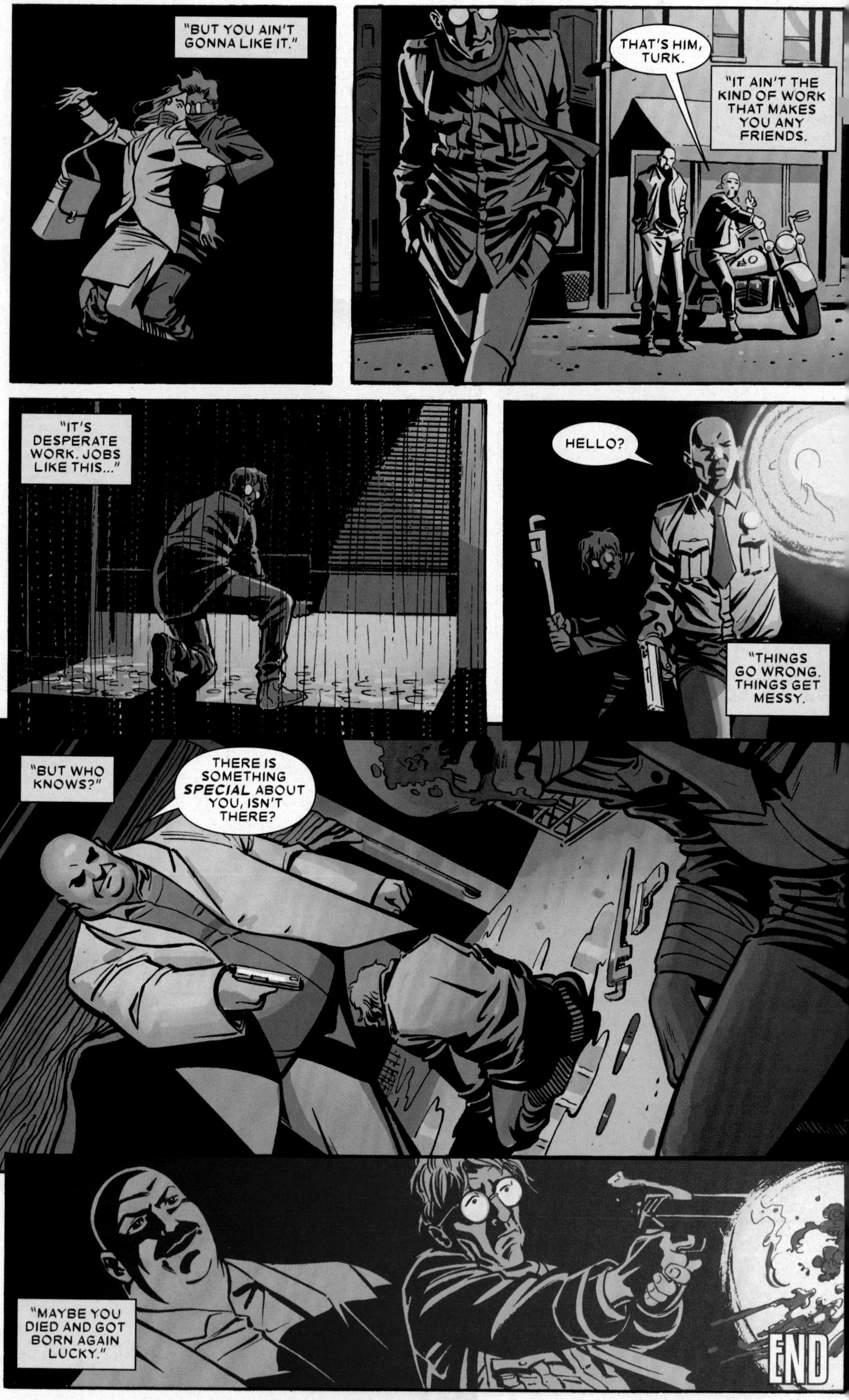
"BUT YOU AIN'T GONNA LIKE IT."
THAT'S HIM, TURK.
"IT AIN'T THE KIND OF WORK THAT MAKES YOU ANY FRIENDS.
"IT'S DESPERATE WORK. JOBS LIKE THIS..."
HELLO?
"THINGS GO WRONG. THINGS GET MESSY.
"BUT WHO KNOWS?"
THERE IS SOMETHING SPECIAL ABOUT YOU, ISN'T THERE?
"MAYBE YOU DIED AND GOT BORN AGAIN LUCKY."
END

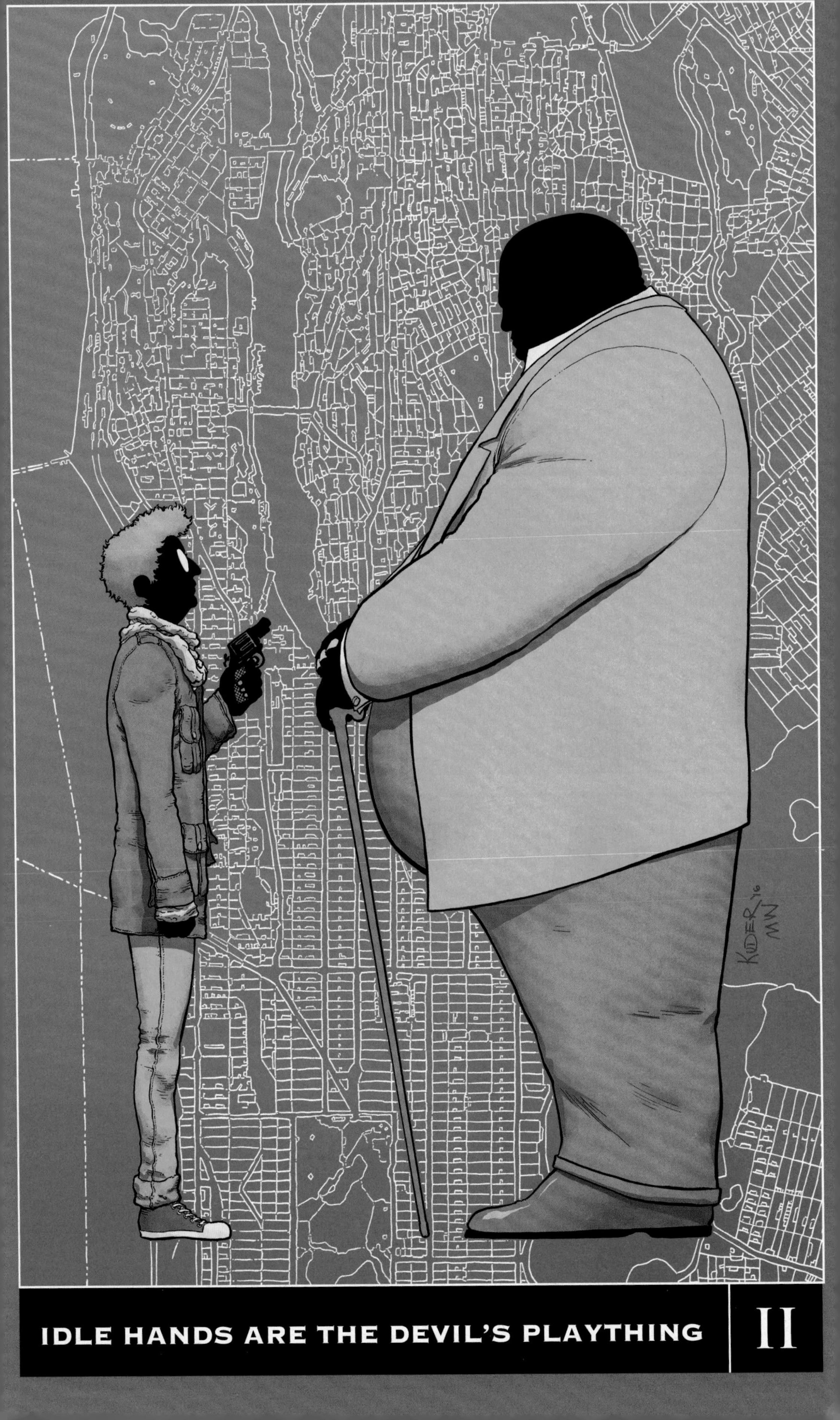

IDLE HANDS ARE THE DEVIL'S PLAYTHING | II

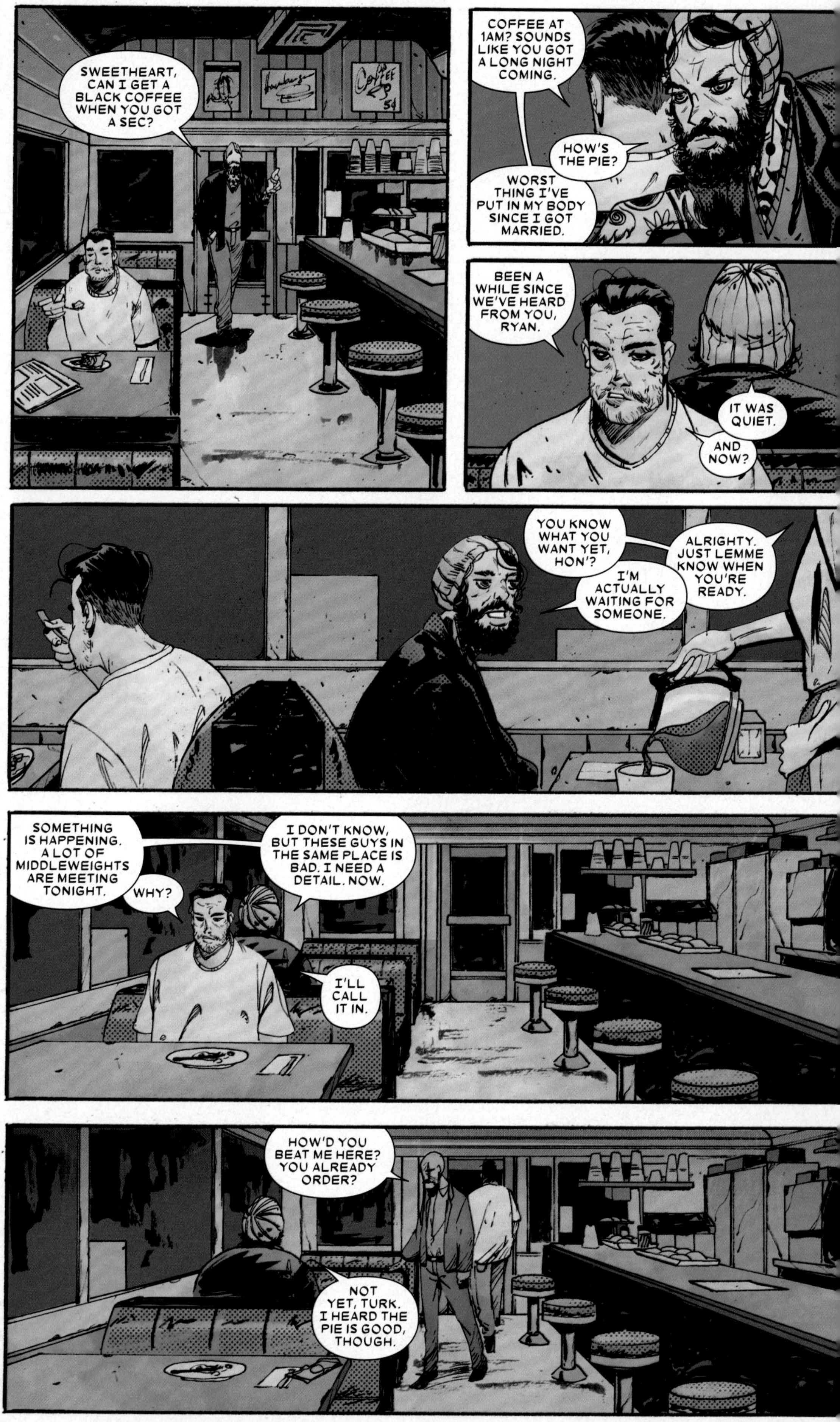
SWEETHEART, CAN I GET A BLACK COFFEE WHEN YOU GOT A SEC?
COFFEE AT 1AM? SOUNDS LIKE YOU GOT A LONG NIGHT COMING.
HOW'S THE PIE?
WORST THING I'VE PUT IN MY BODY SINCE I GOT MARRIED.
BEEN A WHILE SINCE WE'VE HEARD FROM YOU, RYAN.
IT WAS QUIET.
AND NOW?
YOU KNOW WHAT YOU WANT YET, HON'?
I'M ACTUALLY WAITING FOR SOMEONE.
ALRIGHTY. JUST LEMME KNOW WHEN YOU'RE READY.
SOMETHING IS HAPPENING. A LOT OF MIDDLEWEIGHTS ARE MEETING TONIGHT.
WHY?
I DON'T KNOW, BUT THESE GUYS IN THE SAME PLACE IS BAD. I NEED A DETAIL. NOW.
I'LL CALL IT IN.
HOW'D YOU BEAT ME HERE? YOU ALREADY ORDER?
NOT YET, TURK. I HEARD THE PIE IS GOOD, THOUGH.

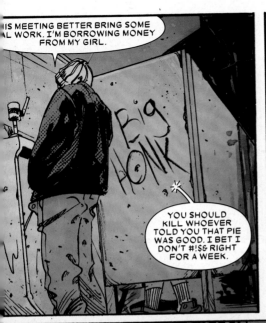

IS MEETING BETTER BRING SOME REAL WORK. I'M BORROWING MONEY FROM MY GIRL.

YOU SHOULD KILL WHOEVER TOLD YOU THAT PIE WAS GOOD. I BET I DON'T #!$& RIGHT FOR A WEEK.

SO WHAT IS IT?

WHAT?

THE WORK.

PICK PICK

YOU'LL SEE.

I DON'T LOVE SURPRISES, TURK.

WELL THEN, FRIENDO...

...YOU'RE IN FOR A LONG NIGHT.

AHH, MR. TURK. MR. GUDMUNSDOTTIR. GLAD YOU COULD FINALLY JOIN US.

THANK YOU ALL FOR COMING. I KNOW WORKING HAS PROVEN VERY DIFFICULT FOR YOU ALL RECENTLY. AND I'M SURE YOU'RE ALL AWARE THAT IT HAS BEEN...*LESS DIFFICULT* FOR ME.

IT'S NOTHING TO BE ASHAMED OF. THE SHOE COULD JUST AS EASILY BE ON THE OTHER FOOT. I COULD BE HERE LOOKING TO FOLLOW ONE OF YOU RIGHT NOW. BUT IT ISN'T. AND I'M NOT.

WITH THAT SAID, I'LL MAKE IT SIMPLE. IF YOU WANT TO WORK AGAIN, WANT TO AVOID THIS NEW SCRUTINY, THERE IS ONLY ONE OPTION: YOU WORK FOR ME.

HALF THE HOODS IN THE CITY HAVE BEEN LOCKED UP ALREADY. WHAT ARE YOU DOING THAT THEY AREN'T, FATMAN?

SONUVA--

NOW, NOW. EASY, GROTTO. I UNDERSTAND THIS IS AN UNCOMFORTABLE OFFER FOR YOU, TOMBSTONE. MANY OF US DON'T PLAY WELL TOGETHER.

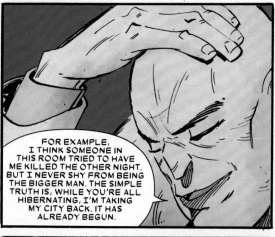

FOR EXAMPLE, I THINK SOMEONE IN THIS ROOM TRIED TO HAVE ME KILLED THE OTHER NIGHT. BUT I NEVER SHY FROM BEING THE BIGGER MAN. THE SIMPLE TRUTH IS, WHILE YOU'RE ALL HIBERNATING, I'M TAKING MY CITY BACK. IT HAS ALREADY BEGUN.

HOW ARE YOU AVOIDING THE CAPES?

THE "HOW" IS A TRICK I WON'T BE SHARING, CRIME MASTER. IT'S NOT YOUR CONCERN.

I THIN IT IS

I ONLY EXPLAIN MYSELF TO THE PEOPLE I TRUST. AND THAT IS A *VERY* SHORT LIST, AND YOU ARE *VERY* FAR FROM BEING ON IT.

BUT I AM HAPPY TO GIVE AN EXAMPLE OF *WHY* WORKING FOR ME WOULD BENEFIT YOU.

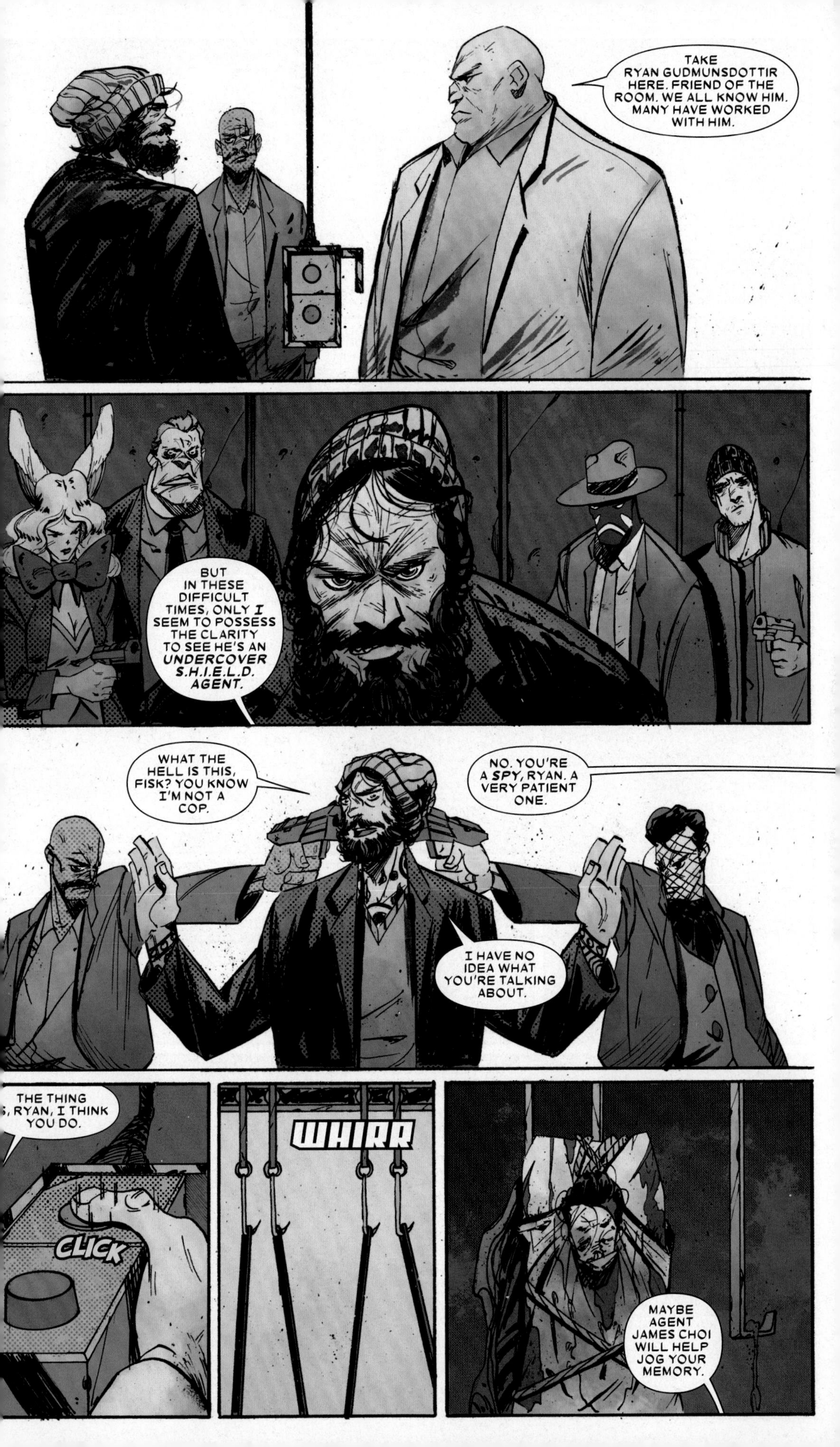
TAKE RYAN GUDMUNSDOTTIR HERE. FRIEND OF THE ROOM. WE ALL KNOW HIM. MANY HAVE WORKED WITH HIM.
BUT IN THESE DIFFICULT TIMES, ONLY *I* SEEM TO POSSESS THE CLARITY TO SEE HE'S AN ***UNDERCOVER S.H.I.E.L.D. AGENT.***
WHAT THE HELL IS THIS, FISK? YOU KNOW I'M NOT A COP.
NO. YOU'RE A ***SPY***, RYAN. A VERY PATIENT ONE.
I HAVE NO IDEA WHAT YOU'RE TALKING ABOUT.
THE THING IS, RYAN, I THINK YOU DO.
CLICK
WHIRR
MAYBE AGENT JAMES CHOI WILL HELP JOG YOUR MEMORY.

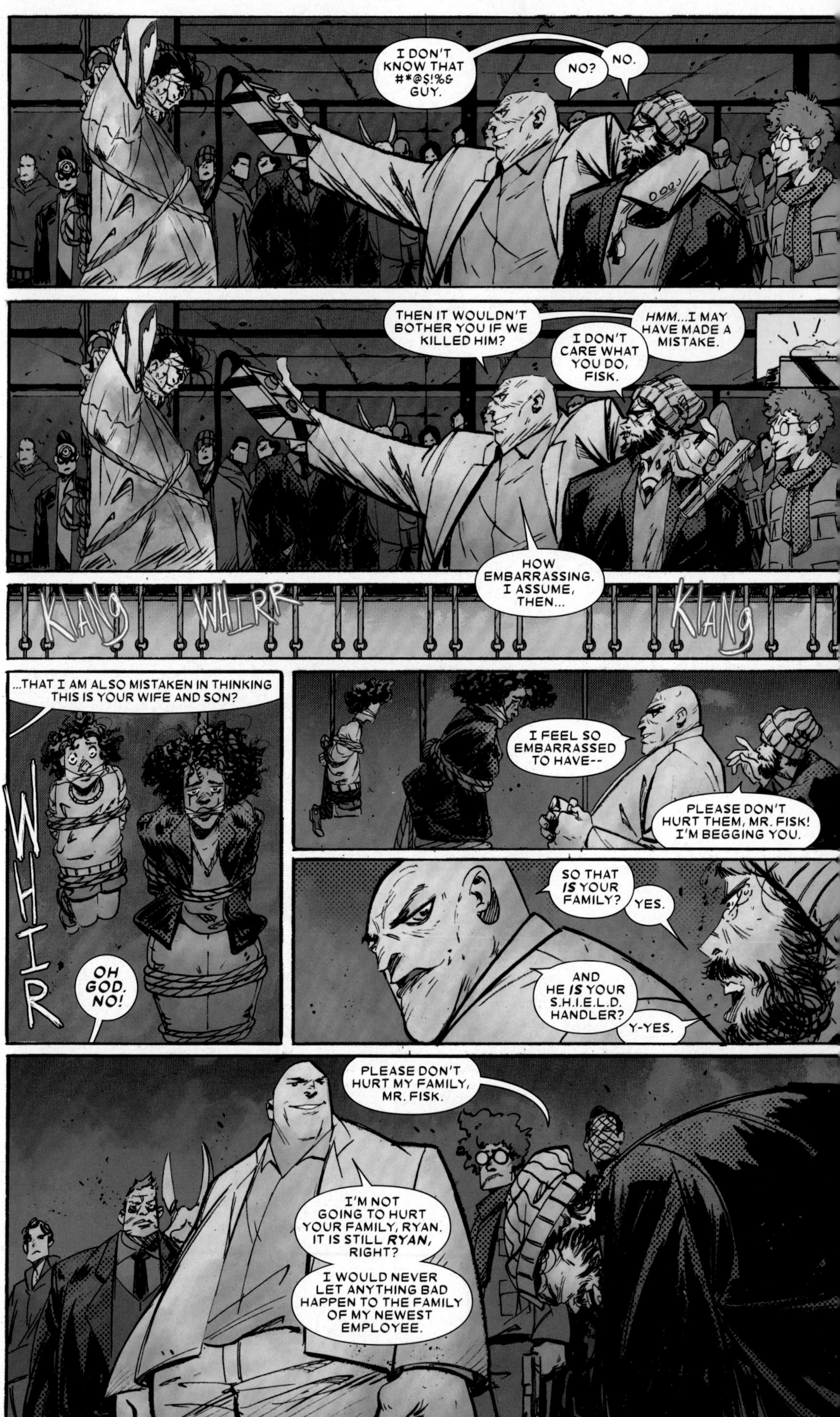
I DON'T KNOW THAT #*@$!%& GUY.
NO?
NO.
THEN IT WOULDN'T BOTHER YOU IF WE KILLED HIM?
I DON'T CARE WHAT YOU DO, FISK.
HMM...I MAY HAVE MADE A MISTAKE.
HOW EMBARRASSING. I ASSUME, THEN...
KLANG
WHIRR
KLANG
...THAT I AM ALSO MISTAKEN IN THINKING THIS IS YOUR WIFE AND SON?
WHIR
OH GOD. NO!
I FEEL SO EMBARRASSED TO HAVE--
PLEASE DON'T HURT THEM, MR. FISK! I'M BEGGING YOU.
SO THAT IS YOUR FAMILY?
YES.
AND HE IS YOUR S.H.I.E.L.D. HANDLER?
Y-YES.
PLEASE DON'T HURT MY FAMILY, MR. FISK.
I'M NOT GOING TO HURT YOUR FAMILY, RYAN. IT IS STILL RYAN, RIGHT?
I WOULD NEVER LET ANYTHING BAD HAPPEN TO THE FAMILY OF MY NEWEST EMPLOYEE.

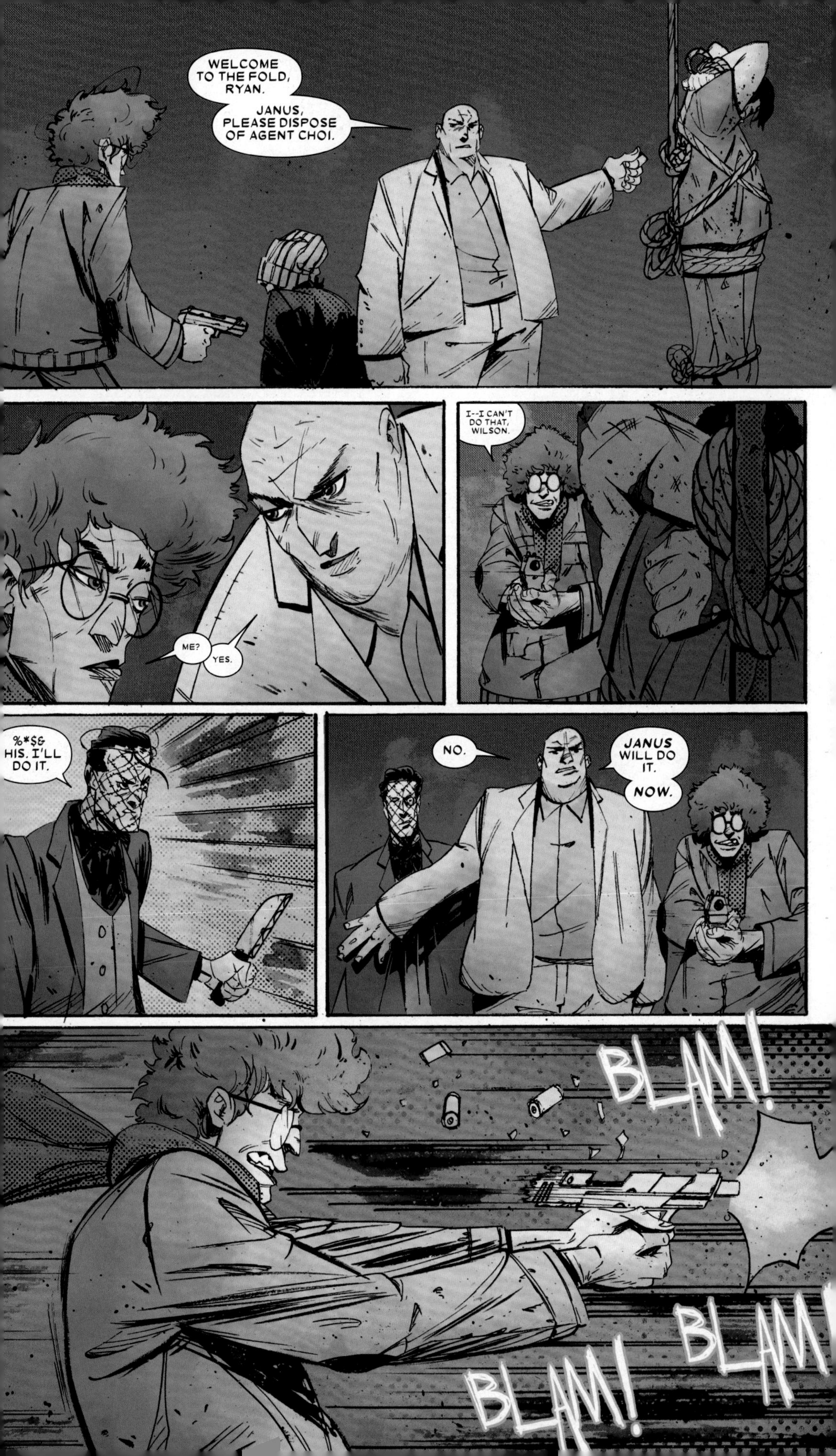
WELCOME TO THE FOLD, RYAN.
JANUS, PLEASE DISPOSE OF AGENT CHOI.
ME?
YES.
I--I CAN'T DO THAT, WILSON.
%*$& HIS. I'LL DO IT.
NO.
JANUS WILL DO IT.
NOW.
BLAM!
BLAM!
BLAM!

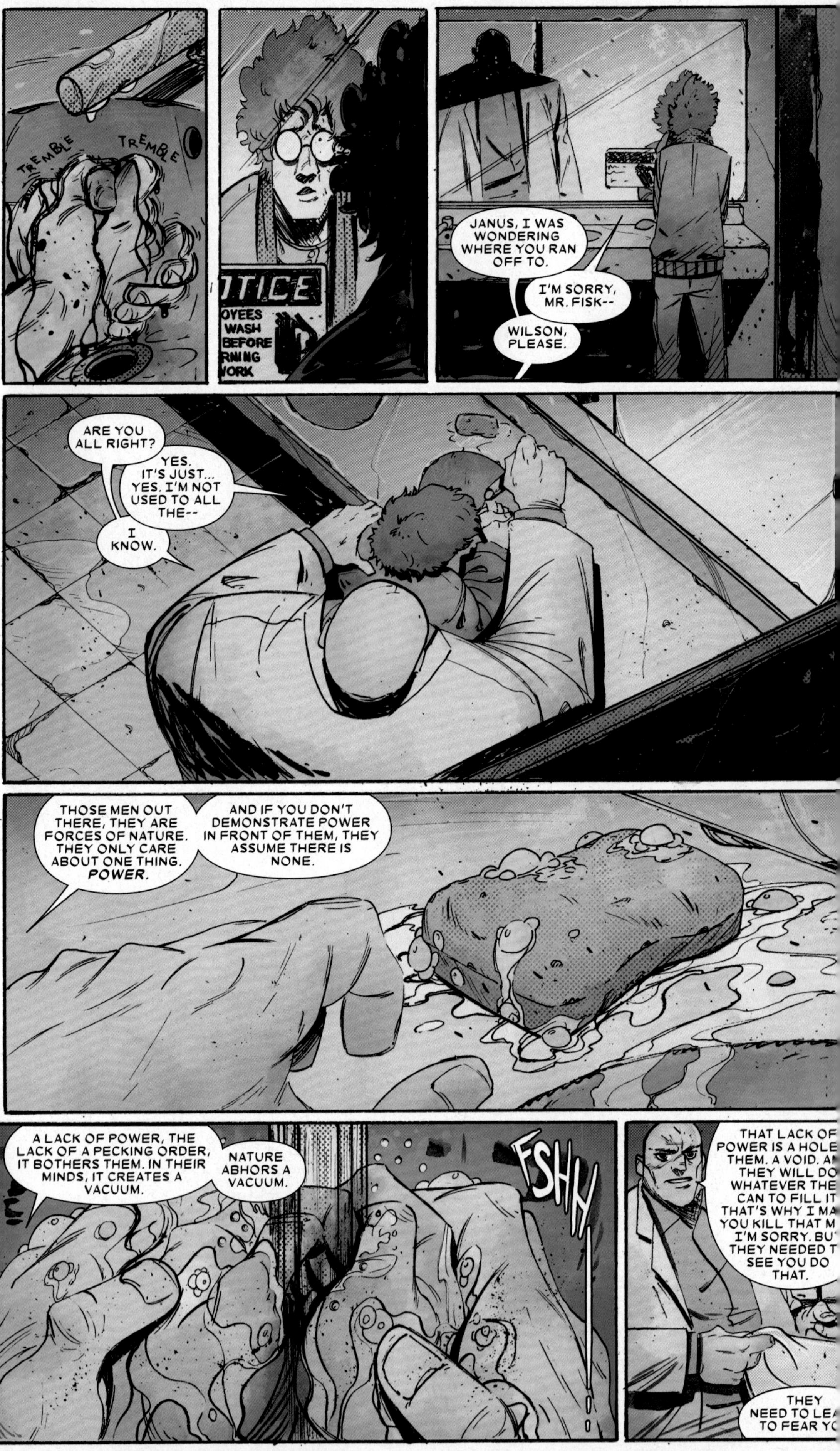
TREMBLE
TREMBLE
JANUS, I WAS WONDERING WHERE YOU RAN OFF TO.
I'M SORRY, MR. FISK--
WILSON, PLEASE.
ARE YOU ALL RIGHT?
YES. IT'S JUST... YES. I'M NOT USED TO ALL THE--
I KNOW.
THOSE MEN OUT THERE, THEY ARE FORCES OF NATURE. THEY ONLY CARE ABOUT ONE THING. POWER.
AND IF YOU DON'T DEMONSTRATE POWER IN FRONT OF THEM, THEY ASSUME THERE IS NONE.
A LACK OF POWER, THE LACK OF A PECKING ORDER, IT BOTHERS THEM. IN THEIR MINDS, IT CREATES A VACUUM.
NATURE ABHORS A VACUUM.
FSHHH
THAT LACK OF POWER IS A HOLE THEM. A VOID. A THEY WILL DO WHATEVER THE CAN TO FILL IT THAT'S WHY I MA YOU KILL THAT M I'M SORRY. BU THEY NEEDED T SEE YOU DO THAT.
THEY NEED TO LEA TO FEAR Y

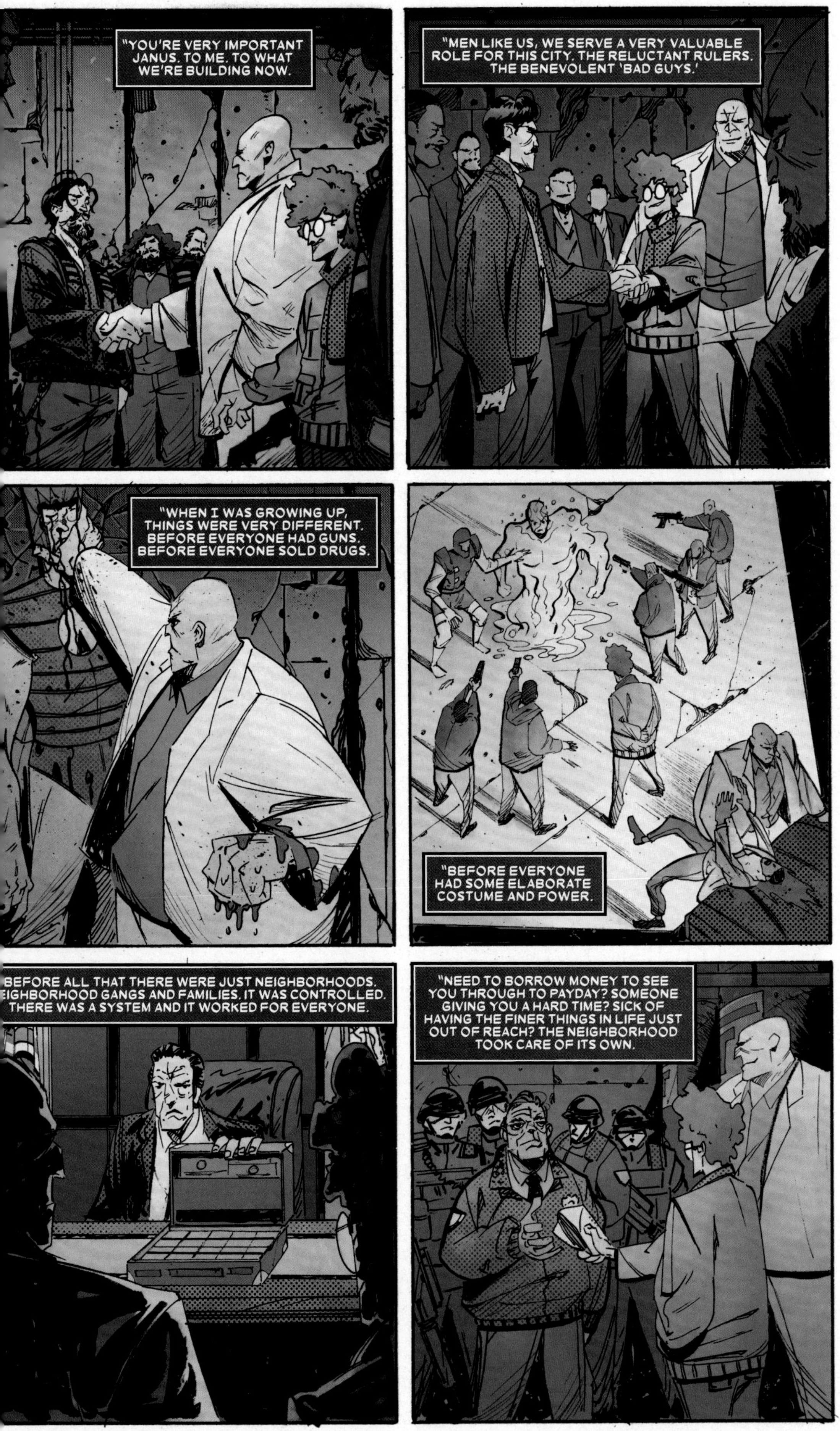
"YOU'RE VERY IMPORTANT JANUS. TO ME. TO WHAT WE'RE BUILDING NOW.
"MEN LIKE US, WE SERVE A VERY VALUABLE ROLE FOR THIS CITY. THE RELUCTANT RULERS. THE BENEVOLENT 'BAD GUYS.'
"WHEN I WAS GROWING UP, THINGS WERE VERY DIFFERENT. BEFORE EVERYONE HAD GUNS. BEFORE EVERYONE SOLD DRUGS.
"BEFORE EVERYONE HAD SOME ELABORATE COSTUME AND POWER.
BEFORE ALL THAT THERE WERE JUST NEIGHBORHOODS. EIGHBORHOOD GANGS AND FAMILIES. IT WAS CONTROLLED. THERE WAS A SYSTEM AND IT WORKED FOR EVERYONE.
"NEED TO BORROW MONEY TO SEE YOU THROUGH TO PAYDAY? SOMEONE GIVING YOU A HARD TIME? SICK OF HAVING THE FINER THINGS IN LIFE JUST OUT OF REACH? THE NEIGHBORHOOD TOOK CARE OF ITS OWN.

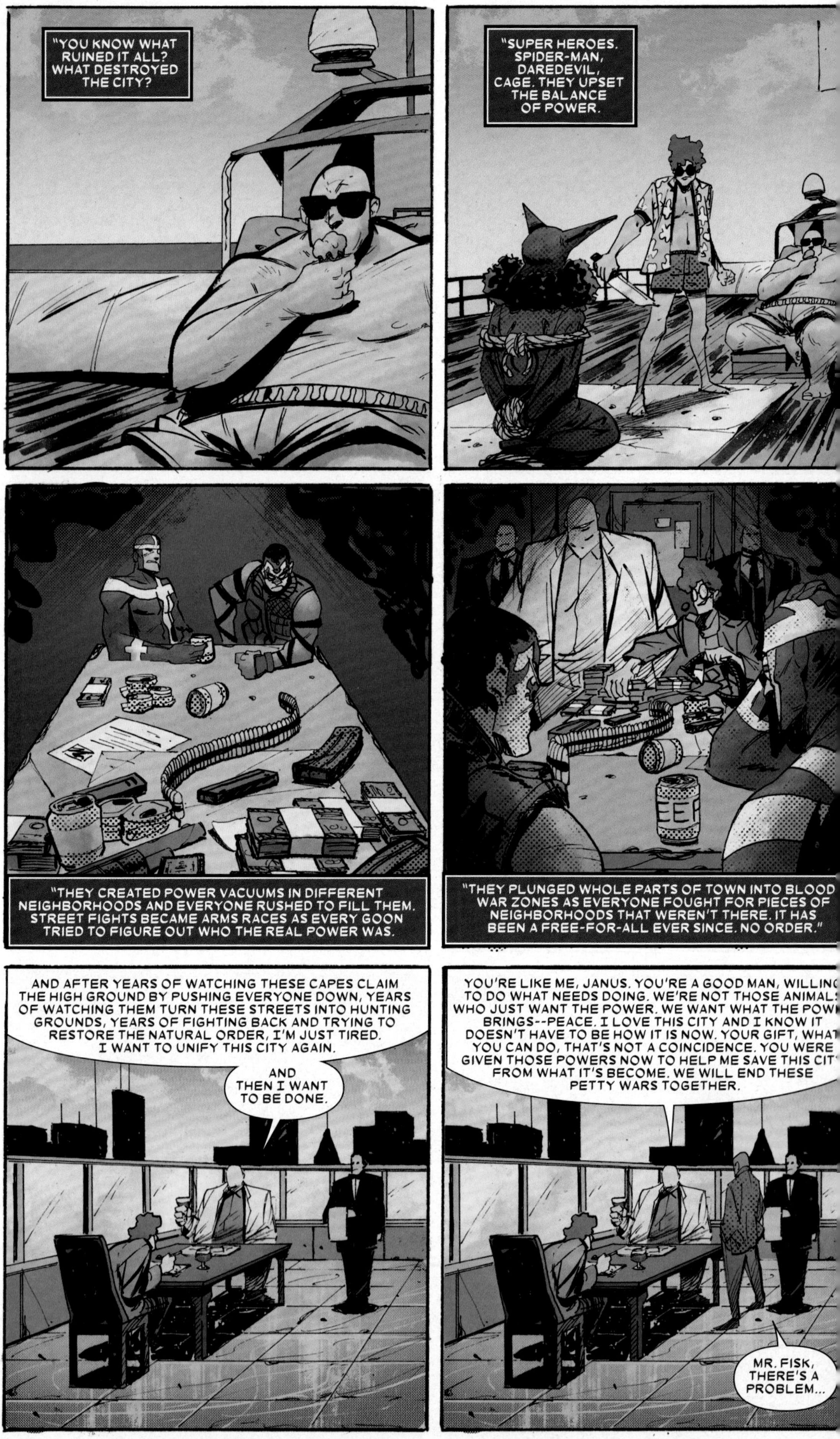
"YOU KNOW WHAT RUINED IT ALL? WHAT DESTROYED THE CITY?
"SUPER HEROES. SPIDER-MAN, DAREDEVIL, CAGE. THEY UPSET THE BALANCE OF POWER.
"THEY CREATED POWER VACUUMS IN DIFFERENT NEIGHBORHOODS AND EVERYONE RUSHED TO FILL THEM. STREET FIGHTS BECAME ARMS RACES AS EVERY GOON TRIED TO FIGURE OUT WHO THE REAL POWER WAS.
"THEY PLUNGED WHOLE PARTS OF TOWN INTO BLOOD WAR ZONES AS EVERYONE FOUGHT FOR PIECES OF NEIGHBORHOODS THAT WEREN'T THERE. IT HAS BEEN A FREE-FOR-ALL EVER SINCE. NO ORDER."
AND AFTER YEARS OF WATCHING THESE CAPES CLAIM THE HIGH GROUND BY PUSHING EVERYONE DOWN, YEARS OF WATCHING THEM TURN THESE STREETS INTO HUNTING GROUNDS, YEARS OF FIGHTING BACK AND TRYING TO RESTORE THE NATURAL ORDER, I'M JUST TIRED. I WANT TO UNIFY THIS CITY AGAIN.
AND THEN I WANT TO BE DONE.
YOU'RE LIKE ME, JANUS. YOU'RE A GOOD MAN, WILLIN TO DO WHAT NEEDS DOING. WE'RE NOT THOSE ANIMAL WHO JUST WANT THE POWER. WE WANT WHAT THE POW BRINGS--PEACE. I LOVE THIS CITY AND I KNOW IT DOESN'T HAVE TO BE HOW IT IS NOW. YOUR GIFT, WHAT YOU CAN DO, THAT'S NOT A COINCIDENCE. YOU WERE GIVEN THOSE POWERS NOW TO HELP ME SAVE THIS CIT FROM WHAT IT'S BECOME. WE WILL END THESE PETTY WARS TOGETHER.
MR. FISK, THERE'S A PROBLEM...

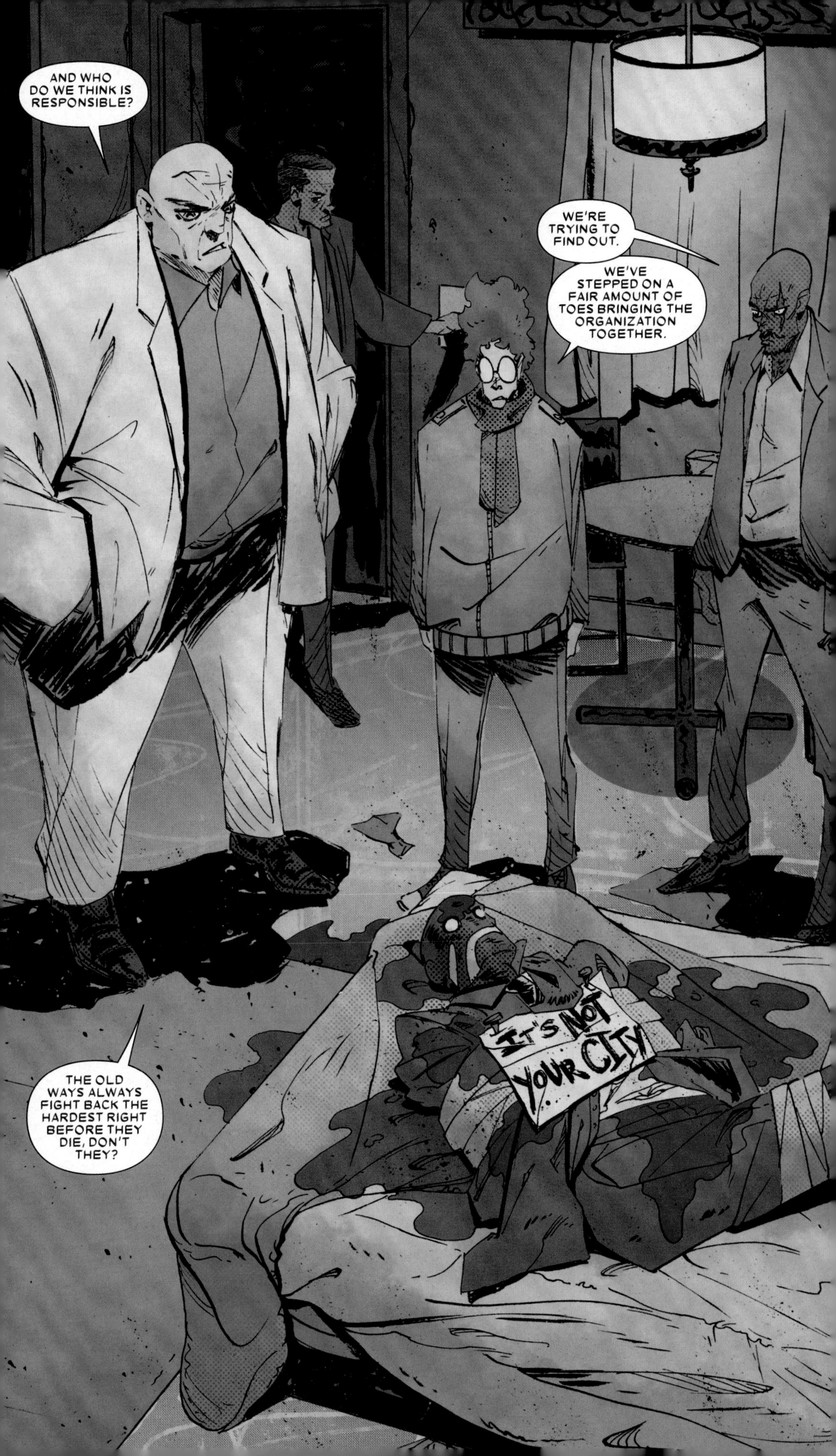
AND WHO DO WE THINK IS RESPONSIBLE?
WE'RE TRYING TO FIND OUT.
WE'VE STEPPED ON A FAIR AMOUNT OF TOES BRINGING THE ORGANIZATION TOGETHER.
IT'S NOT YOUR CITY
THE OLD WAYS ALWAYS FIGHT BACK THE HARDEST RIGHT BEFORE THEY DIE, DON'T THEY?

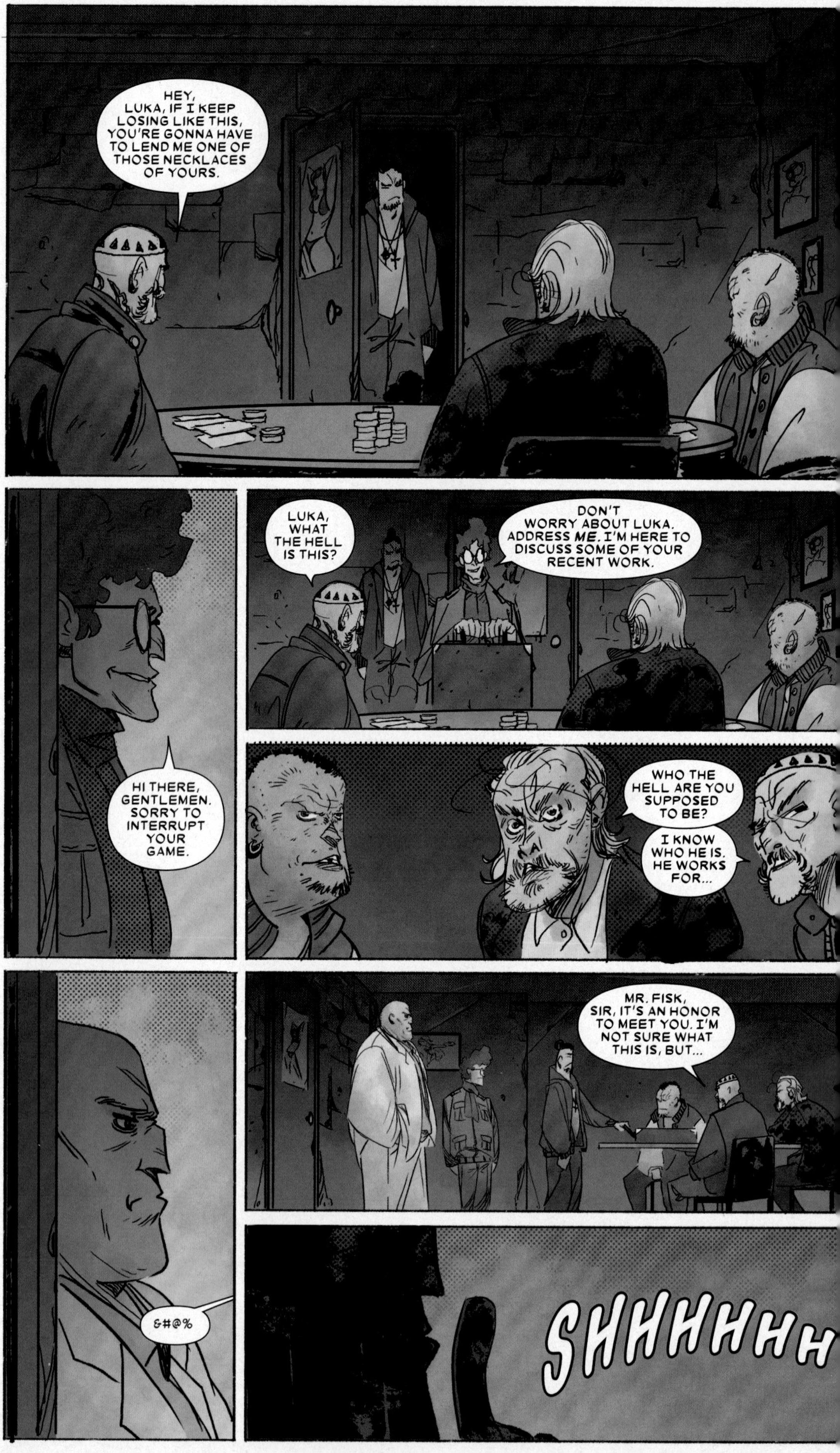
HEY, LUKA, IF I KEEP LOSING LIKE THIS, YOU'RE GONNA HAVE TO LEND ME ONE OF THOSE NECKLACES OF YOURS.
HI THERE, GENTLEMEN. SORRY TO INTERRUPT YOUR GAME.
LUKA, WHAT THE HELL IS THIS?
DON'T WORRY ABOUT LUKA. ADDRESS ME. I'M HERE TO DISCUSS SOME OF YOUR RECENT WORK.
WHO THE HELL ARE YOU SUPPOSED TO BE?
I KNOW WHO HE IS. HE WORKS FOR...
&#@%
MR. FISK, SIR, IT'S AN HONOR TO MEET YOU. I'M NOT SURE WHAT THIS IS, BUT...
SHHHHHH

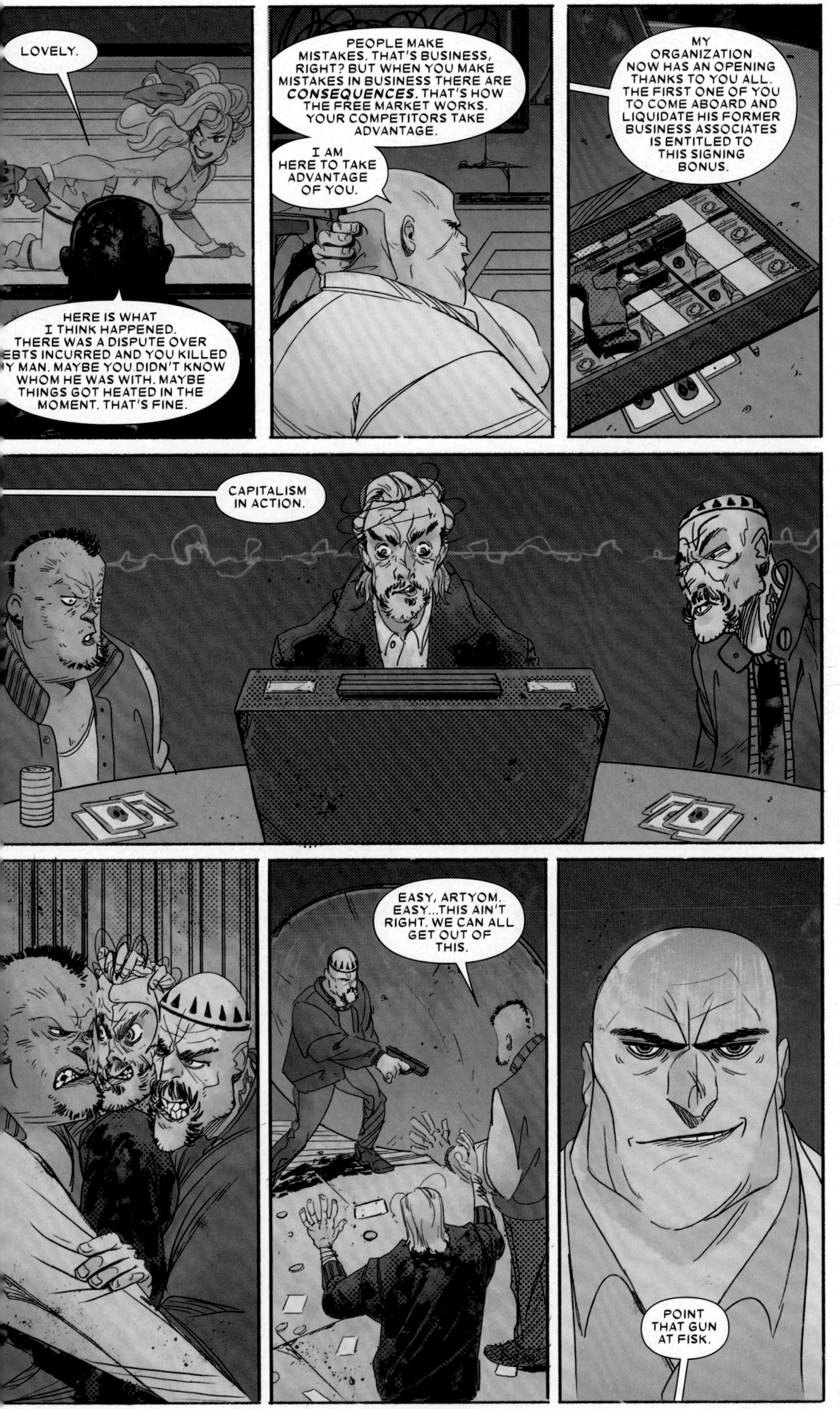

LOVELY.
HERE IS WHAT I THINK HAPPENED. THERE WAS A DISPUTE OVER EBTS INCURRED AND YOU KILLED Y MAN. MAYBE YOU DIDN'T KNOW WHOM HE WAS WITH. MAYBE THINGS GOT HEATED IN THE MOMENT. THAT'S FINE.
PEOPLE MAKE MISTAKES. THAT'S BUSINESS, RIGHT? BUT WHEN YOU MAKE MISTAKES IN BUSINESS THERE ARE CONSEQUENCES. THAT'S HOW THE FREE MARKET WORKS. YOUR COMPETITORS TAKE ADVANTAGE.
I AM HERE TO TAKE ADVANTAGE OF YOU.
MY ORGANIZATION NOW HAS AN OPENING THANKS TO YOU ALL. THE FIRST ONE OF YOU TO COME ABOARD AND LIQUIDATE HIS FORMER BUSINESS ASSOCIATES IS ENTITLED TO THIS SIGNING BONUS.
CAPITALISM IN ACTION.
EASY, ARTYOM. EASY...THIS AIN'T RIGHT. WE CAN ALL GET OUT OF THIS.
POINT THAT GUN AT FISK.

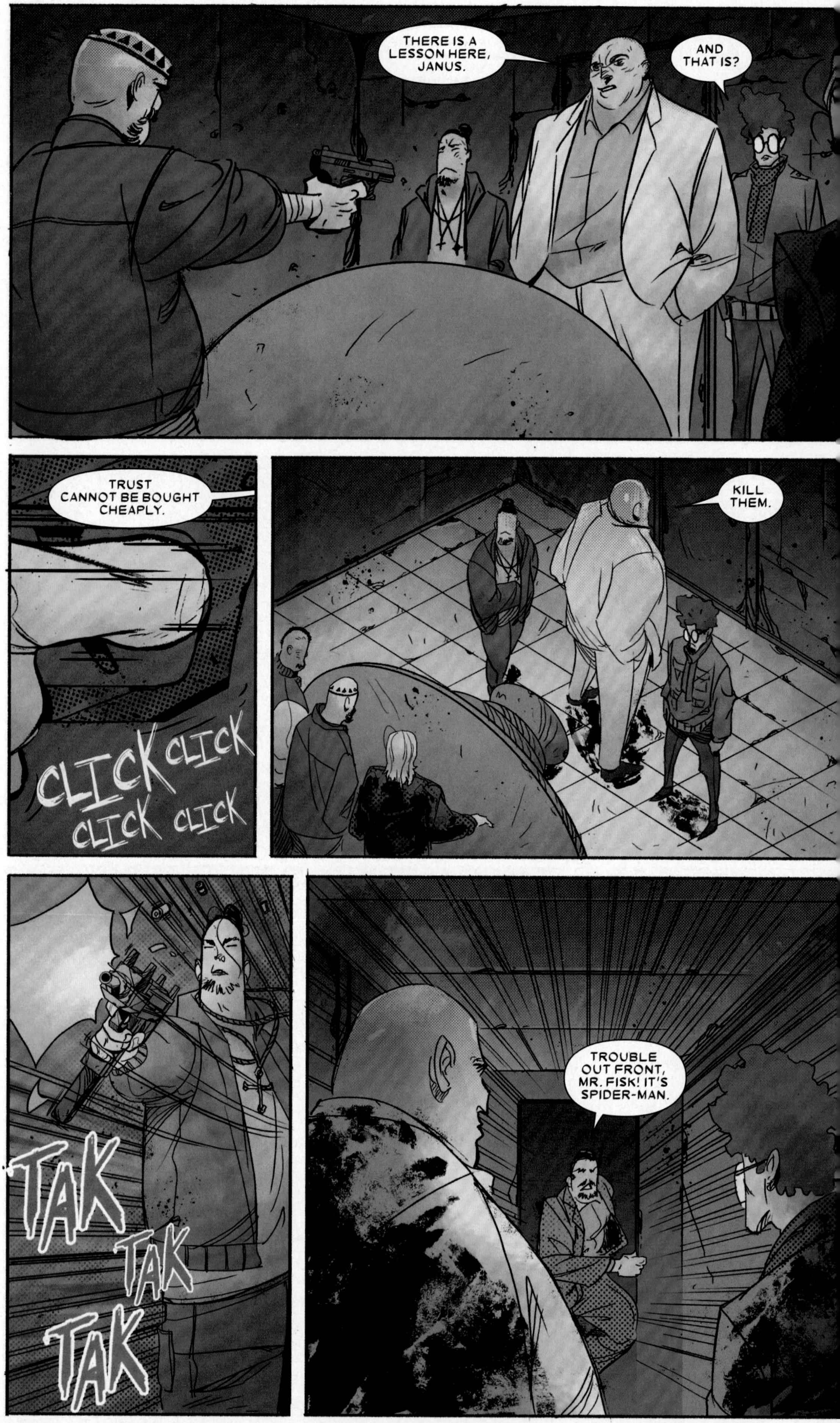
THERE IS A LESSON HERE, JANUS.
AND THAT IS?
TRUST CANNOT BE BOUGHT CHEAPLY.
CLICK CLICK CLICK CLICK
KILL THEM.
TAK TAK TAK
TROUBLE OUT FRONT, MR. FISK! IT'S SPIDER-MAN.

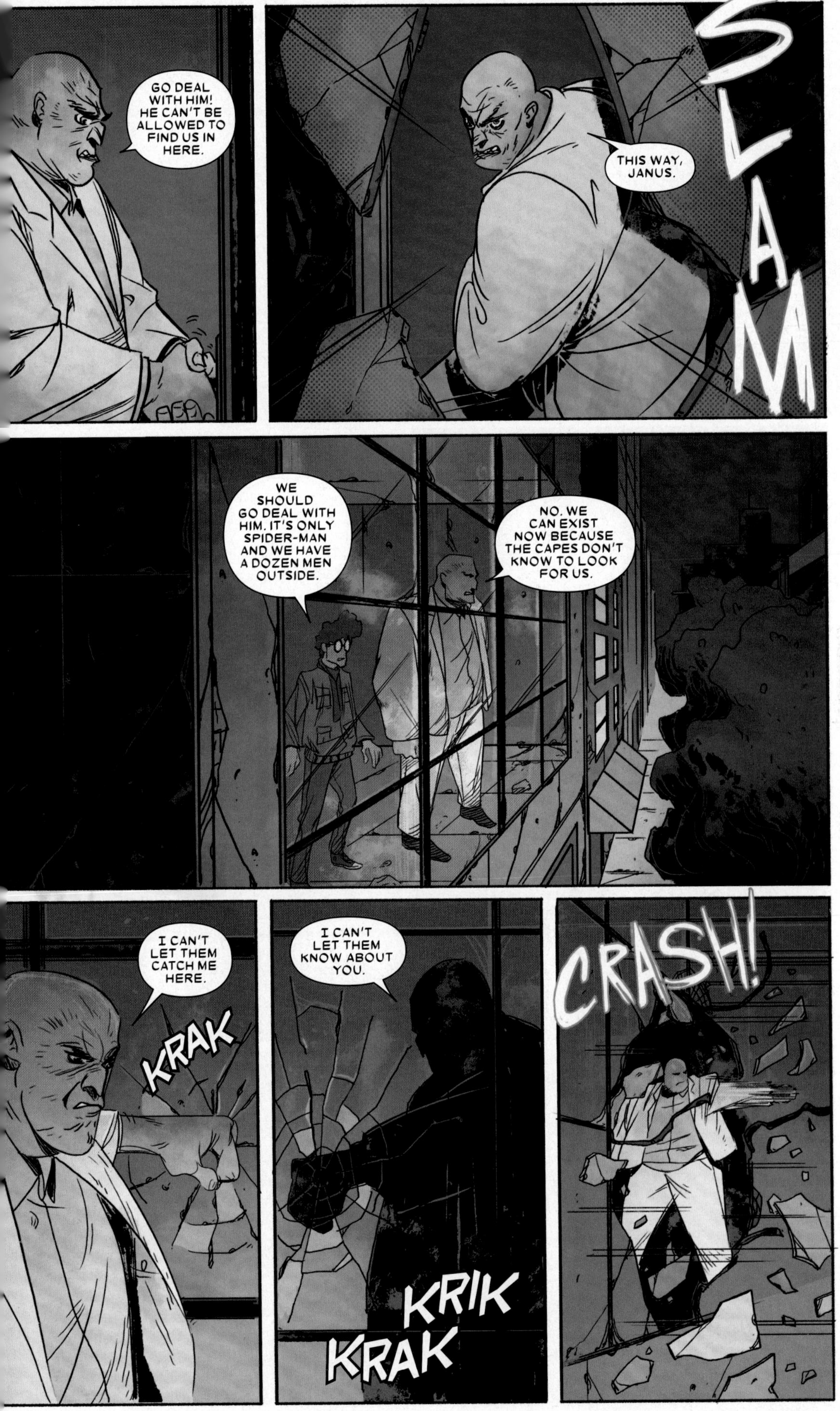
GO DEAL WITH HIM! HE CAN'T BE ALLOWED TO FIND US IN HERE.
THIS WAY, JANUS.
SLAM
WE SHOULD GO DEAL WITH HIM. IT'S ONLY SPIDER-MAN AND WE HAVE A DOZEN MEN OUTSIDE.
NO. WE CAN EXIST NOW BECAUSE THE CAPES DON'T KNOW TO LOOK FOR US.
I CAN'T LET THEM CATCH ME HERE.
KRAK
I CAN'T LET THEM KNOW ABOUT YOU.
KRIK
KRAK
CRASH!

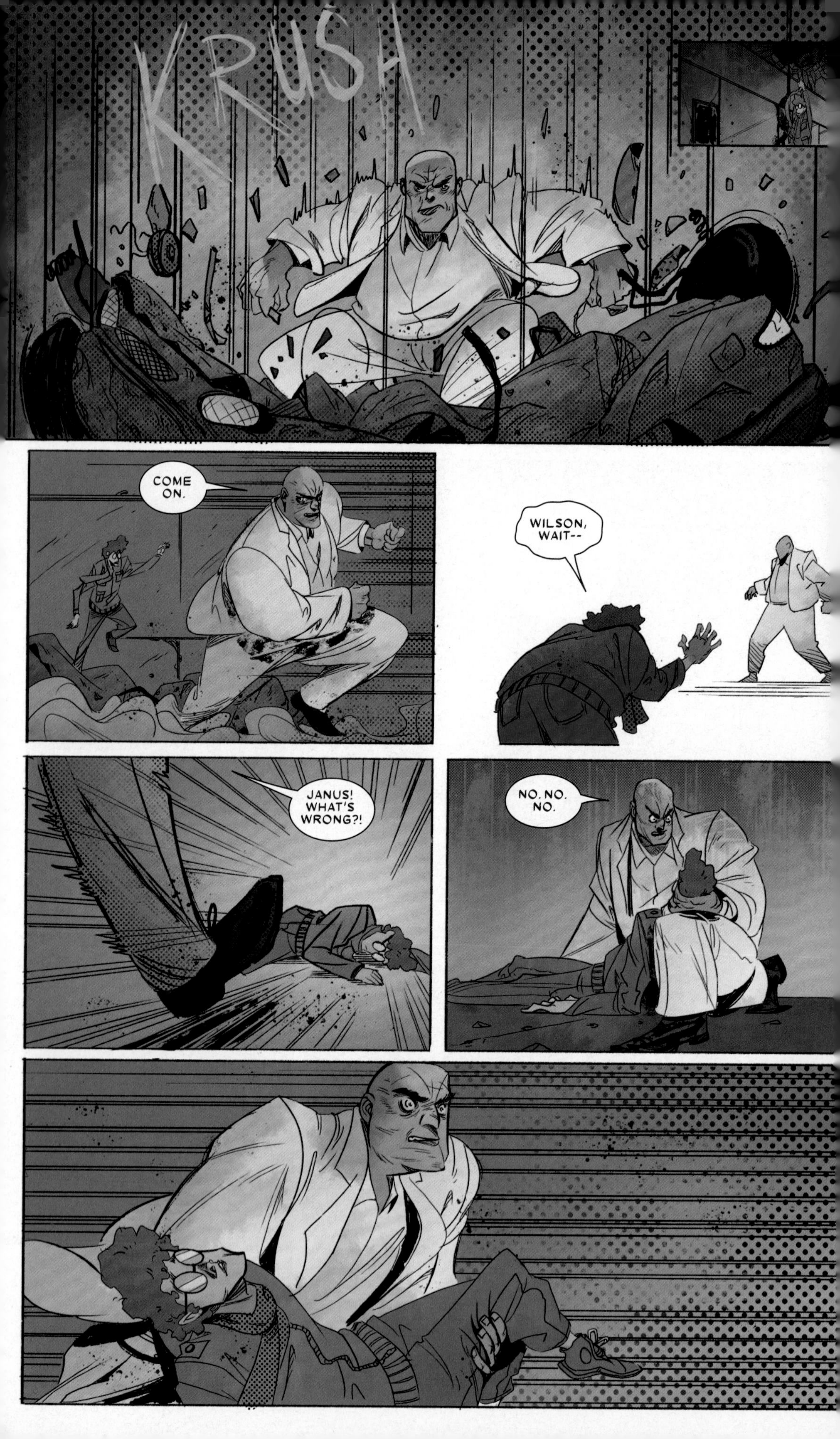
KRUSH
COME ON.
WILSON, WAIT--
JANUS! WHAT'S WRONG?!
NO. NO. NO.

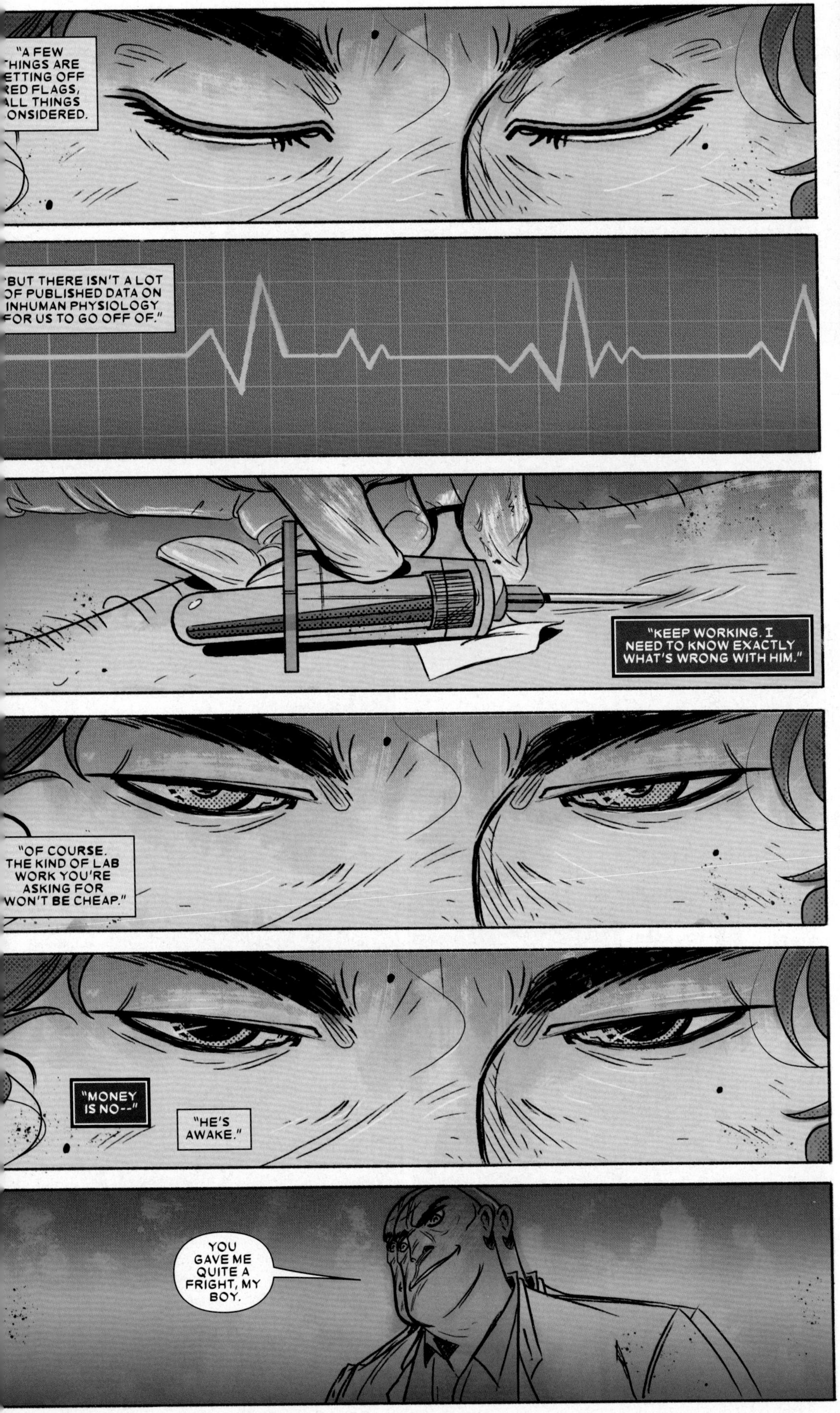
"A FEW
THINGS ARE
ETTING OFF
RED FLAGS,
ALL THINGS
ONSIDERED.
"BUT THERE ISN'T A LOT
OF PUBLISHED DATA ON
INHUMAN PHYSIOLOGY
FOR US TO GO OFF OF."
"KEEP WORKING. I NEED TO KNOW EXACTLY WHAT'S WRONG WITH HIM."
"OF COURSE. THE KIND OF LAB WORK YOU'RE ASKING FOR
WON'T BE CHEAP."
"MONEY IS NO--"
"HE'S AWAKE."
YOU GAVE ME QUITE A FRIGHT, MY BOY.

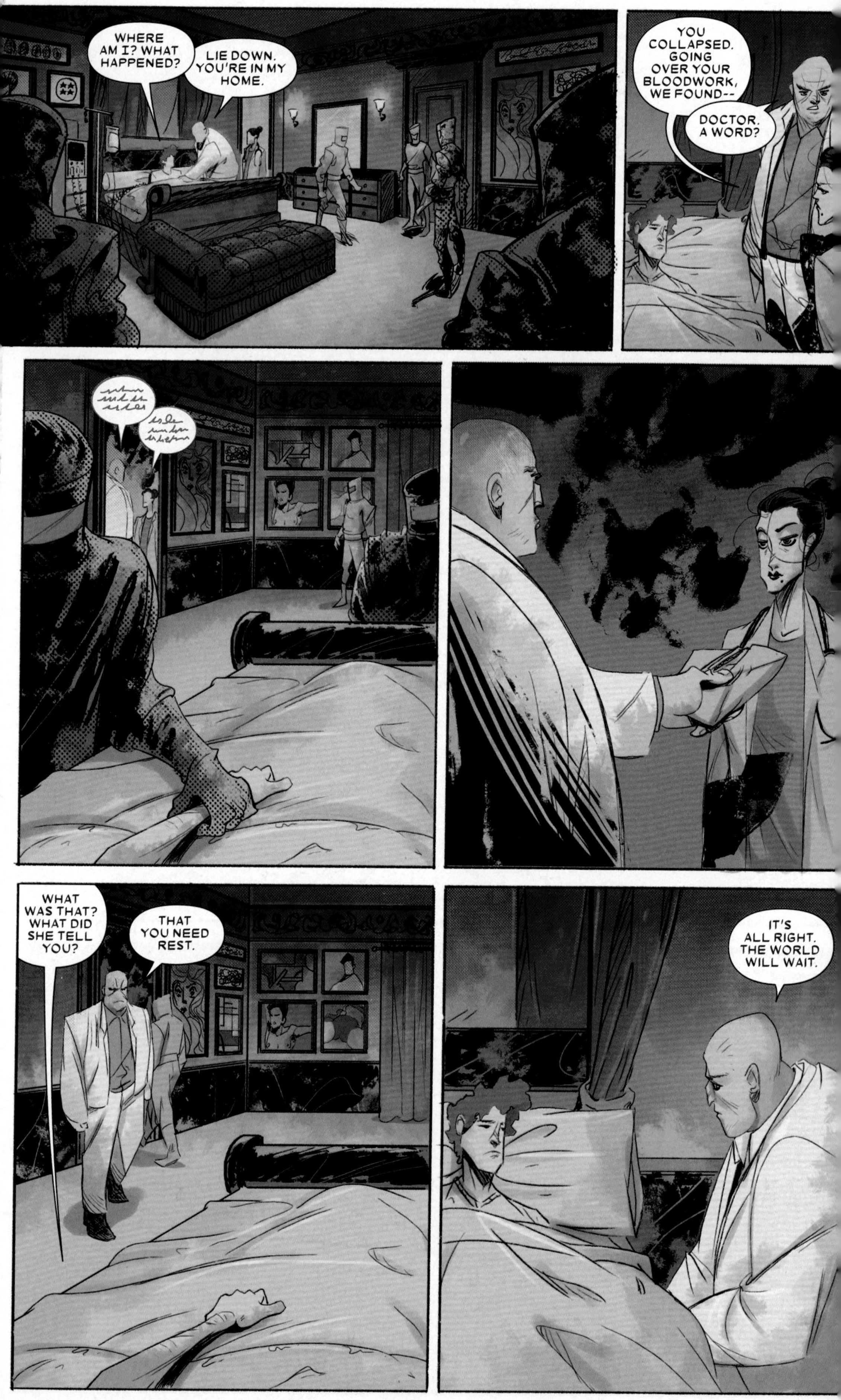
WHERE AM I? WHAT HAPPENED?
LIE DOWN. YOU'RE IN MY HOME.
YOU COLLAPSED. GOING OVER YOUR BLOODWORK, WE FOUND--
DOCTOR. A WORD?
WHAT WAS THAT? WHAT DID SHE TELL YOU?
THAT YOU NEED REST.
IT'S ALL RIGHT. THE WORLD WILL WAIT.

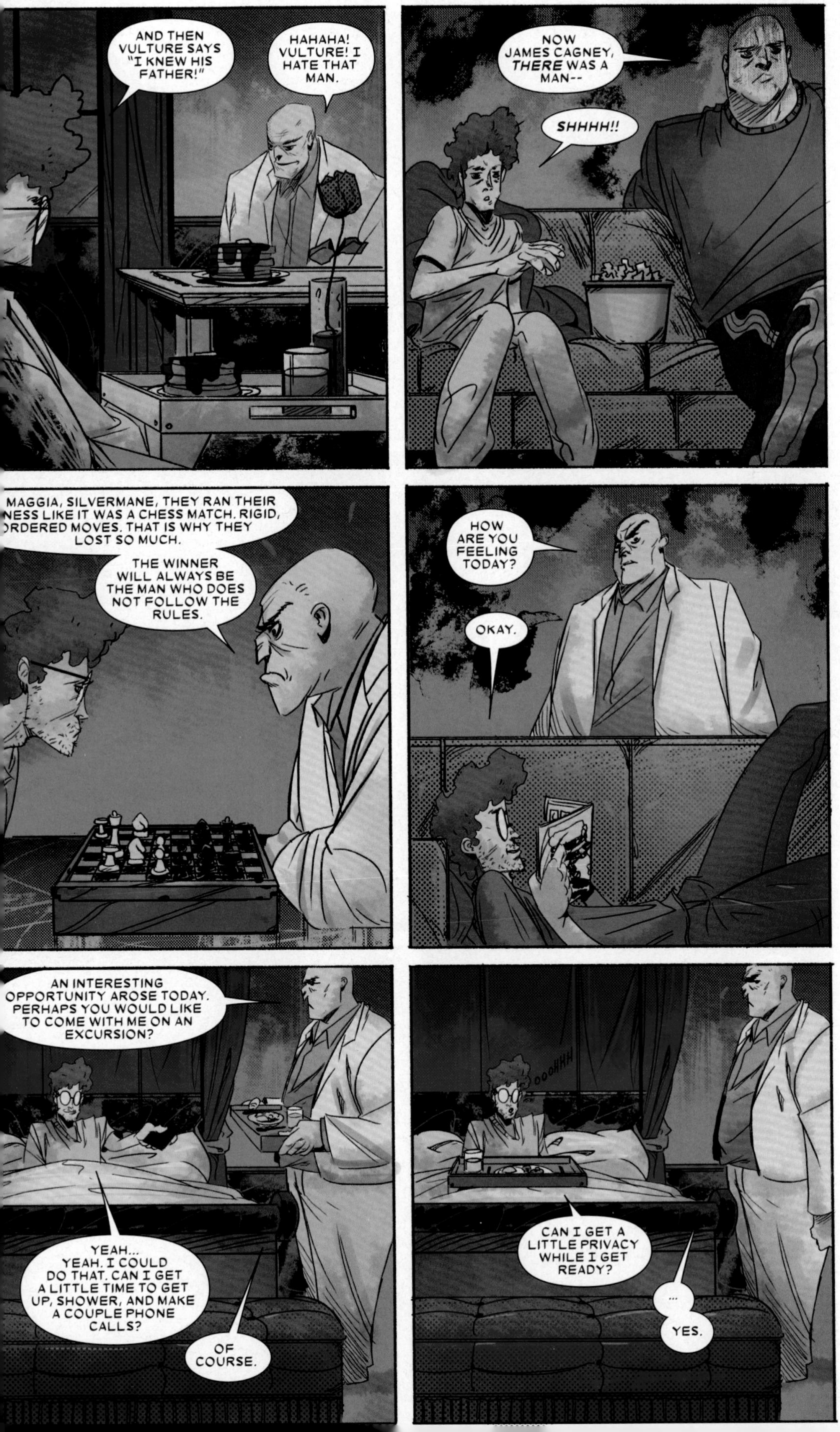
AND THEN VULTURE SAYS "I KNEW HIS FATHER!"
HAHAHA! VULTURE! I HATE THAT MAN.
NOW JAMES CAGNEY, THERE WAS A MAN--
SHHHH!!
MAGGIA, SILVERMANE, THEY RAN THEIR NESS LIKE IT WAS A CHESS MATCH. RIGID, ORDERED MOVES. THAT IS WHY THEY LOST SO MUCH.
THE WINNER WILL ALWAYS BE THE MAN WHO DOES NOT FOLLOW THE RULES.
HOW ARE YOU FEELING TODAY?
OKAY.
AN INTERESTING OPPORTUNITY AROSE TODAY. PERHAPS YOU WOULD LIKE TO COME WITH ME ON AN EXCURSION?
YEAH... YEAH. I COULD DO THAT. CAN I GET A LITTLE TIME TO GET UP, SHOWER, AND MAKE A COUPLE PHONE CALLS?
OF COURSE.
CAN I GET A LITTLE PRIVACY WHILE I GET READY?
...
YES.

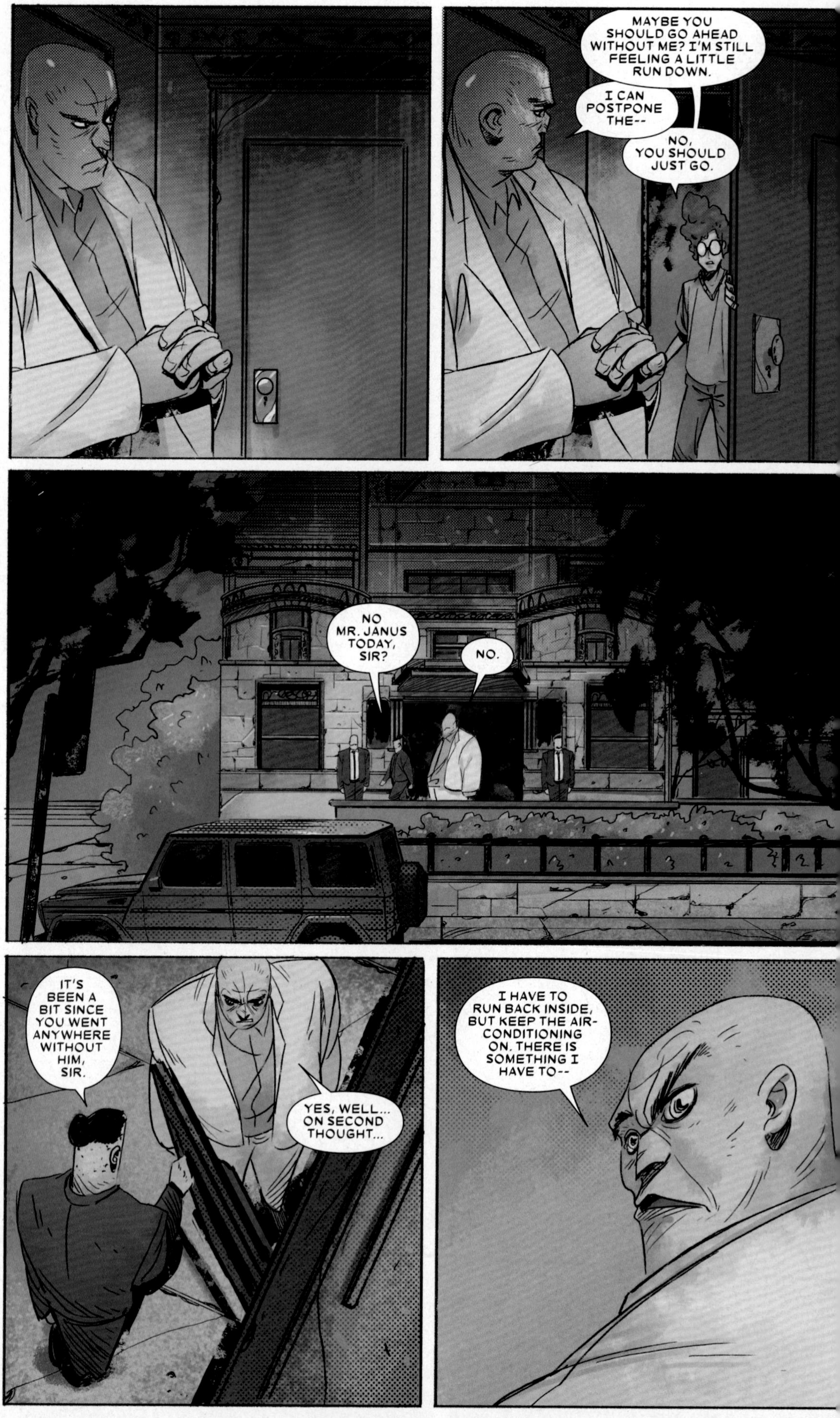
MAYBE YOU SHOULD GO AHEAD WITHOUT ME? I'M STILL FEELING A LITTLE RUN DOWN.
I CAN POSTPONE THE--
NO, YOU SHOULD JUST GO.
NO MR. JANUS TODAY, SIR?
NO.
IT'S BEEN A BIT SINCE YOU WENT ANYWHERE WITHOUT HIM, SIR.
YES, WELL... ON SECOND THOUGHT...
I HAVE TO RUN BACK INSIDE, BUT KEEP THE AIR-CONDITIONING ON. THERE IS SOMETHING I HAVE TO--

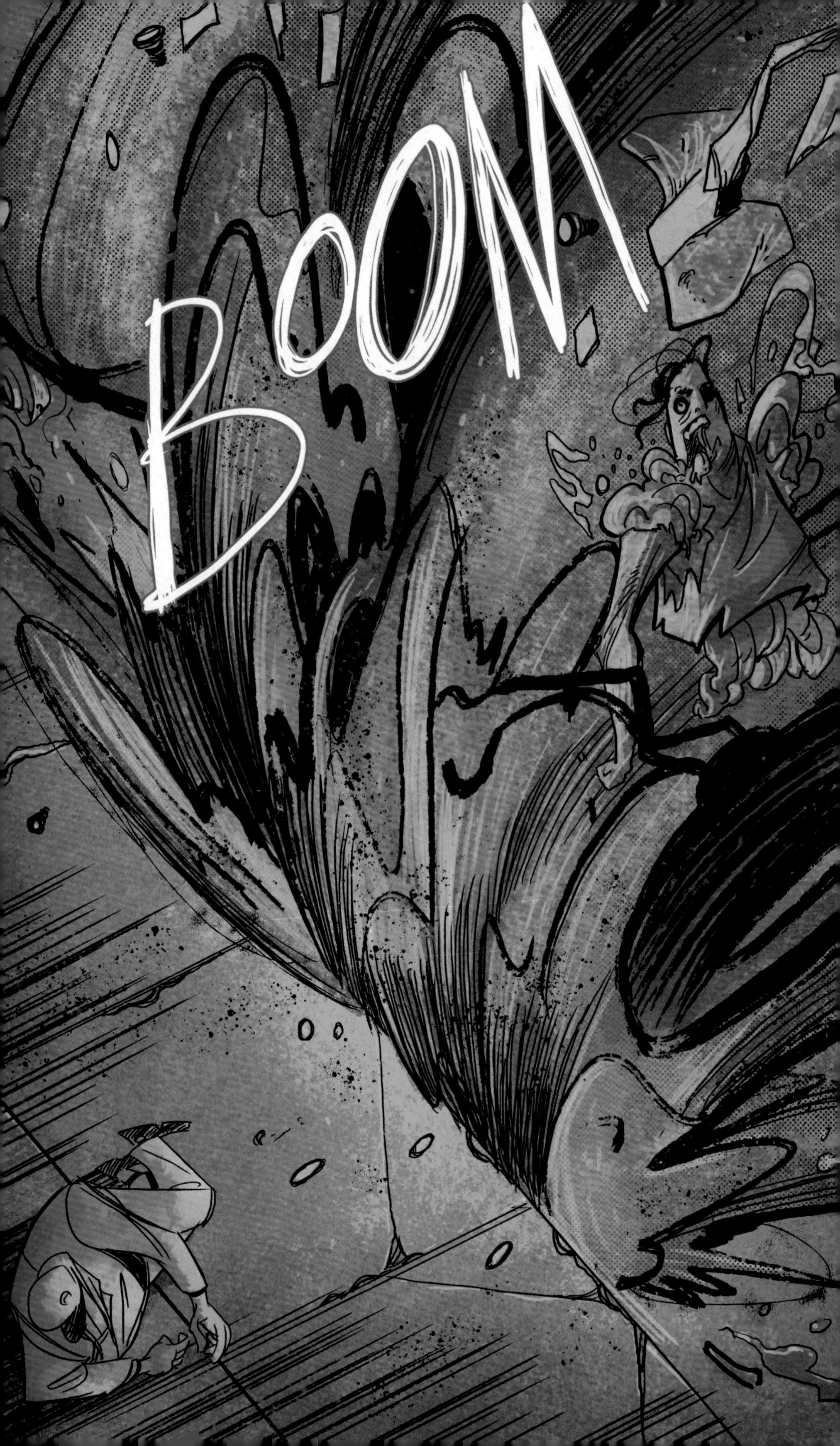
BOOM

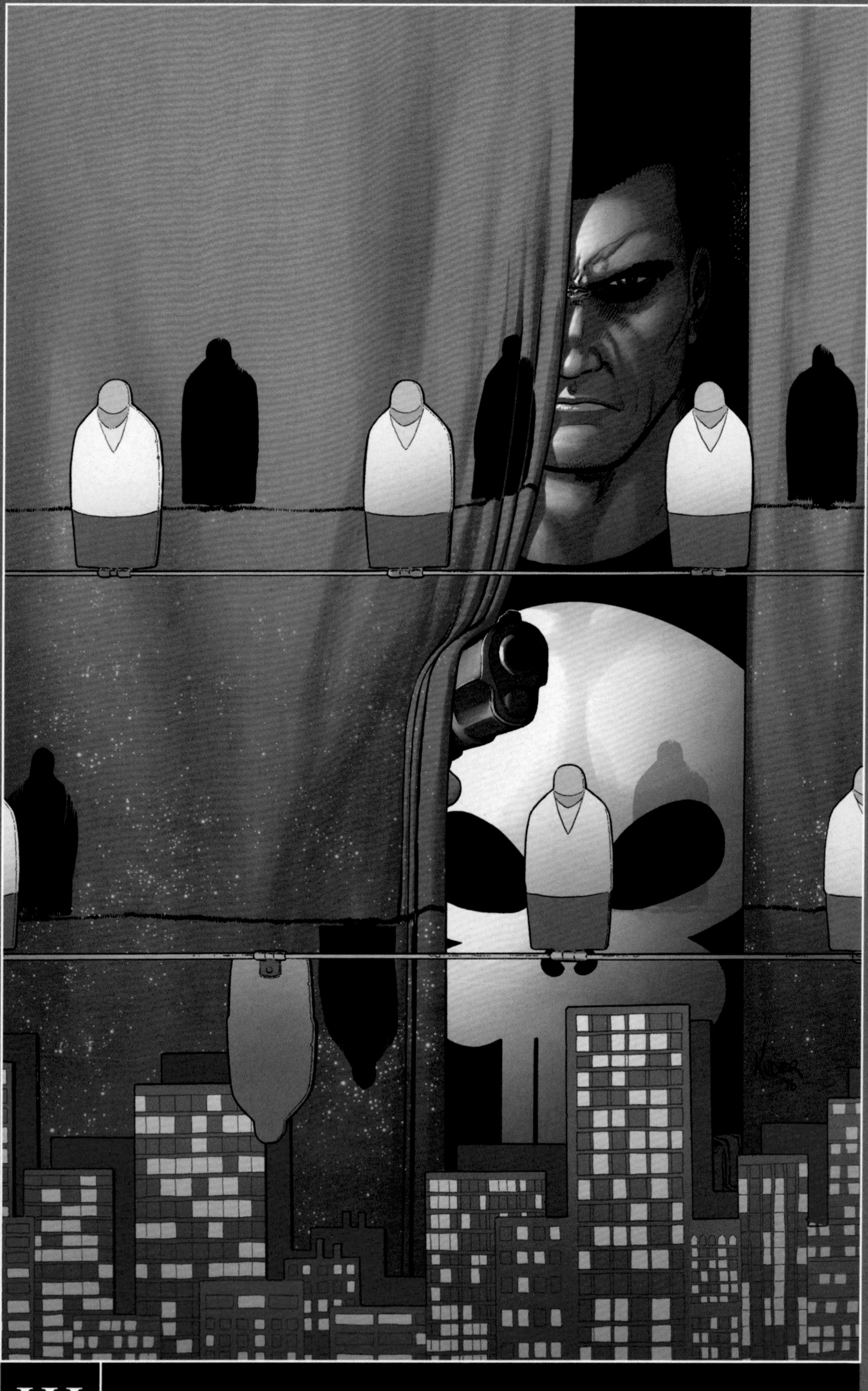

III RED IN TOOTH AND CLAW

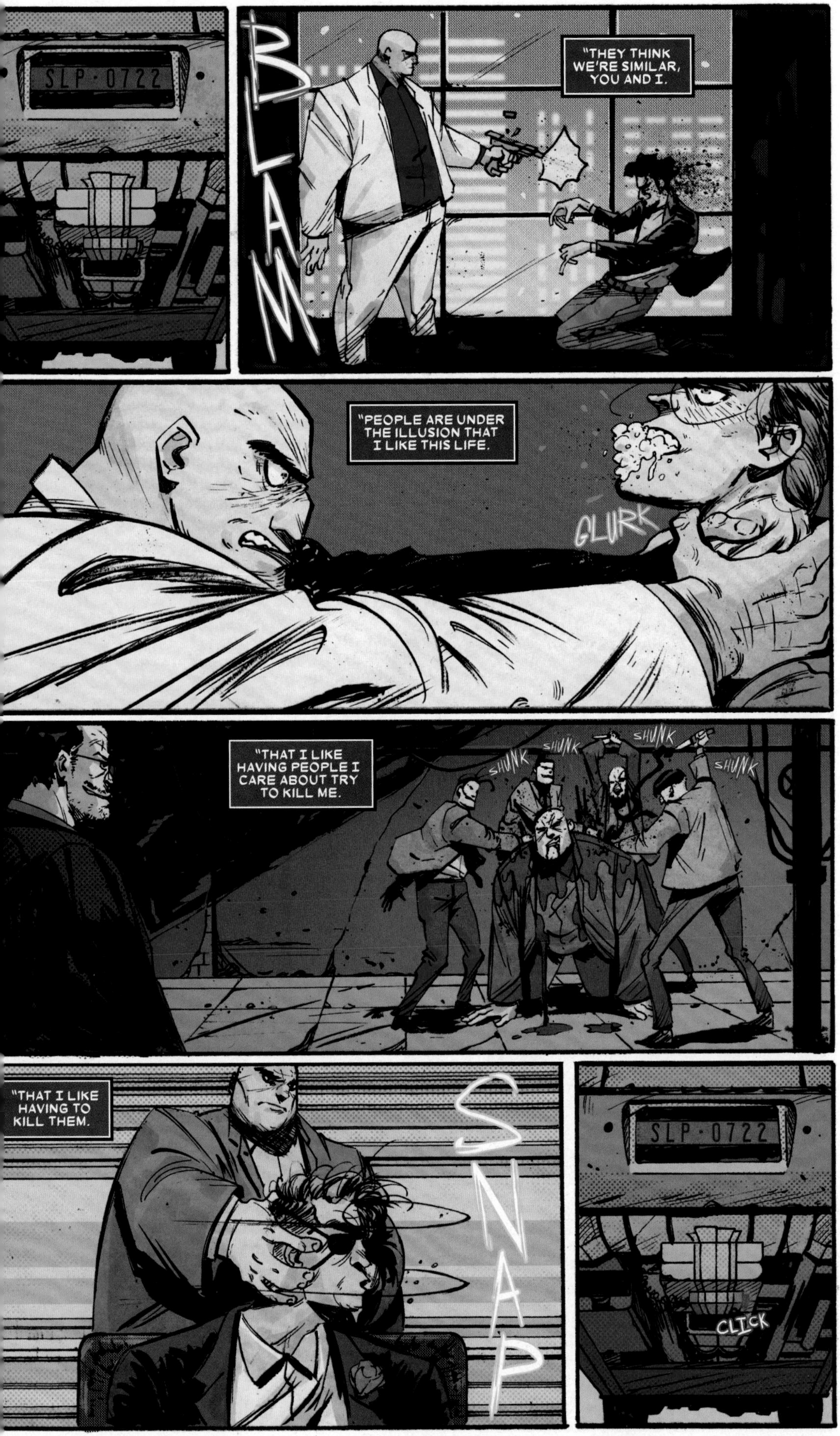
SLP·0722
BLAM
"THEY THINK WE'RE SIMILAR, YOU AND I.
"PEOPLE ARE UNDER THE ILLUSION THAT I LIKE THIS LIFE.
GLURK
"THAT I LIKE HAVING PEOPLE I CARE ABOUT TRY TO KILL ME.
SHUNK
SHUNK
SHUNK
SHUNK
"THAT I LIKE HAVING TO KILL THEM.
SNAP
SLP·0722
CLICK

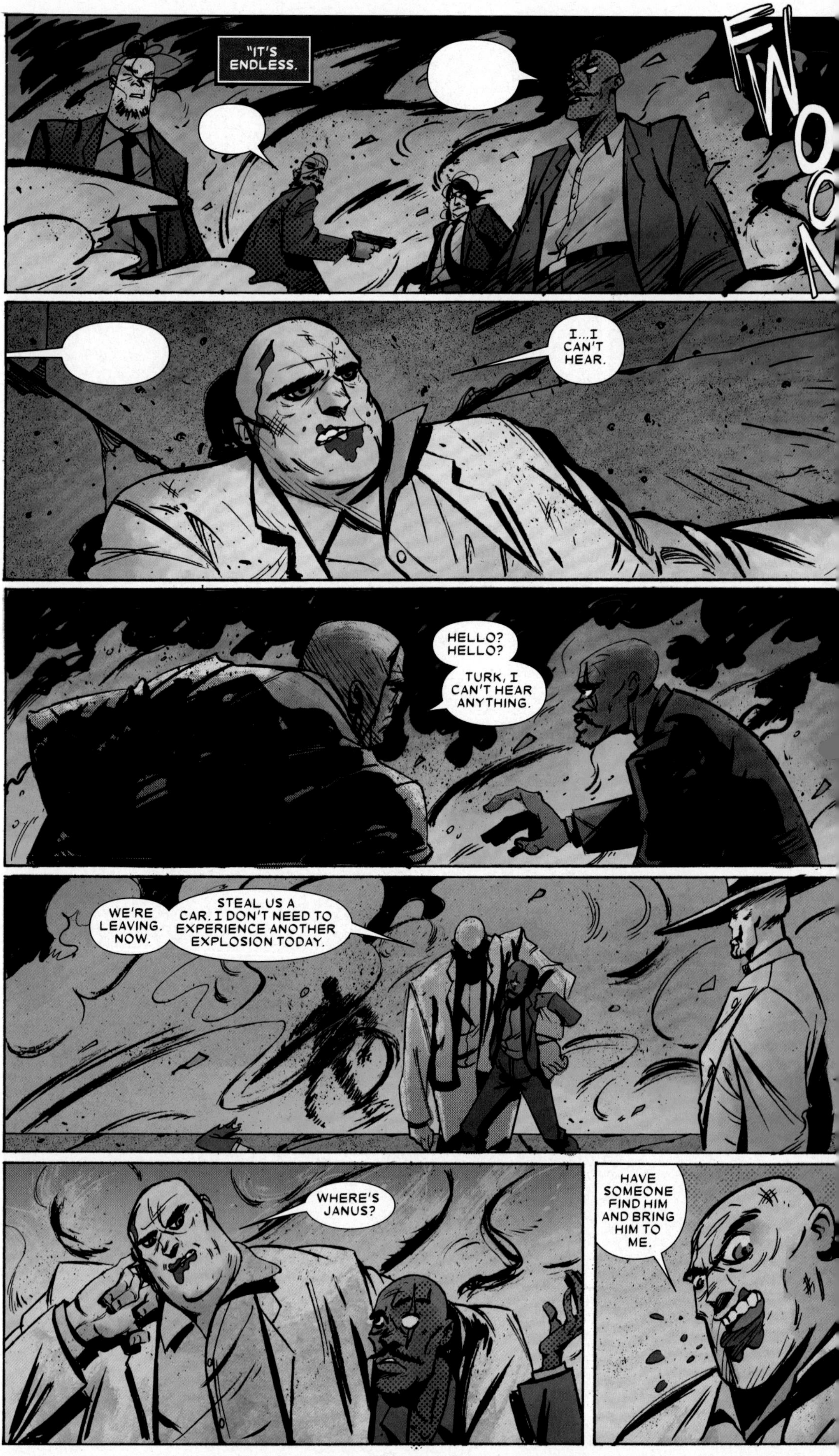
"IT'S ENDLESS.
FWOOM
I...I CAN'T HEAR.
HELLO? HELLO?
TURK, I CAN'T HEAR ANYTHING.
WE'RE LEAVING. NOW.
STEAL US A CAR. I DON'T NEED TO EXPERIENCE ANOTHER EXPLOSION TODAY.
WHERE'S JANUS?
HAVE SOMEONE FIND HIM AND BRING HIM TO ME.

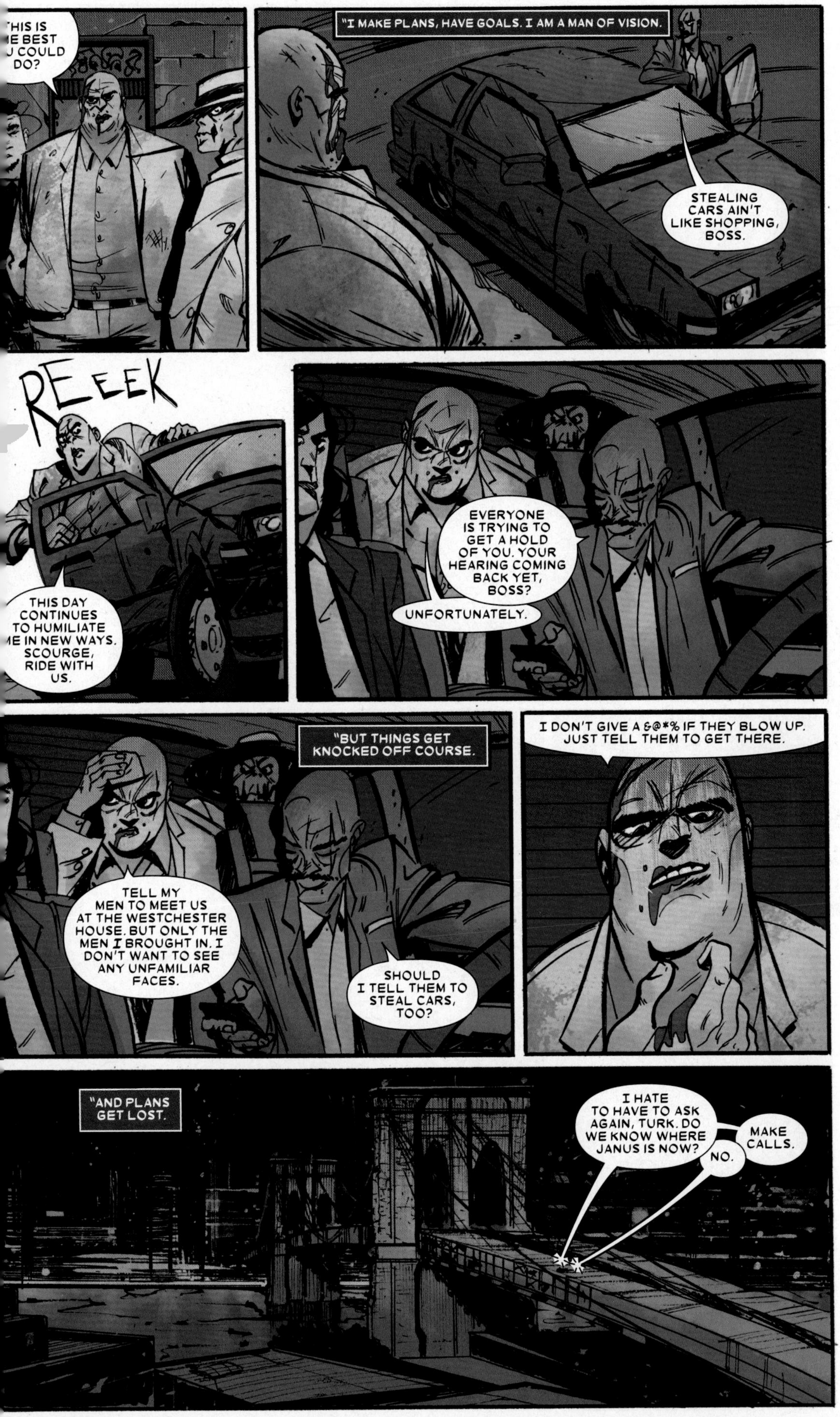
THIS IS
E BEST
U COULD
DO?
"I MAKE PLANS, HAVE GOALS. I AM A MAN OF VISION.
STEALING CARS AIN'T LIKE SHOPPING, BOSS.
REEEK
THIS DAY CONTINUES TO HUMILIATE
E IN NEW WAYS. SCOURGE, RIDE WITH US.
EVERYONE IS TRYING TO GET A HOLD OF YOU. YOUR HEARING COMING BACK YET, BOSS?
UNFORTUNATELY.
"BUT THINGS GET KNOCKED OFF COURSE.
TELL MY MEN TO MEET US AT THE WESTCHESTER HOUSE. BUT ONLY THE MEN I BROUGHT IN. I DON'T WANT TO SEE ANY UNFAMILIAR FACES.
SHOULD I TELL THEM TO STEAL CARS, TOO?
I DON'T GIVE A &@*% IF THEY BLOW UP. JUST TELL THEM TO GET THERE.
"AND PLANS GET LOST.
I HATE TO HAVE TO ASK AGAIN, TURK. DO WE KNOW WHERE JANUS IS NOW?
NO.
MAKE CALLS.

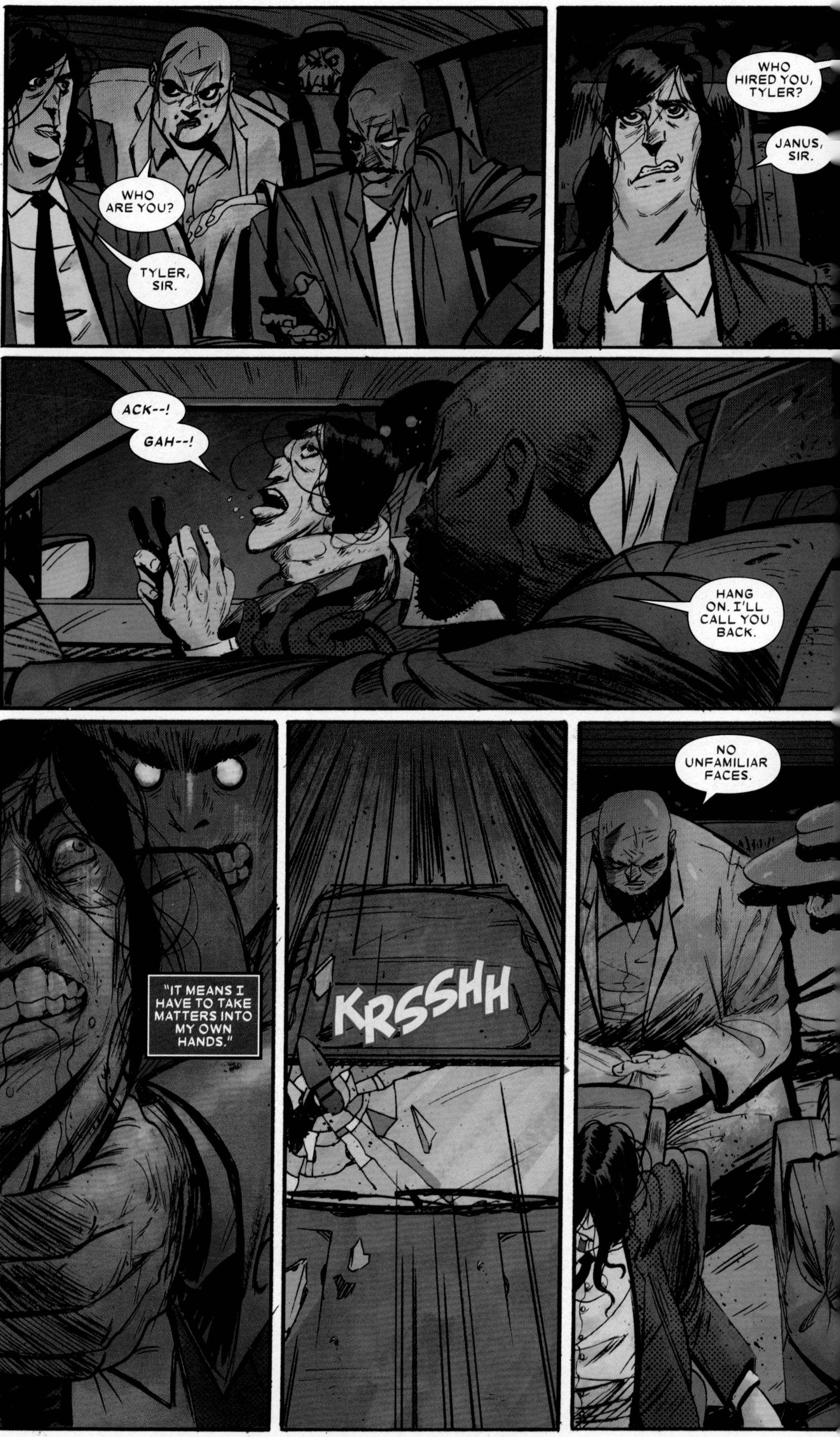
WHO ARE YOU?
TYLER, SIR.
WHO HIRED YOU, TYLER?
JANUS, SIR.
ACK--!
GAH--!
HANG ON. I'LL CALL YOU BACK.
"IT MEANS I HAVE TO TAKE MATTERS INTO MY OWN HANDS."
KRSSHH
NO UNFAMILIAR FACES.

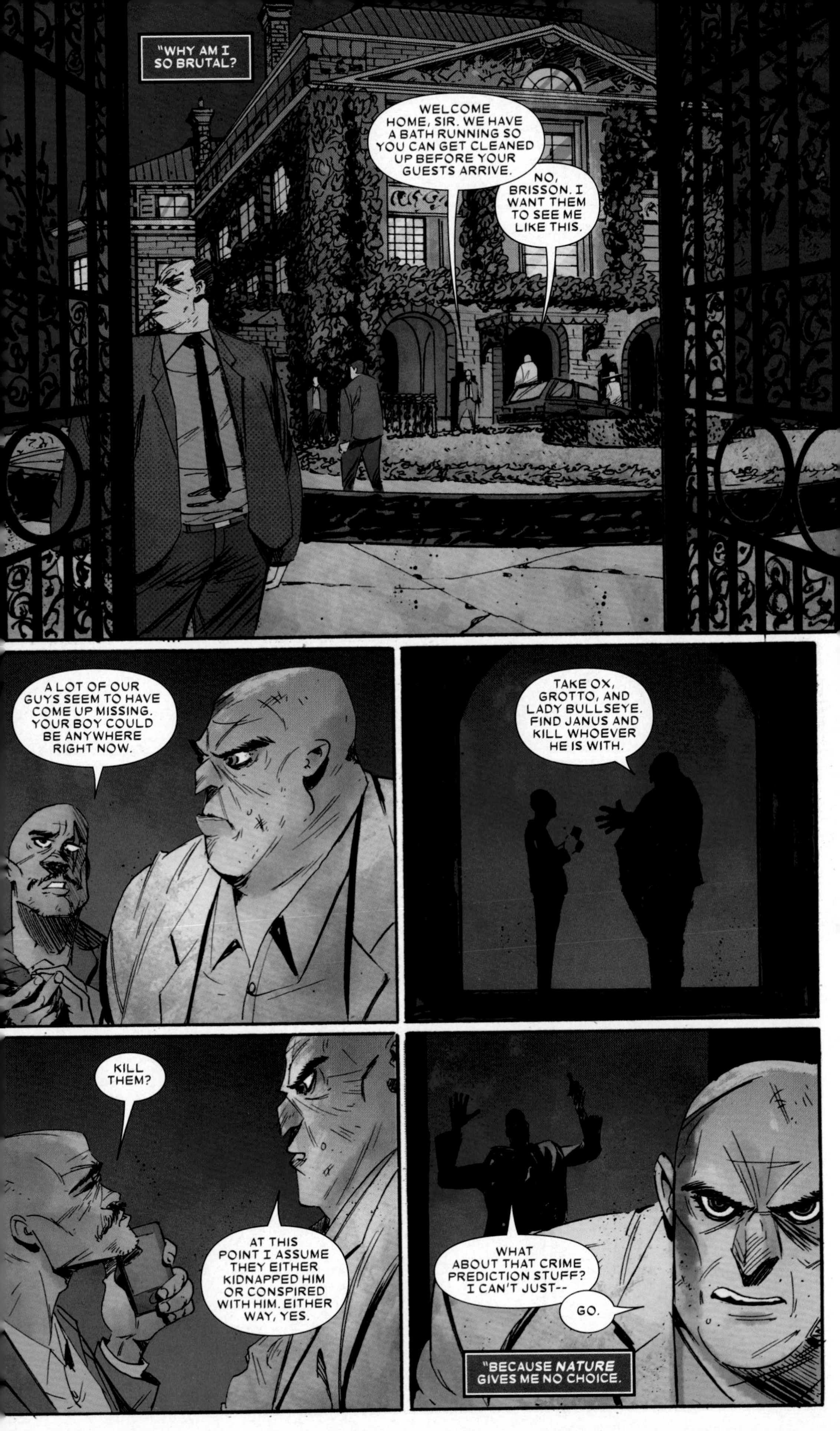
"WHY AM I SO BRUTAL?
WELCOME HOME, SIR. WE HAVE A BATH RUNNING SO YOU CAN GET CLEANED UP BEFORE YOUR GUESTS ARRIVE.
NO, BRISSON. I WANT THEM TO SEE ME LIKE THIS.
A LOT OF OUR GUYS SEEM TO HAVE COME UP MISSING. YOUR BOY COULD BE ANYWHERE RIGHT NOW.
TAKE OX, GROTTO, AND LADY BULLSEYE. FIND JANUS AND KILL WHOEVER HE IS WITH.
KILL THEM?
AT THIS POINT I ASSUME THEY EITHER KIDNAPPED HIM OR CONSPIRED WITH HIM. EITHER WAY, YES.
WHAT ABOUT THAT CRIME PREDICTION STUFF? I CAN'T JUST--
GO.
"BECAUSE NATURE GIVES ME NO CHOICE.

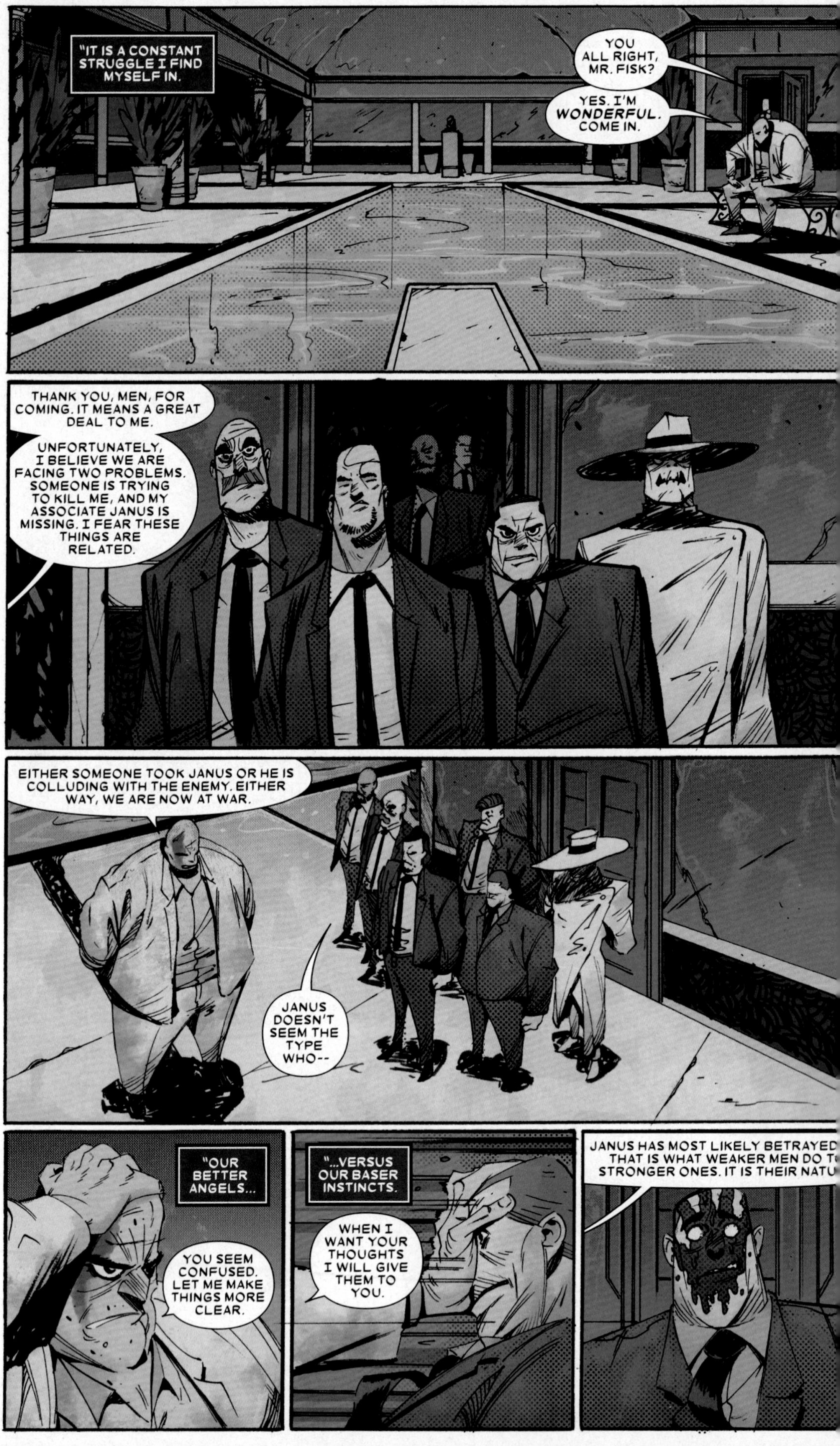
"IT IS A CONSTANT STRUGGLE I FIND MYSELF IN.
YOU ALL RIGHT, MR. FISK?
YES. I'M WONDERFUL. COME IN.
THANK YOU, MEN, FOR COMING. IT MEANS A GREAT DEAL TO ME.
UNFORTUNATELY, I BELIEVE WE ARE FACING TWO PROBLEMS. SOMEONE IS TRYING TO KILL ME, AND MY ASSOCIATE JANUS IS MISSING. I FEAR THESE THINGS ARE RELATED.
EITHER SOMEONE TOOK JANUS OR HE IS COLLUDING WITH THE ENEMY. EITHER WAY, WE ARE NOW AT WAR.
JANUS DOESN'T SEEM THE TYPE WHO--
"OUR BETTER ANGELS...
YOU SEEM CONFUSED. LET ME MAKE THINGS MORE CLEAR.
"...VERSUS OUR BASER INSTINCTS.
WHEN I WANT YOUR THOUGHTS I WILL GIVE THEM TO YOU.
JANUS HAS MOST LIKELY BETRAYED
THAT IS WHAT WEAKER MEN DO T
STRONGER ONES. IT IS THEIR NATU

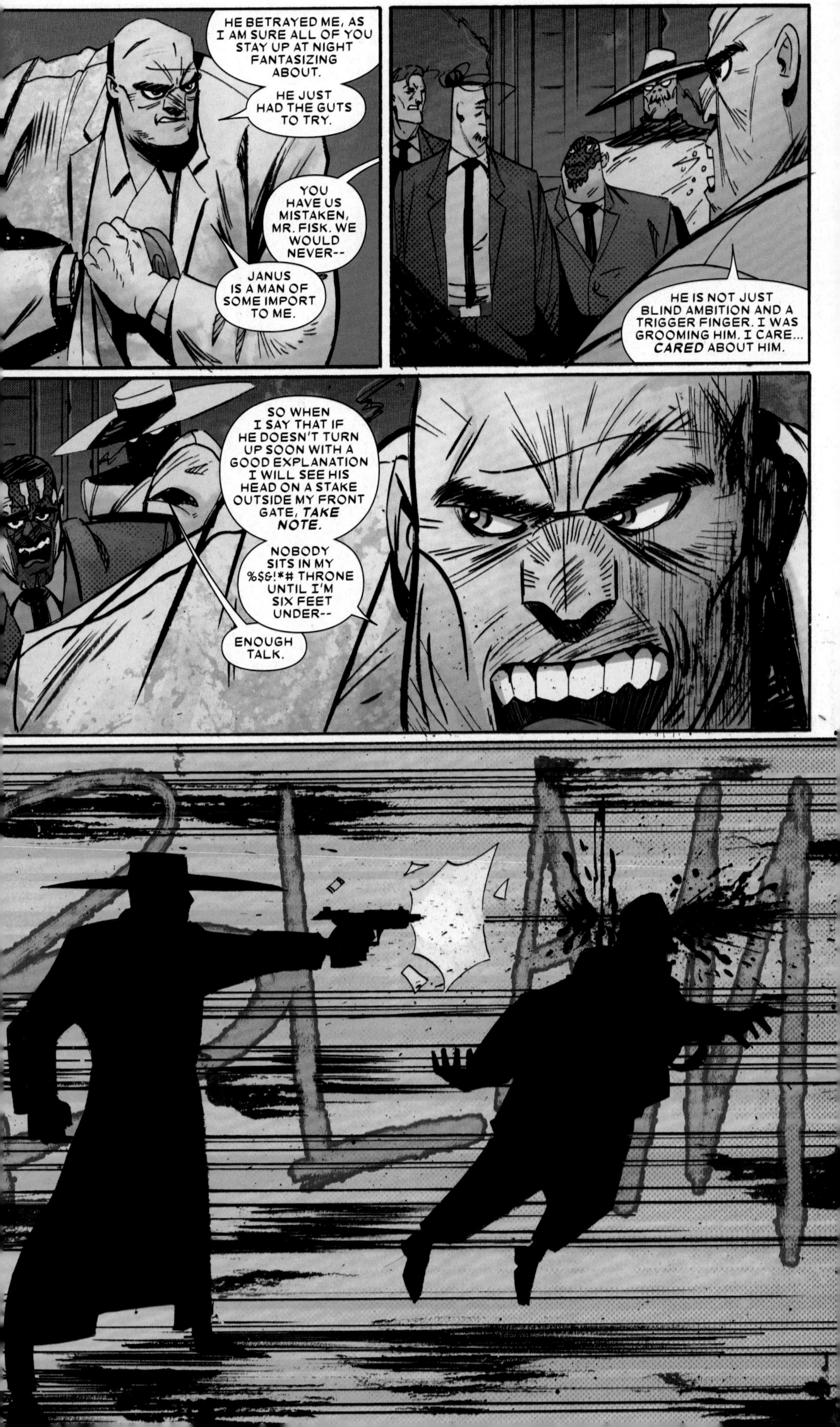
HE BETRAYED ME, AS I AM SURE ALL OF YOU STAY UP AT NIGHT FANTASIZING ABOUT.
HE JUST HAD THE GUTS TO TRY.
YOU HAVE US MISTAKEN, MR. FISK. WE WOULD NEVER--
JANUS IS A MAN OF SOME IMPORT TO ME.
HE IS NOT JUST BLIND AMBITION AND A TRIGGER FINGER. I WAS GROOMING HIM. I CARE... CARED ABOUT HIM.
SO WHEN I SAY THAT IF HE DOESN'T TURN UP SOON WITH A GOOD EXPLANATION I WILL SEE HIS HEAD ON A STAKE OUTSIDE MY FRONT GATE, TAKE NOTE.
NOBODY SITS IN MY %$&!*# THRONE UNTIL I'M SIX FEET UNDER--
ENOUGH TALK.

STOP HIM!

DON'T LET HIM GET TO MR. FISK!

BLAM

OOOF

HE'S TOO STRONG!

KSHUNK!

"I'VE SPENT MY LIFE TRYING TO RISE ABOVE THIS NATURE.

"CLAWING. TRYING TO PULL EVERYONE I CAN WITH ME.

HOLD HIM.

"BUT NATURE ALWAYS DRAGS US BACK DOWN.

NOW, NOW, SCOURGE. WHAT HAS GOTTEN INTO YOU?

RRRIP

OH.

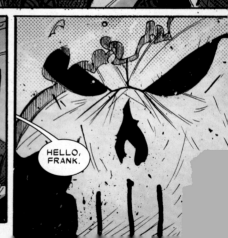

HELLO, FRANK.

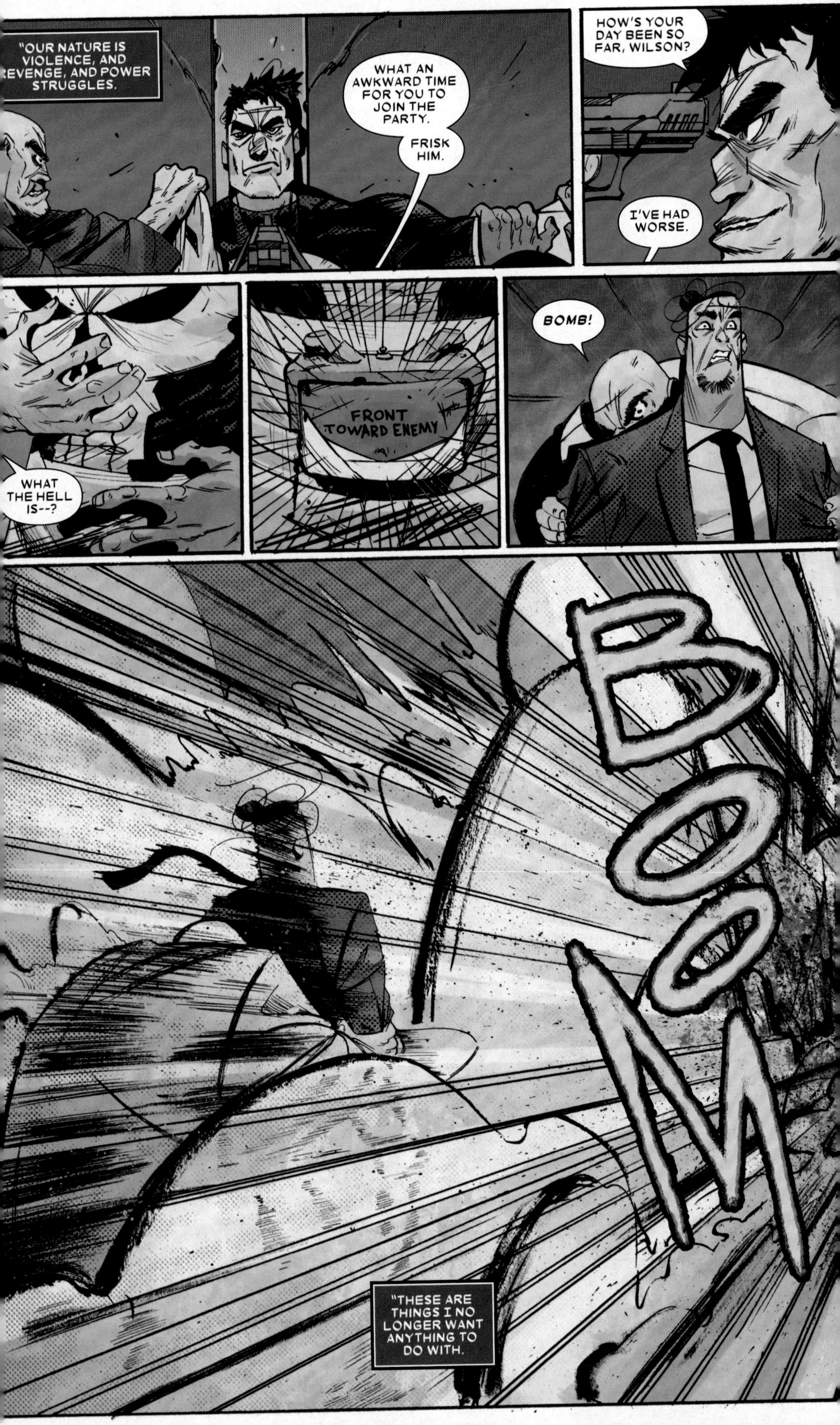
"OUR NATURE IS VIOLENCE, AND REVENGE, AND POWER STRUGGLES.
WHAT AN AWKWARD TIME FOR YOU TO JOIN THE PARTY.
FRISK HIM.
HOW'S YOUR DAY BEEN SO FAR, WILSON?
I'VE HAD WORSE.
WHAT THE HELL IS--?
FRONT TOWARD ENEMY
BOMB!
BOOM
"THESE ARE THINGS I NO LONGER WANT ANYTHING TO DO WITH.

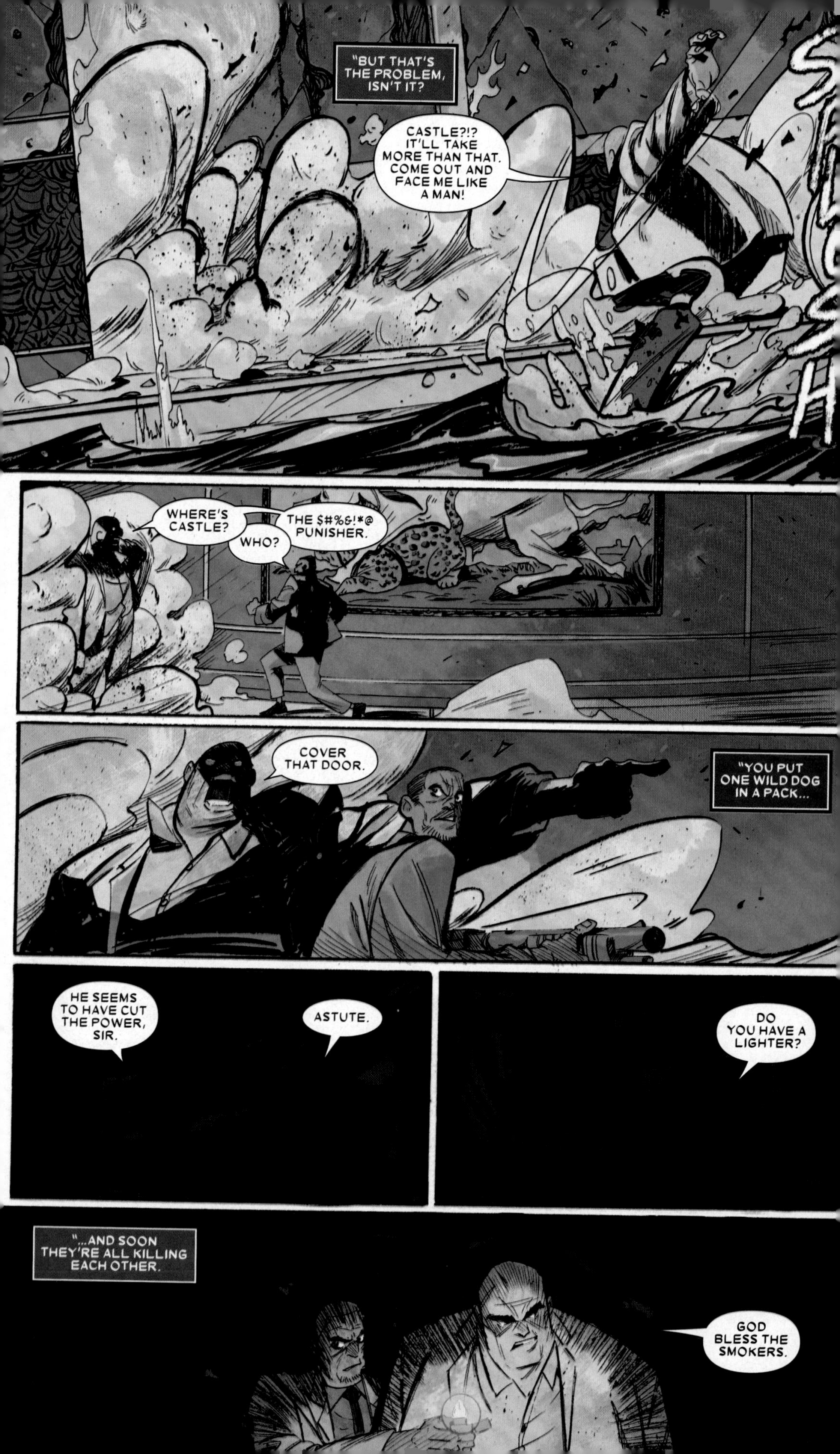
"BUT THAT'S THE PROBLEM, ISN'T IT?
CASTLE?!? IT'LL TAKE MORE THAN THAT. COME OUT AND FACE ME LIKE A MAN!
WHERE'S CASTLE?
WHO?
THE $#%&!*@ PUNISHER.
COVER THAT DOOR.
"YOU PUT ONE WILD DOG IN A PACK...
HE SEEMS TO HAVE CUT THE POWER, SIR.
ASTUTE.
DO YOU HAVE A LIGHTER?
"...AND SOON THEY'RE ALL KILLING EACH OTHER.
GOD BLESS THE SMOKERS.

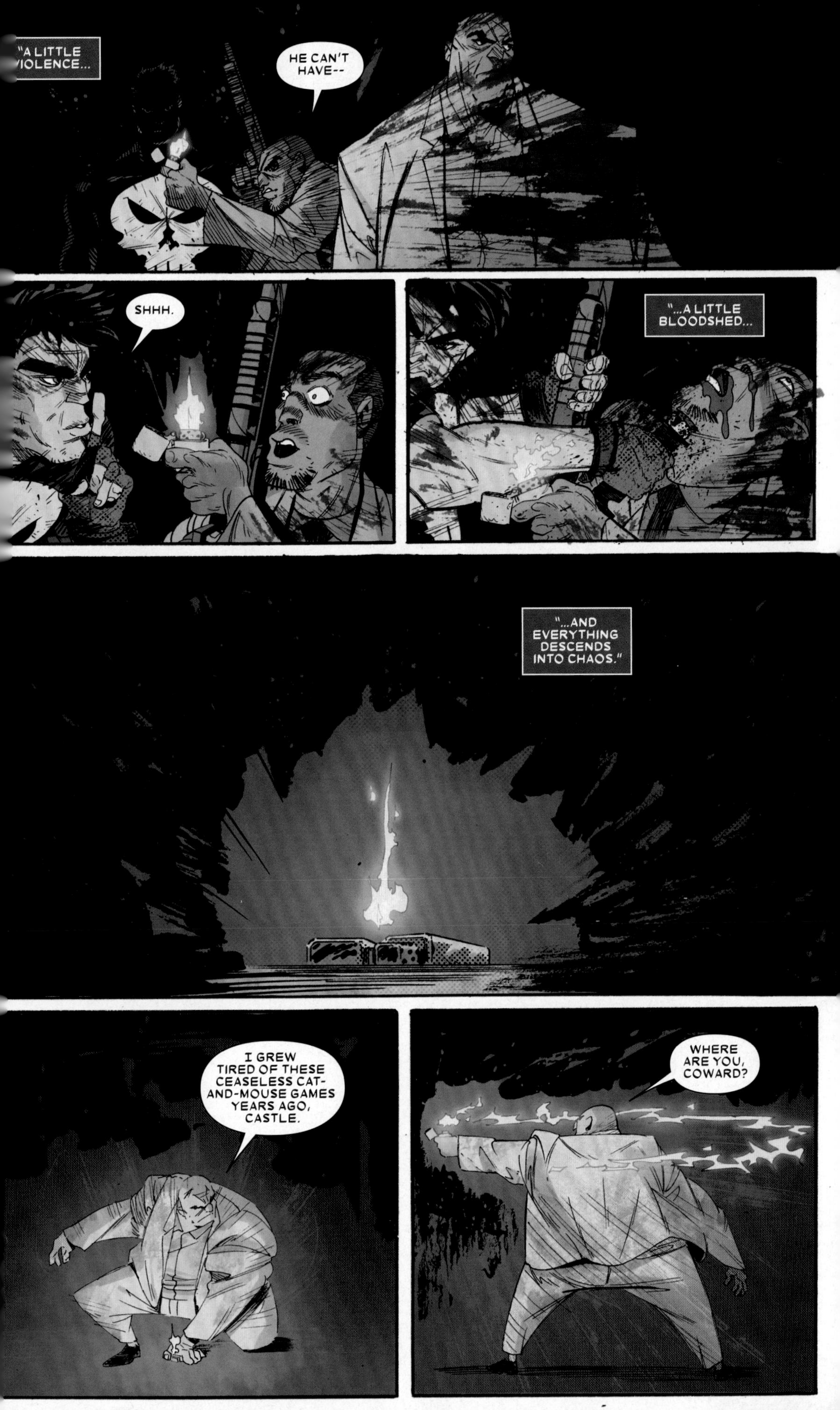
"A LITTLE VIOLENCE...
HE CAN'T HAVE--
SHHH.
"...A LITTLE BLOODSHED...
"...AND EVERYTHING DESCENDS INTO CHAOS."
I GREW TIRED OF THESE CEASELESS CAT-AND-MOUSE GAMES YEARS AGO, CASTLE.
WHERE ARE YOU, COWARD?

"I TRY TO CLEAN UP THIS CITY.

"I TRY TO BRING PEACE BETWEEN WARRING FAMILIES.

BRISSON, WHAT ARE YOU DOING? WE HAVE--

MMMPPH!

"I TRY TO ELEVATE MAN ABOVE HIS NATURE.

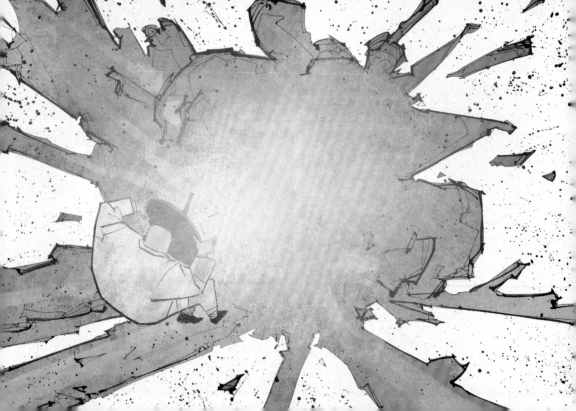

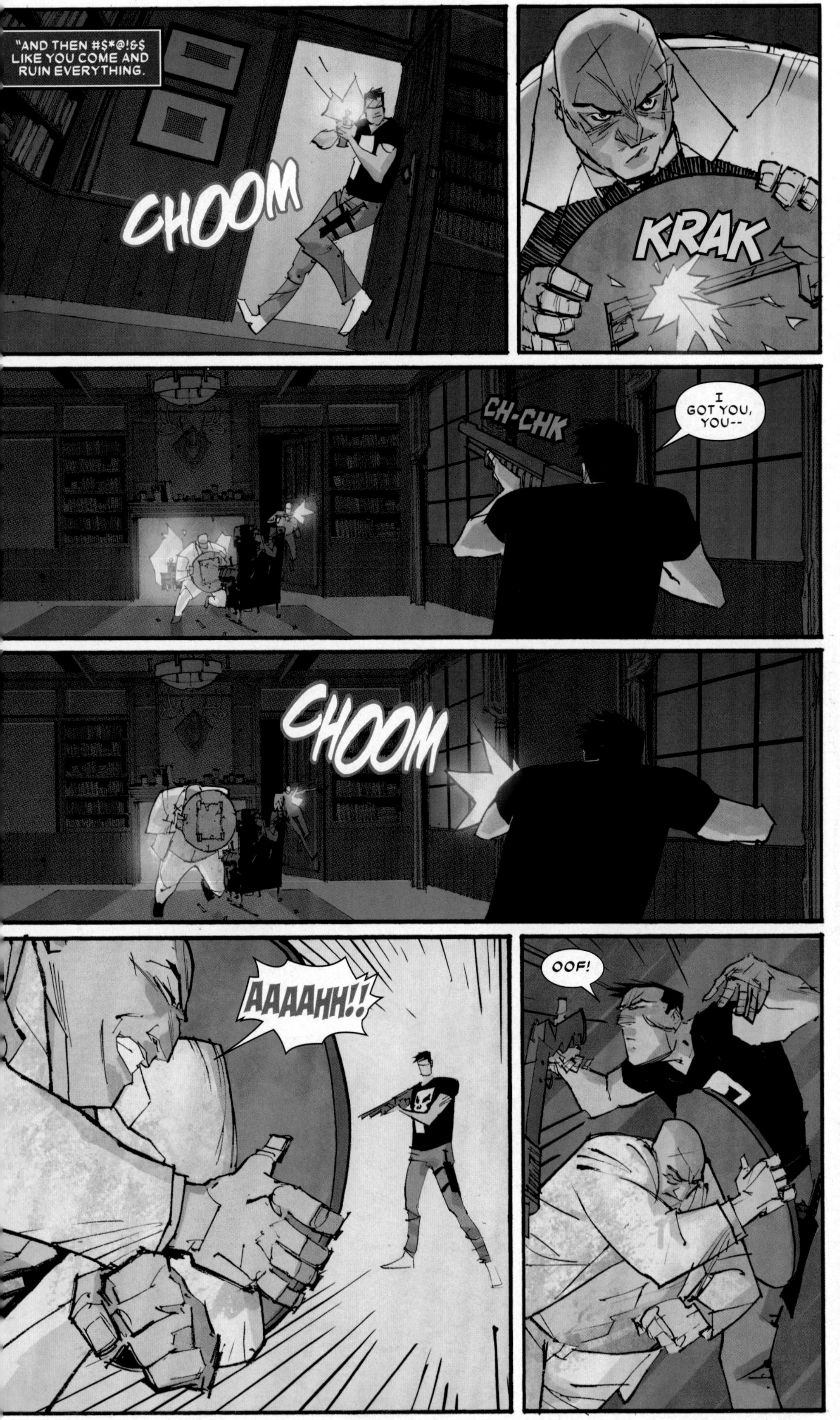

"AND THEN #$*@!&$ LIKE YOU COME AND RUIN EVERYTHING.
CHOOM
KRAK
CH-CHK
I GOT YOU, YOU--
CHOOM
AAAAHH!!
OOF!

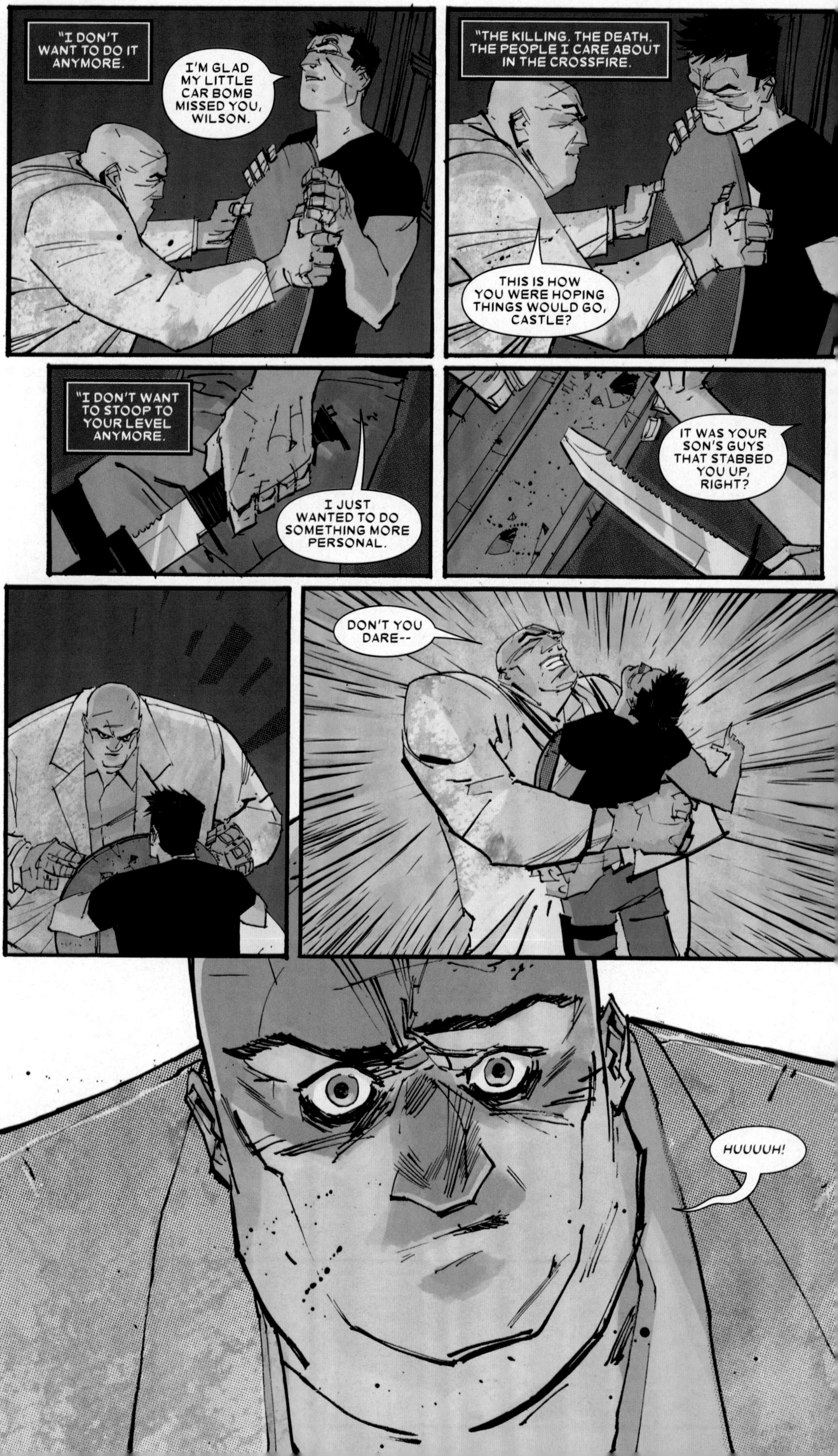
"I DON'T WANT TO DO IT ANYMORE.
I'M GLAD MY LITTLE CAR BOMB MISSED YOU, WILSON.
"THE KILLING. THE DEATH. THE PEOPLE I CARE ABOUT IN THE CROSSFIRE.
THIS IS HOW YOU WERE HOPING THINGS WOULD GO, CASTLE?
"I DON'T WANT TO STOOP TO YOUR LEVEL ANYMORE.
I JUST WANTED TO DO SOMETHING MORE PERSONAL.
IT WAS YOUR SON'S GUYS THAT STABBED YOU UP, RIGHT?
DON'T YOU DARE--
HUUUUH!

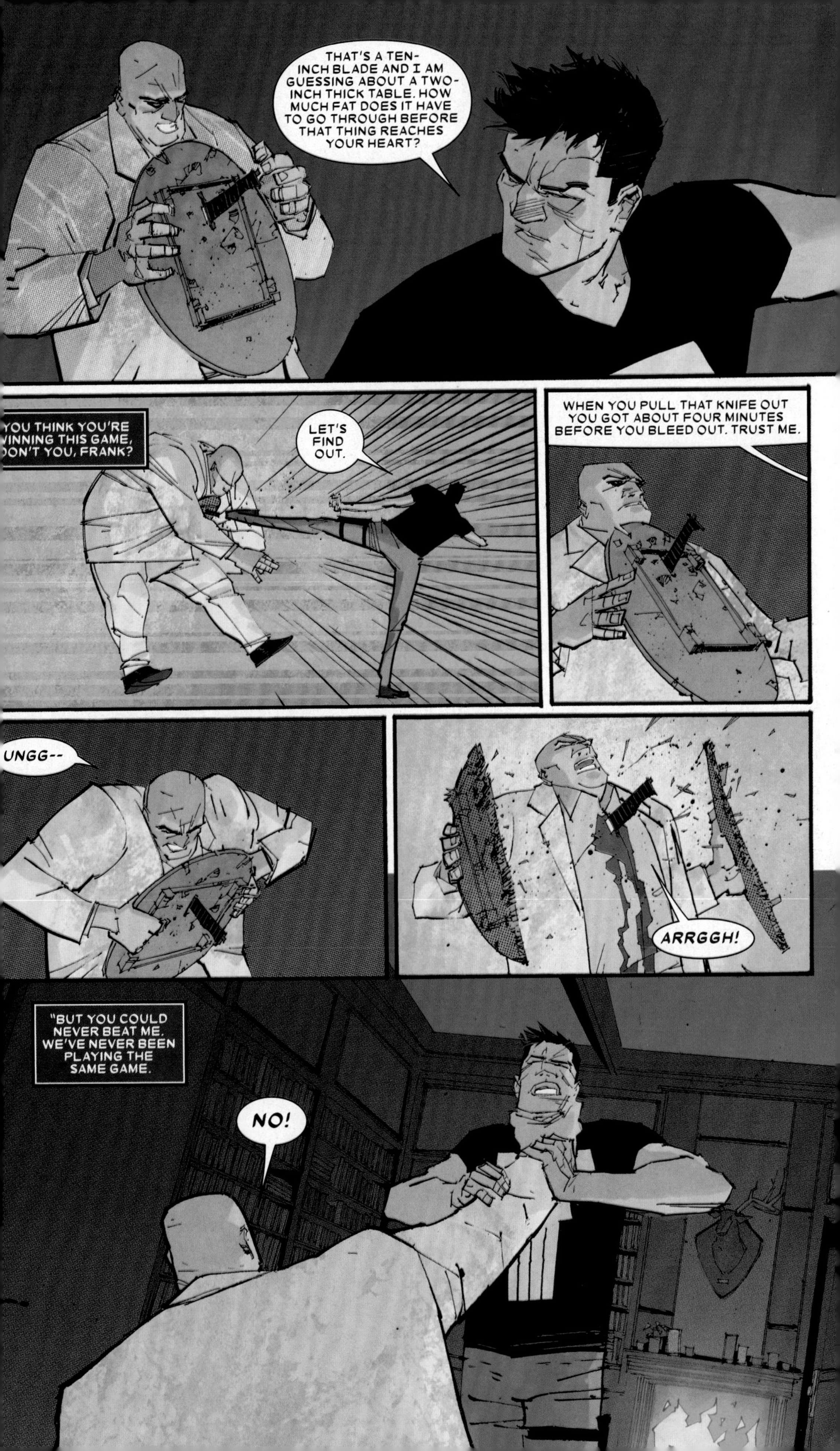
THAT'S A TEN-INCH BLADE AND I AM GUESSING ABOUT A TWO-INCH THICK TABLE. HOW MUCH FAT DOES IT HAVE TO GO THROUGH BEFORE THAT THING REACHES YOUR HEART?
YOU THINK YOU'RE WINNING THIS GAME, DON'T YOU, FRANK?
LET'S FIND OUT.
WHEN YOU PULL THAT KNIFE OUT YOU GOT ABOUT FOUR MINUTES BEFORE YOU BLEED OUT. TRUST ME.
UNGG--
ARRGGH!
"BUT YOU COULD NEVER BEAT ME. WE'VE NEVER BEEN PLAYING THE SAME GAME.
NO!

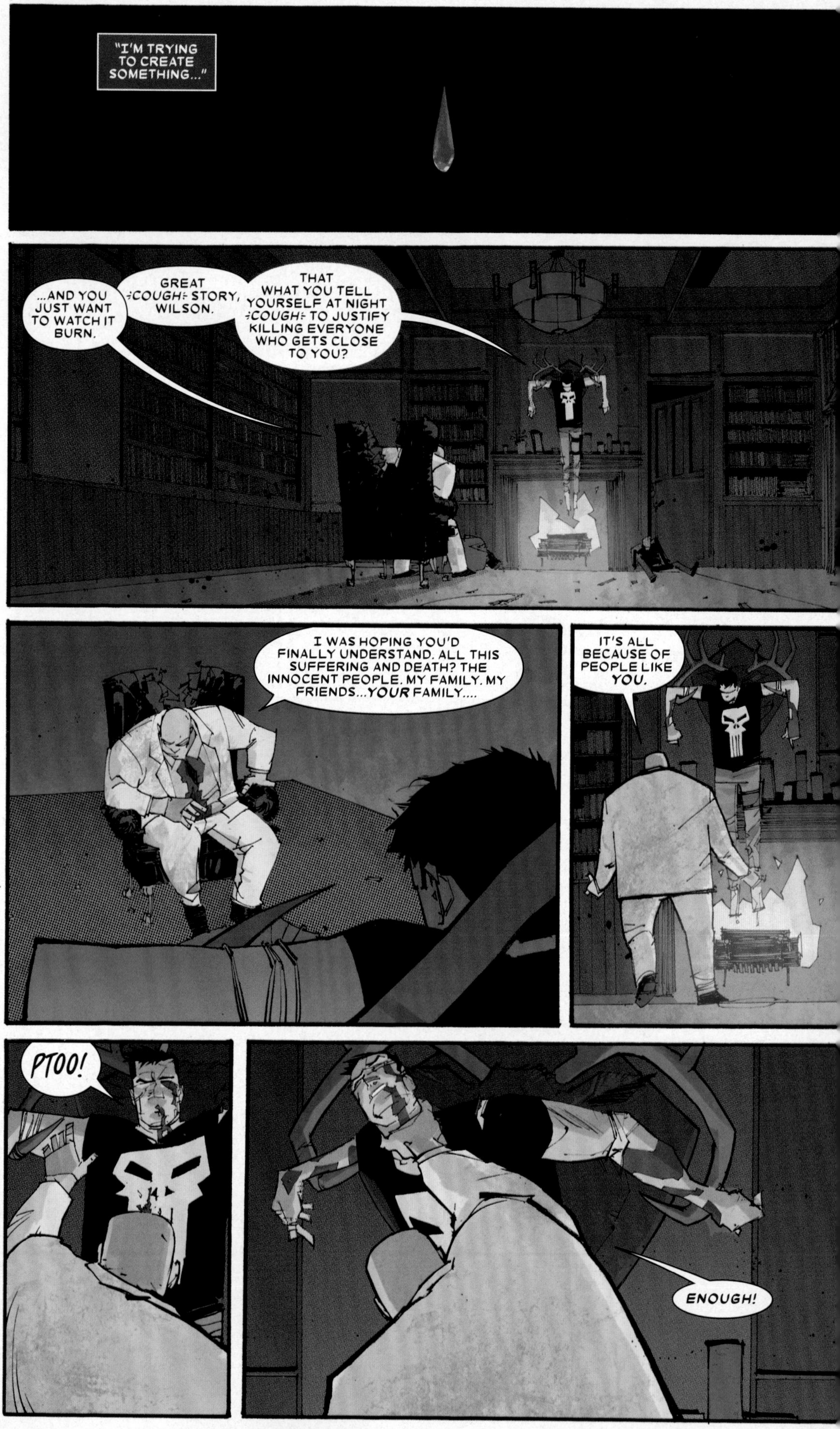
"I'M TRYING TO CREATE SOMETHING..."
...AND YOU JUST WANT TO WATCH IT BURN.
GREAT ÷COUGH÷ STORY, WILSON.
THAT WHAT YOU TELL YOURSELF AT NIGHT ÷COUGH÷ TO JUSTIFY KILLING EVERYONE WHO GETS CLOSE TO YOU?
I WAS HOPING YOU'D FINALLY UNDERSTAND. ALL THIS SUFFERING AND DEATH? THE INNOCENT PEOPLE. MY FAMILY. MY FRIENDS...YOUR FAMILY....
IT'S ALL BECAUSE OF PEOPLE LIKE YOU.
PTOO!
ENOUGH!

BEFORE I DIE I WILL SEE YOU BURN.

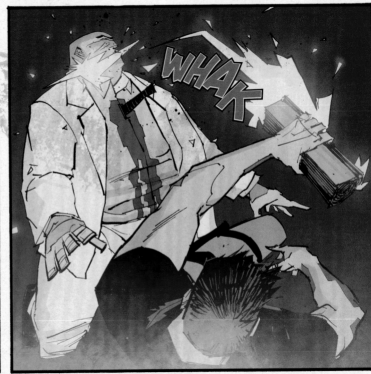

WHAK

NO!

KSSHH

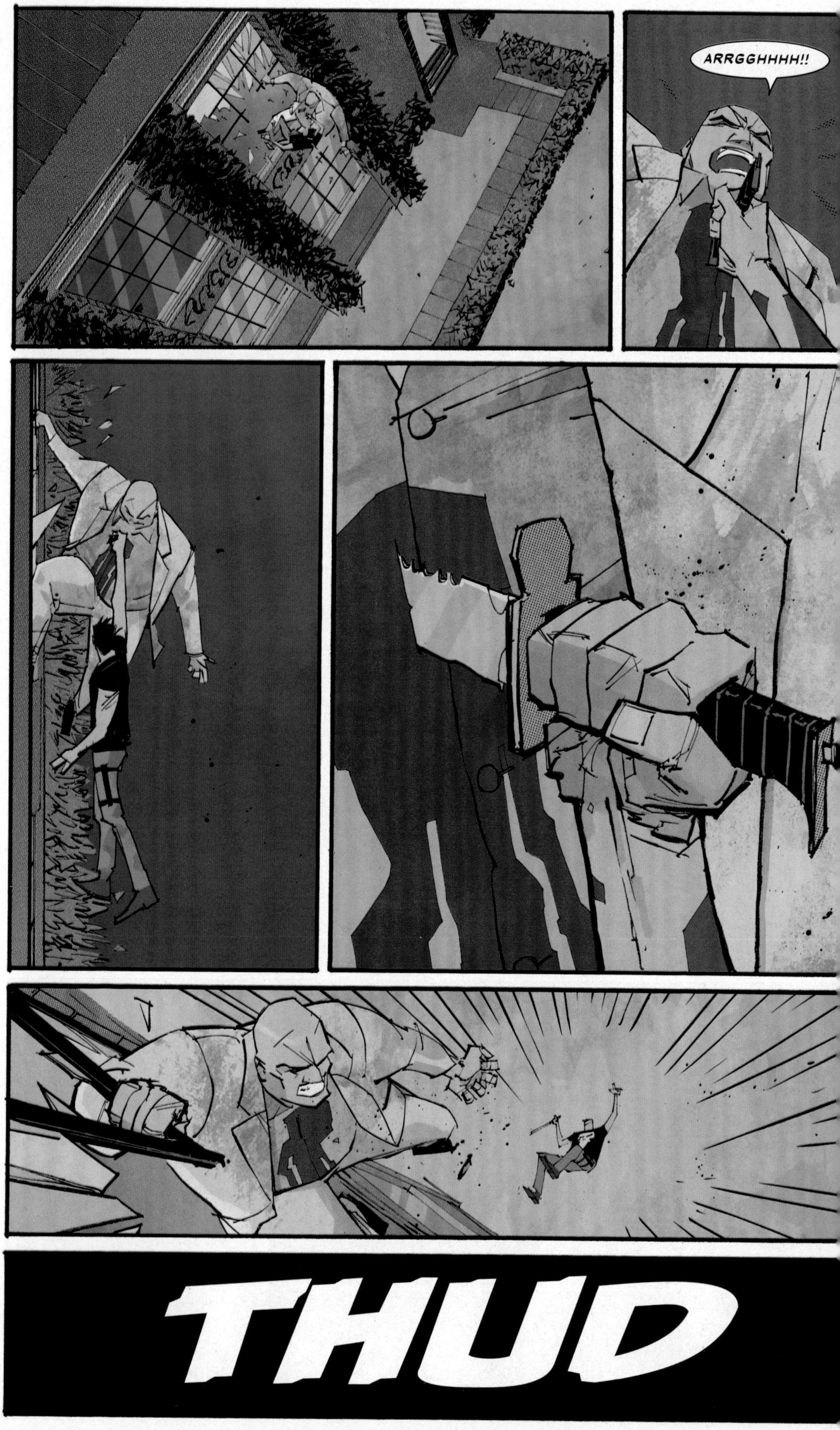
ARRGGHHHH!!
THUD

HAVE TO...

...GET...

UGGGH!

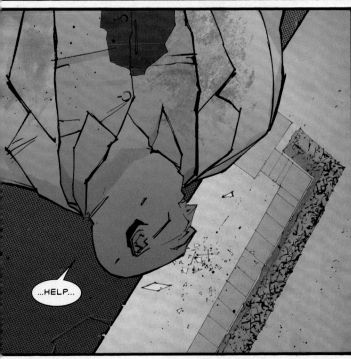

...HELP...

WILSON FISK!

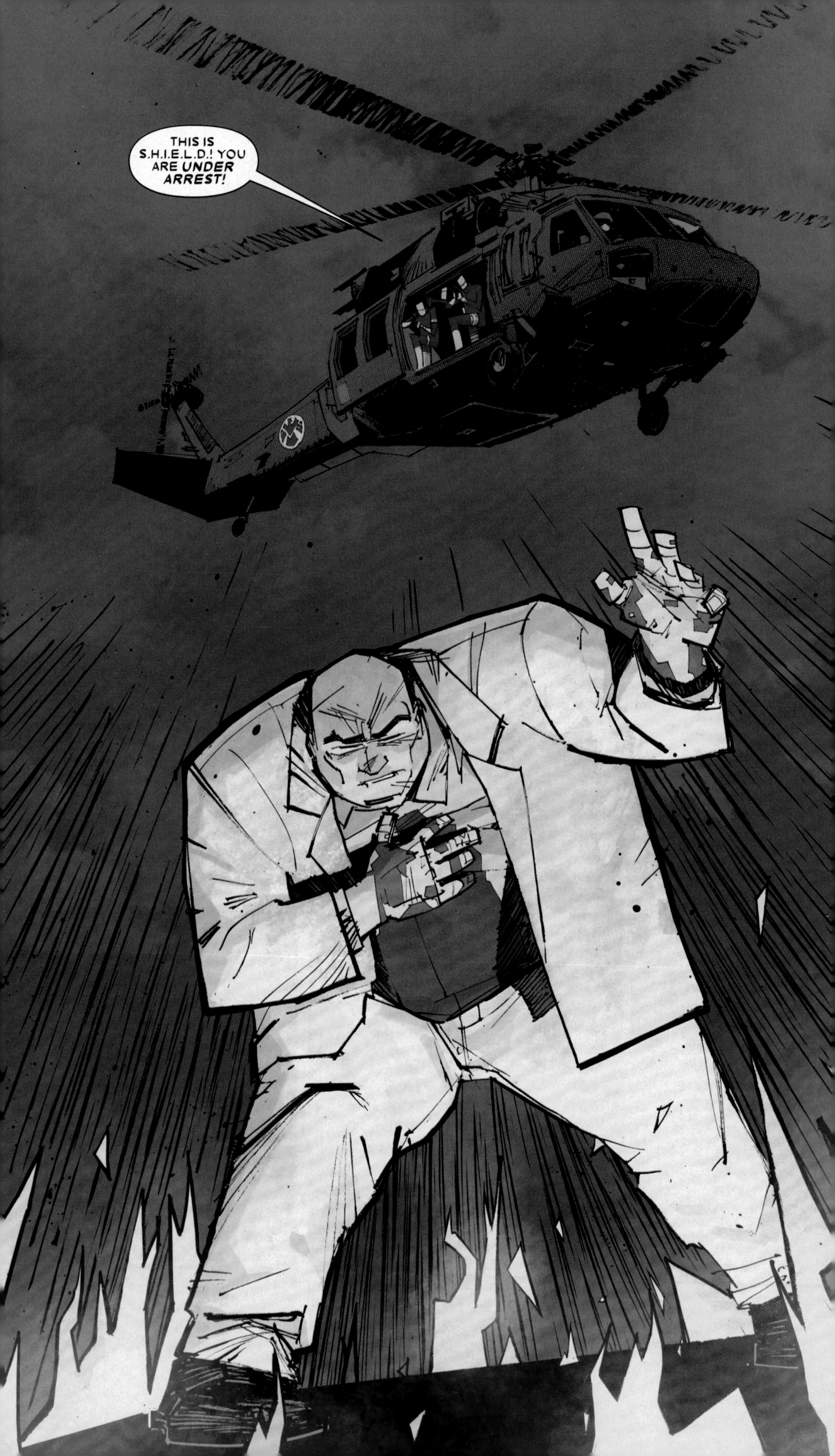
THIS IS S.H.I.E.L.D.! YOU ARE UNDER ARREST!

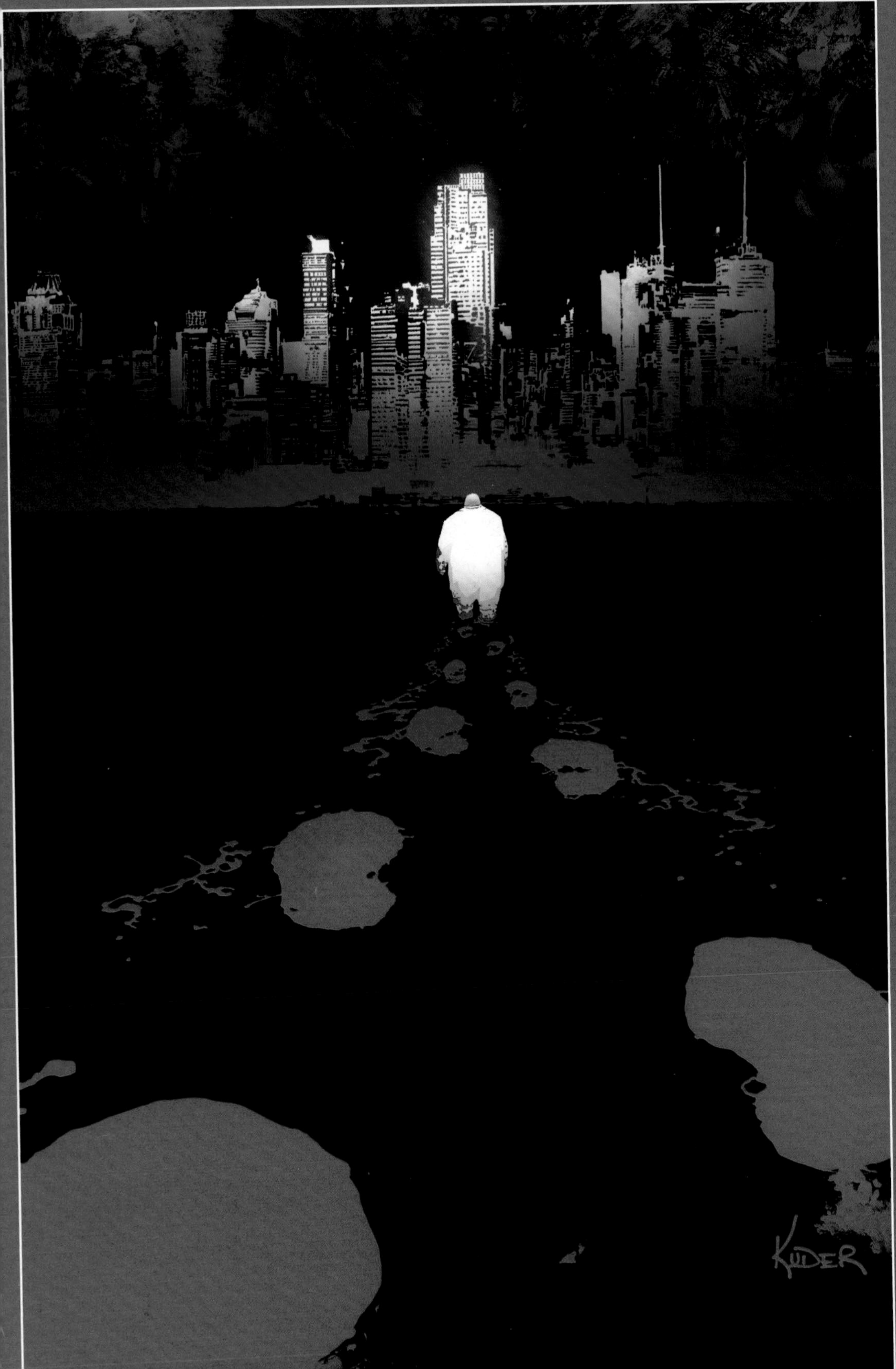
KUDER

WILSON FISK IS DEAD IV

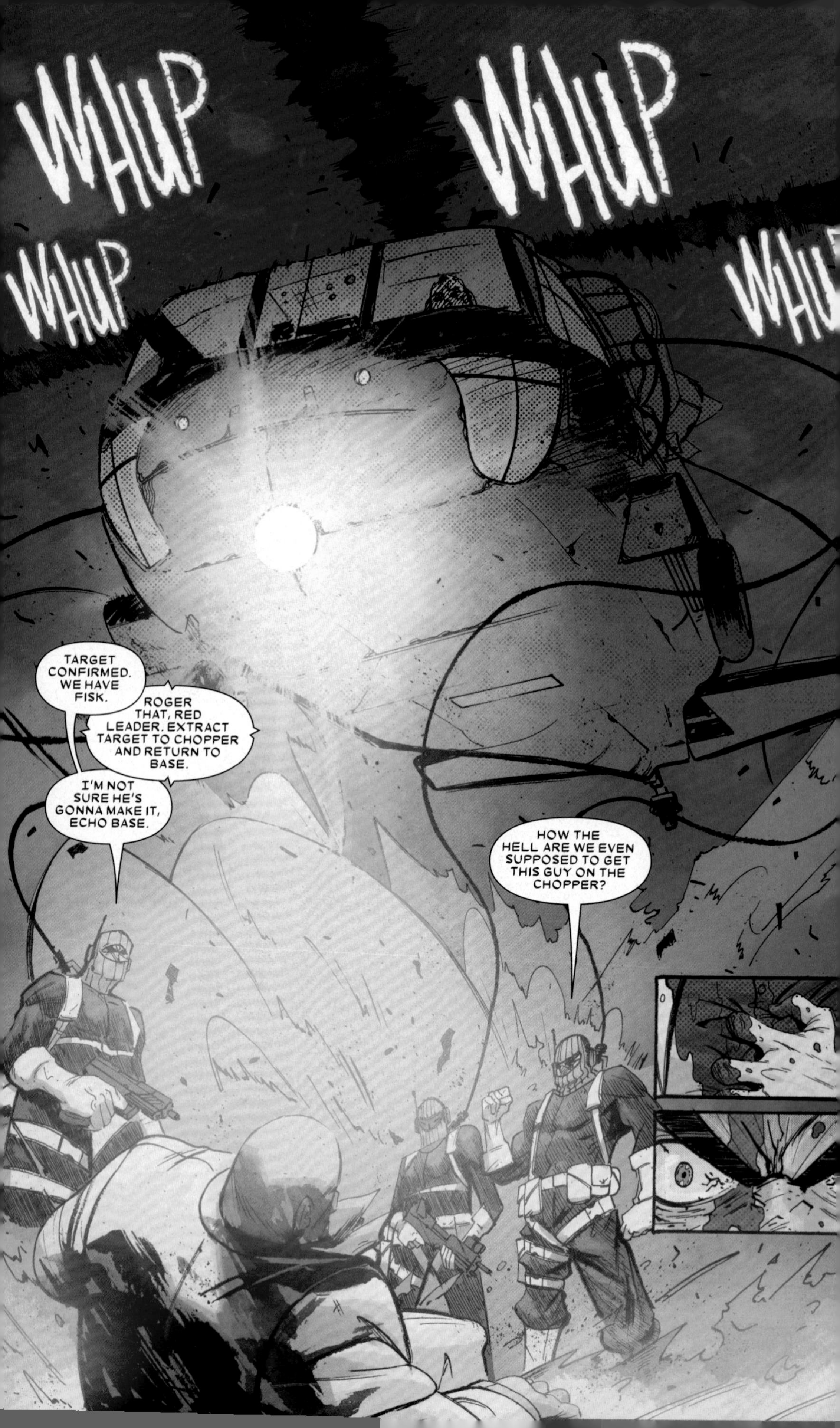
WHUP
WHUP
WHUP
WHU
TARGET CONFIRMED. WE HAVE FISK.
ROGER THAT, RED LEADER. EXTRACT TARGET TO CHOPPER AND RETURN TO BASE.
I'M NOT SURE HE'S GONNA MAKE IT, ECHO BASE.
HOW THE HELL ARE WE EVEN SUPPOSED TO GET THIS GUY ON THE CHOPPER?

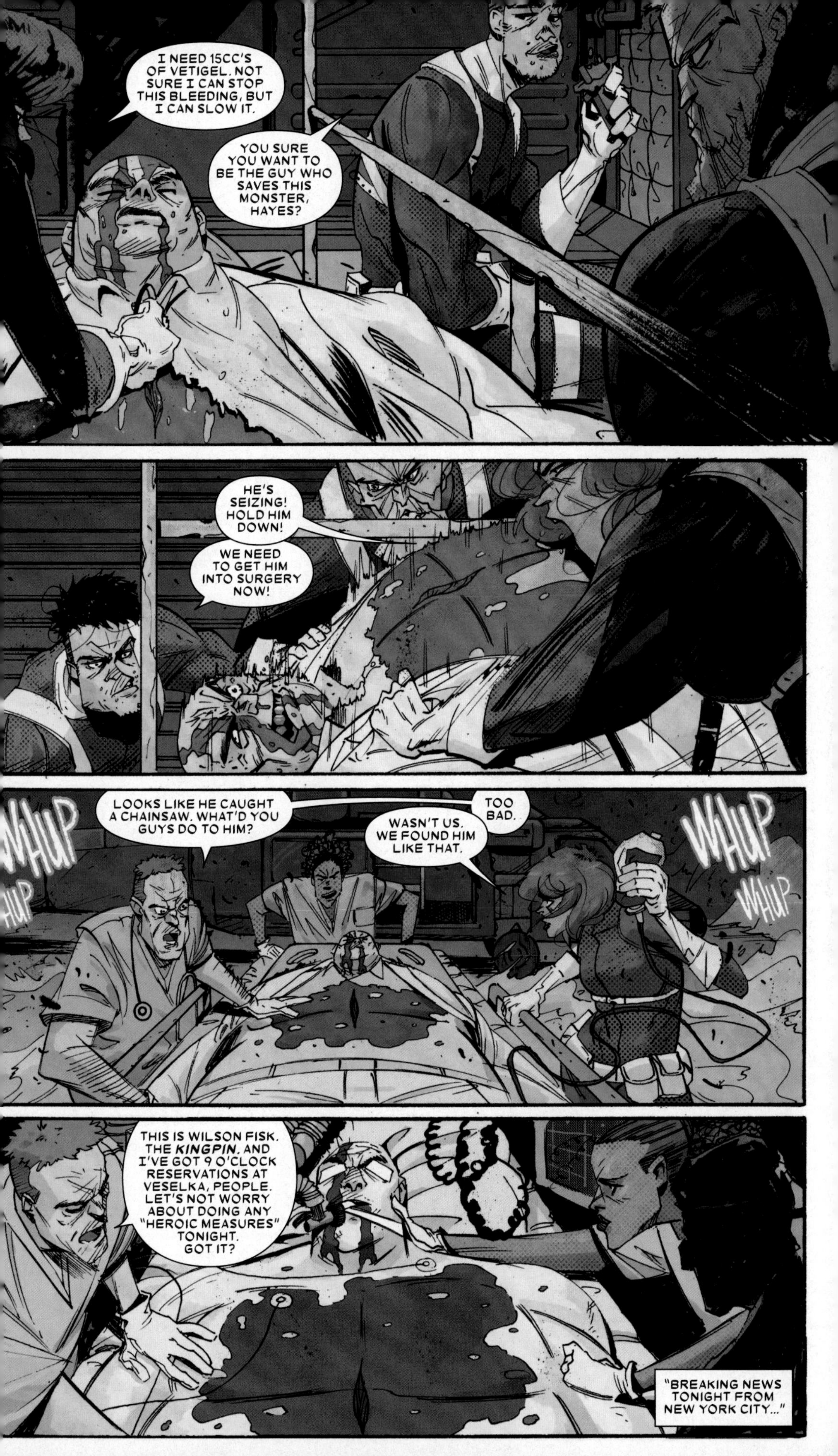

I NEED 15CC'S OF VETIGEL. NOT SURE I CAN STOP THIS BLEEDING, BUT I CAN SLOW IT.
YOU SURE YOU WANT TO BE THE GUY WHO SAVES THIS MONSTER, HAYES?
HE'S SEIZING! HOLD HIM DOWN!
WE NEED TO GET HIM INTO SURGERY NOW!
WHUP
WHUP
LOOKS LIKE HE CAUGHT A CHAINSAW. WHAT'D YOU GUYS DO TO HIM?
TOO BAD.
WASN'T US. WE FOUND HIM LIKE THAT.
WHUP
WHUP
THIS IS WILSON FISK. THE KINGPIN, AND I'VE GOT 9 O'CLOCK RESERVATIONS AT VESELKA, PEOPLE. LET'S NOT WORRY ABOUT DOING ANY "HEROIC MEASURES" TONIGHT. GOT IT?
"BREAKING NEWS TONIGHT FROM NEW YORK CITY..."

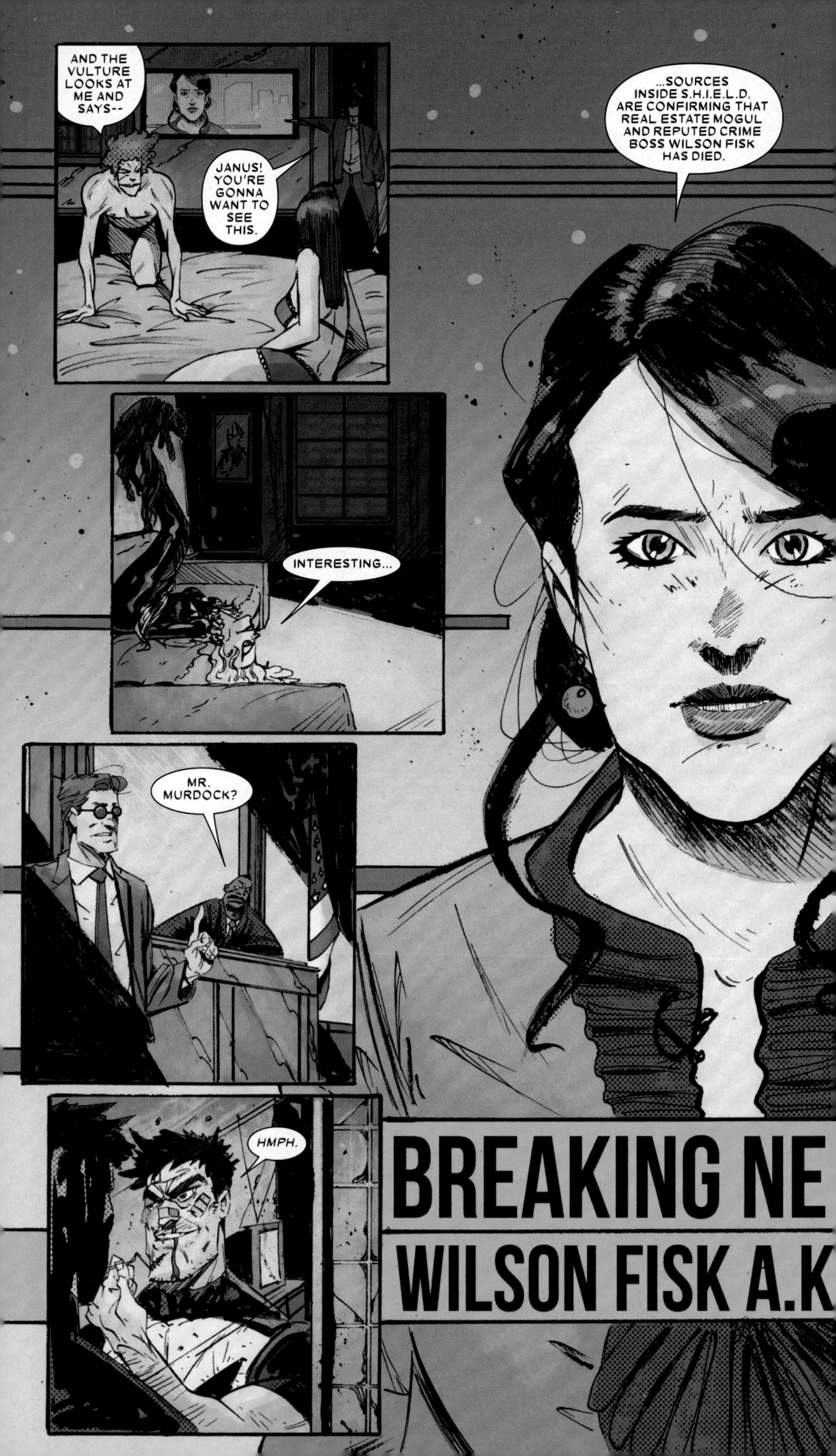
AND THE VULTURE LOOKS AT ME AND SAYS--
JANUS! YOU'RE GONNA WANT TO SEE THIS.
...SOURCES INSIDE S.H.I.E.L.D. ARE CONFIRMING THAT REAL ESTATE MOGUL AND REPUTED CRIME BOSS WILSON FISK HAS DIED.
INTERESTING...
MR. MURDOCK?
HMPH.
BREAKING NE
WILSON FISK A.K

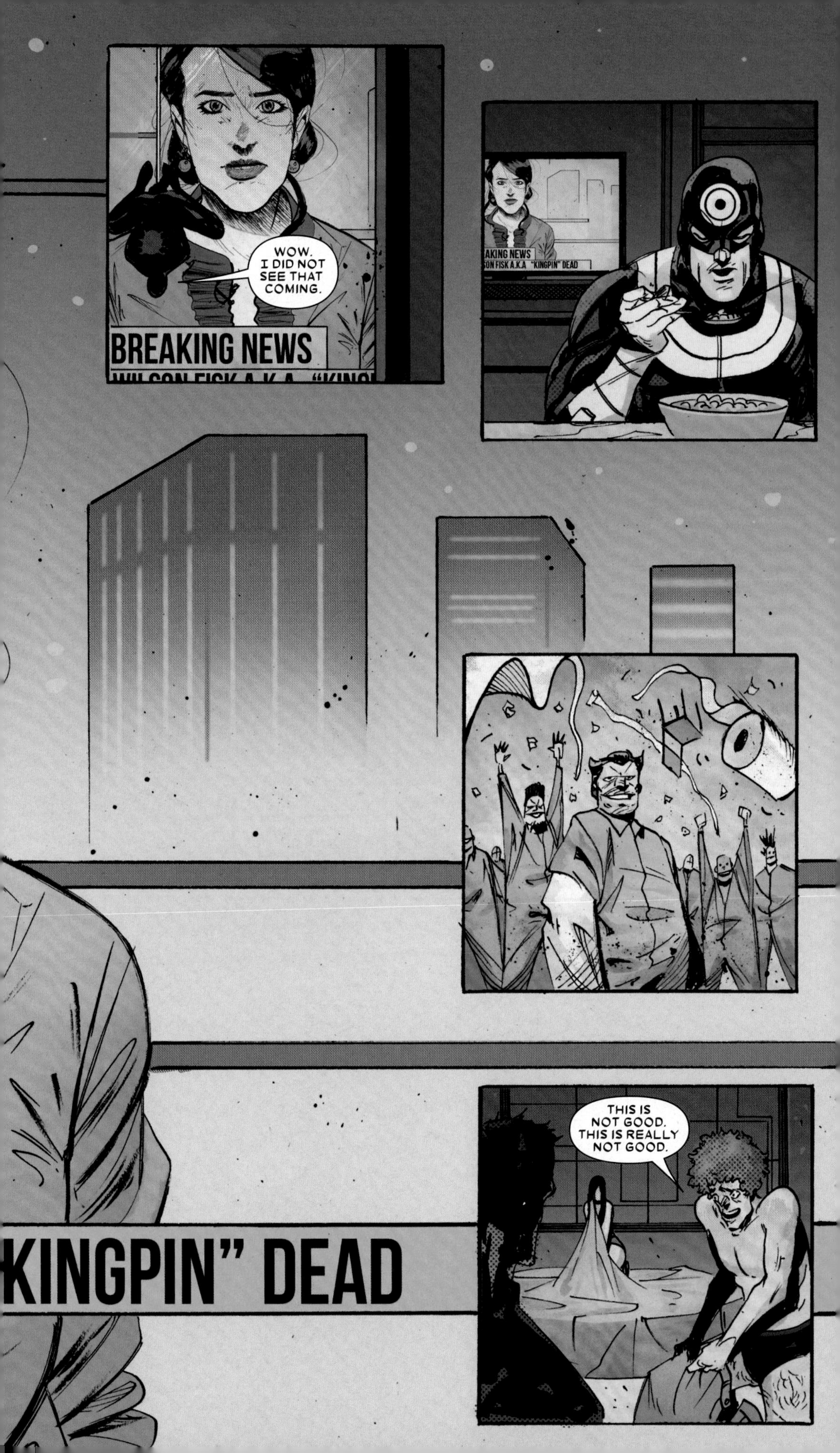

WOW. I DID NOT SEE THAT COMING.
BREAKING NEWS
BREAKING NEWS
SON FISK A.K.A "KINGPIN" DEAD
"KINGPIN" DEAD
THIS IS NOT GOOD. THIS IS REALLY NOT GOOD.

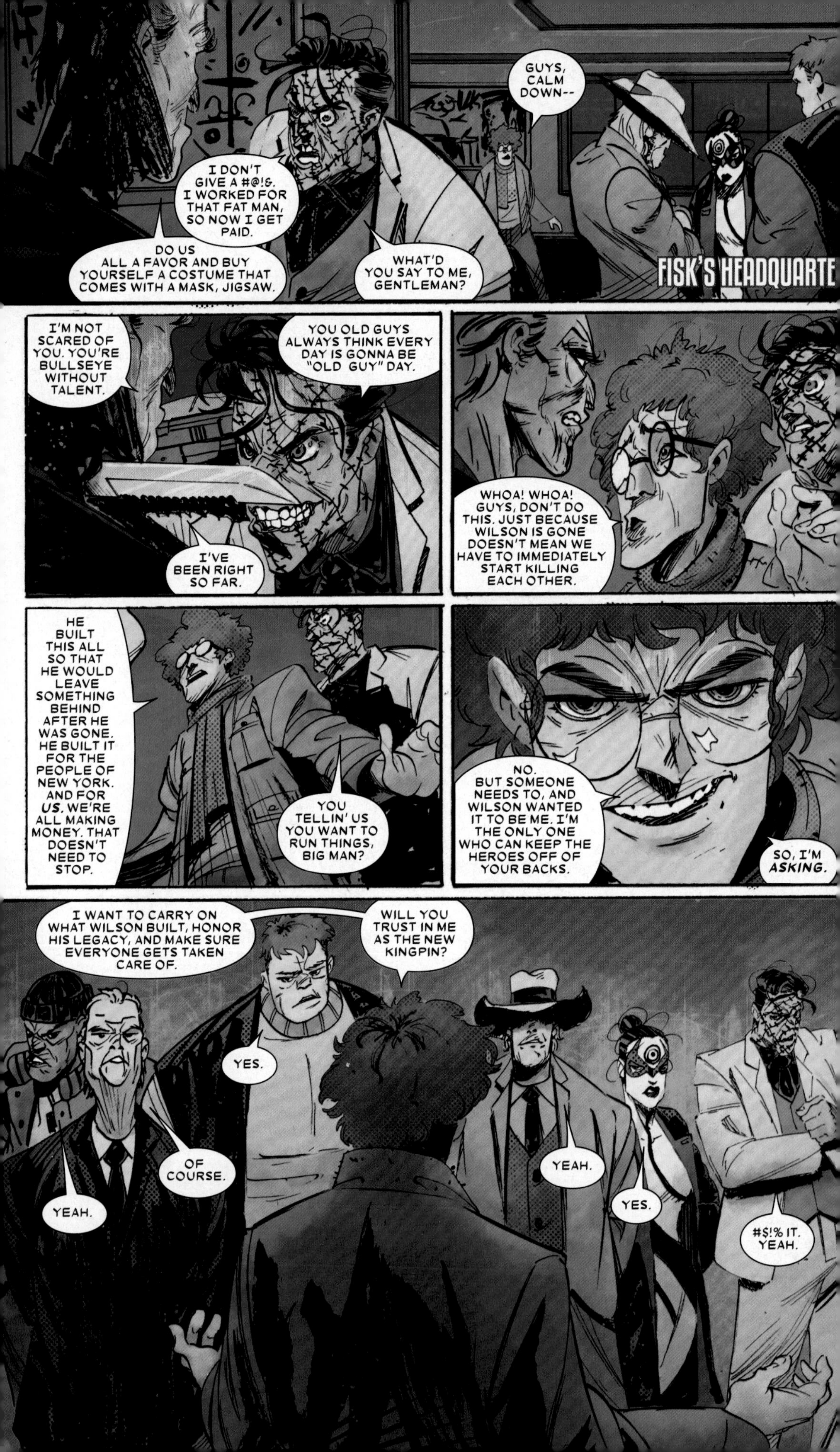
GUYS, CALM DOWN--
I DON'T GIVE A #@!&. I WORKED FOR THAT FAT MAN, SO NOW I GET PAID.
DO US ALL A FAVOR AND BUY YOURSELF A COSTUME THAT COMES WITH A MASK, JIGSAW.
WHAT'D YOU SAY TO ME, GENTLEMAN?
FISK'S HEADQUARTE
I'M NOT SCARED OF YOU. YOU'RE BULLSEYE WITHOUT TALENT.
YOU OLD GUYS ALWAYS THINK EVERY DAY IS GONNA BE "OLD GUY" DAY.
I'VE BEEN RIGHT SO FAR.
WHOA! WHOA! GUYS, DON'T DO THIS. JUST BECAUSE WILSON IS GONE DOESN'T MEAN WE HAVE TO IMMEDIATELY START KILLING EACH OTHER.
HE BUILT THIS ALL SO THAT HE WOULD LEAVE SOMETHING BEHIND AFTER HE WAS GONE. HE BUILT IT FOR THE PEOPLE OF NEW YORK. AND FOR *US*. WE'RE ALL MAKING MONEY. THAT DOESN'T NEED TO STOP.
YOU TELLIN' US YOU WANT TO RUN THINGS, BIG MAN?
NO. BUT SOMEONE NEEDS TO, AND WILSON WANTED IT TO BE ME. I'M THE ONLY ONE WHO CAN KEEP THE HEROES OFF OF YOUR BACKS.
SO, I'M *ASKING*.
I WANT TO CARRY ON WHAT WILSON BUILT, HONOR HIS LEGACY, AND MAKE SURE EVERYONE GETS TAKEN CARE OF.
WILL YOU TRUST IN ME AS THE NEW KINGPIN?
YES.
OF COURSE.
YEAH.
YEAH.
YES.
#$!% IT. YEAH.

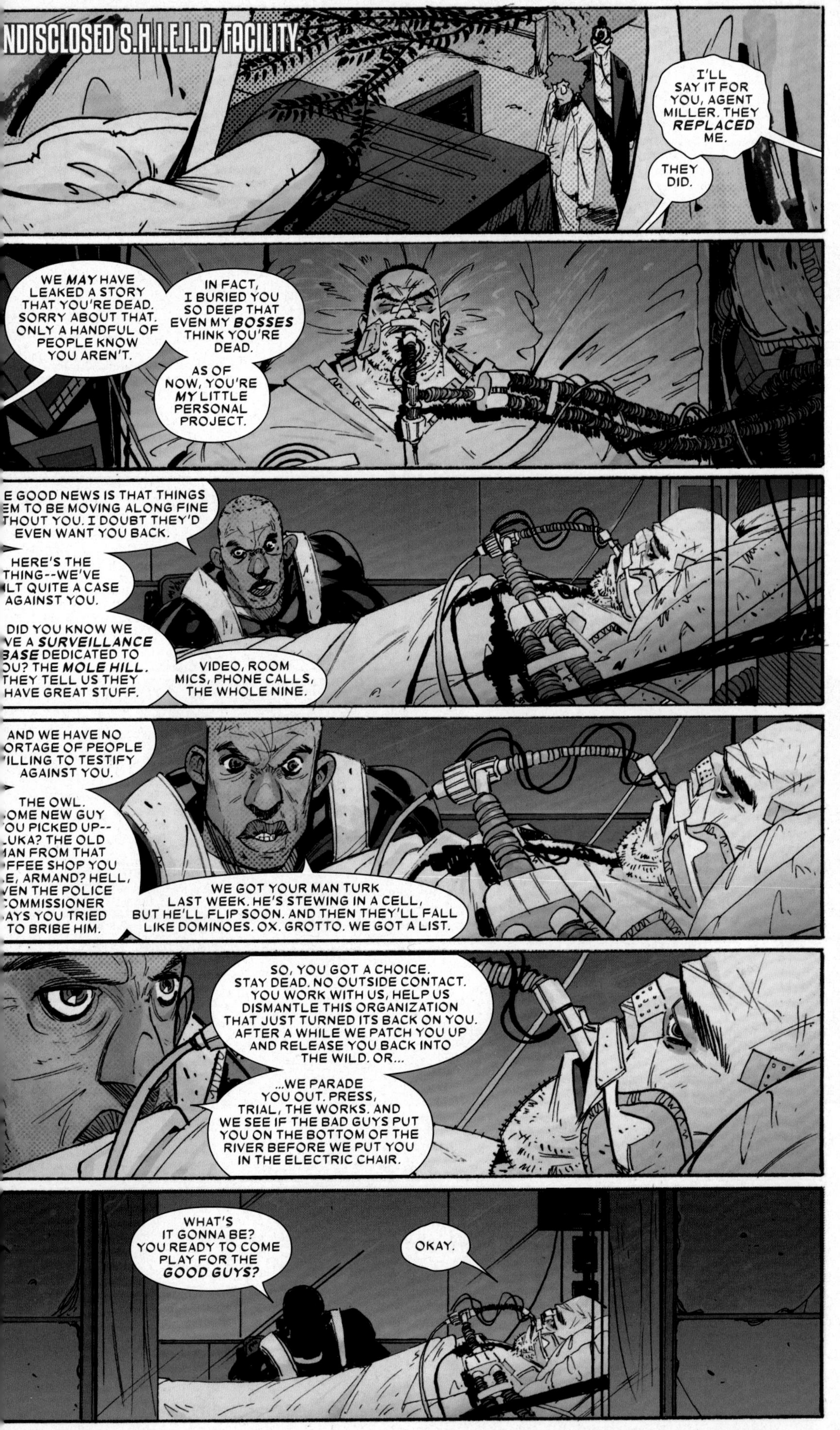
NDISCLOSED S.H.I.E.L.D. FACILITY.
I'LL SAY IT FOR YOU, AGENT MILLER. THEY REPLACED ME.
THEY DID.
WE MAY HAVE LEAKED A STORY THAT YOU'RE DEAD. SORRY ABOUT THAT. ONLY A HANDFUL OF PEOPLE KNOW YOU AREN'T.
IN FACT, I BURIED YOU SO DEEP THAT EVEN MY BOSSES THINK YOU'RE DEAD.
AS OF NOW, YOU'RE MY LITTLE PERSONAL PROJECT.
E GOOD NEWS IS THAT THINGS EM TO BE MOVING ALONG FINE THOUT YOU. I DOUBT THEY'D EVEN WANT YOU BACK.
HERE'S THE THING--WE'VE LT QUITE A CASE AGAINST YOU.
DID YOU KNOW WE VE A SURVEILLANCE BASE DEDICATED TO OU? THE MOLE HILL. THEY TELL US THEY HAVE GREAT STUFF.
VIDEO, ROOM MICS, PHONE CALLS, THE WHOLE NINE.
AND WE HAVE NO ORTAGE OF PEOPLE VILLING TO TESTIFY AGAINST YOU.
THE OWL. OME NEW GUY OU PICKED UP-- LUKA? THE OLD MAN FROM THAT FFEE SHOP YOU E, ARMAND? HELL, VEN THE POLICE COMMISSIONER AYS YOU TRIED TO BRIBE HIM.
WE GOT YOUR MAN TURK LAST WEEK. HE'S STEWING IN A CELL, BUT HE'LL FLIP SOON. AND THEN THEY'LL FALL LIKE DOMINOES. OX. GROTTO. WE GOT A LIST.
SO, YOU GOT A CHOICE. STAY DEAD. NO OUTSIDE CONTACT. YOU WORK WITH US, HELP US DISMANTLE THIS ORGANIZATION THAT JUST TURNED ITS BACK ON YOU. AFTER A WHILE WE PATCH YOU UP AND RELEASE YOU BACK INTO THE WILD. OR...
...WE PARADE YOU OUT. PRESS, TRIAL, THE WORKS. AND WE SEE IF THE BAD GUYS PUT YOU ON THE BOTTOM OF THE RIVER BEFORE WE PUT YOU IN THE ELECTRIC CHAIR.
WHAT'S IT GONNA BE? YOU READY TO COME PLAY FOR THE GOOD GUYS?
OKAY.

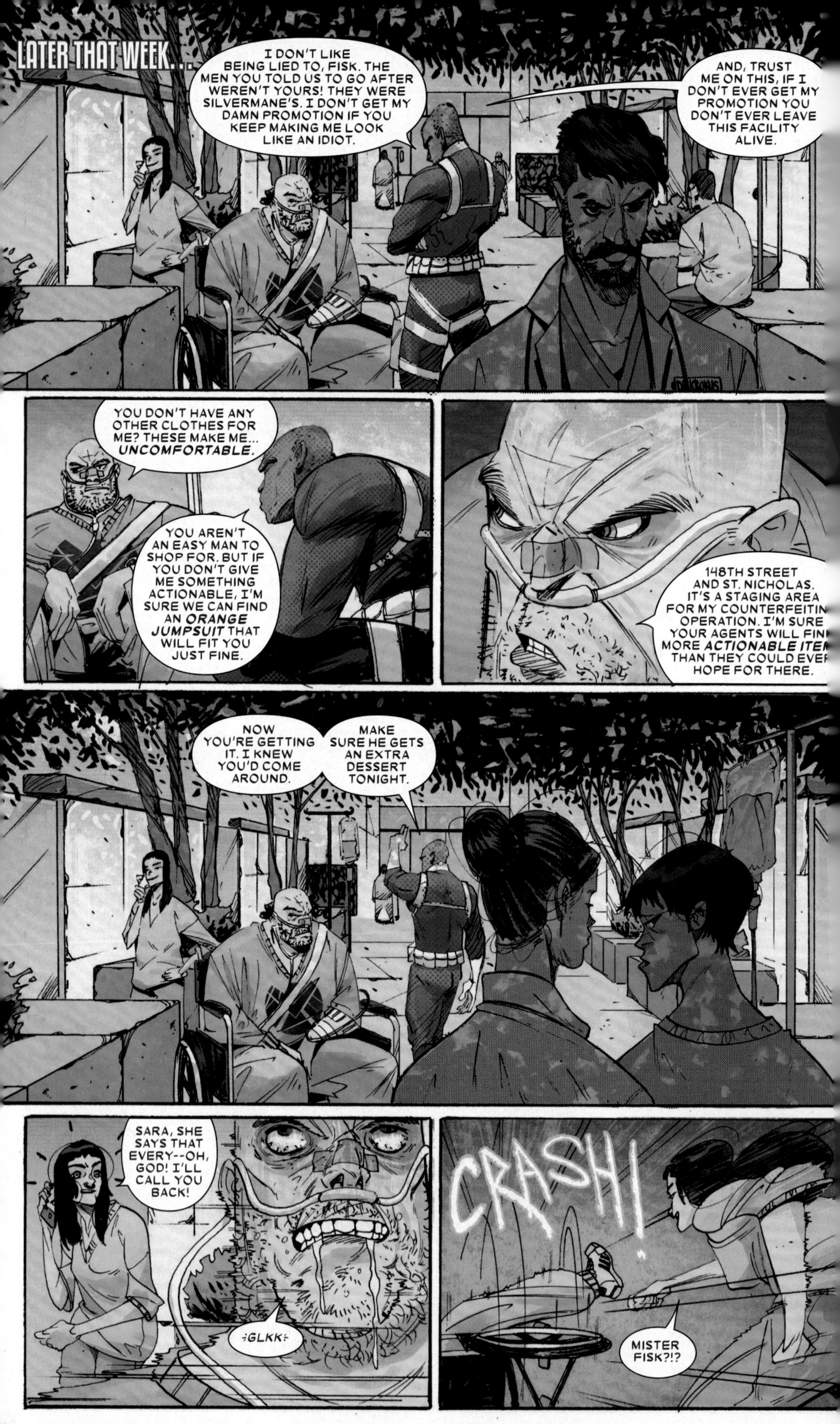
LATER THAT WEEK...
I DON'T LIKE BEING LIED TO, FISK. THE MEN YOU TOLD US TO GO AFTER WEREN'T YOURS! THEY WERE SILVERMANE'S. I DON'T GET MY DAMN PROMOTION IF YOU KEEP MAKING ME LOOK LIKE AN IDIOT.
AND, TRUST ME ON THIS, IF I DON'T EVER GET MY PROMOTION YOU DON'T EVER LEAVE THIS FACILITY ALIVE.
YOU DON'T HAVE ANY OTHER CLOTHES FOR ME? THESE MAKE ME... UNCOMFORTABLE.
YOU AREN'T AN EASY MAN TO SHOP FOR. BUT IF YOU DON'T GIVE ME SOMETHING ACTIONABLE, I'M SURE WE CAN FIND AN ORANGE JUMPSUIT THAT WILL FIT YOU JUST FINE.
148TH STREET AND ST. NICHOLAS. IT'S A STAGING AREA FOR MY COUNTERFEITIN OPERATION. I'M SURE YOUR AGENTS WILL FIN MORE ACTIONABLE ITE THAN THEY COULD EVER HOPE FOR THERE.
NOW YOU'RE GETTING IT. I KNEW YOU'D COME AROUND.
MAKE SURE HE GETS AN EXTRA DESSERT TONIGHT.
SARA, SHE SAYS THAT EVERY--OH, GOD! I'LL CALL YOU BACK!
GLKK
CRASH!
MISTER FISK?!?

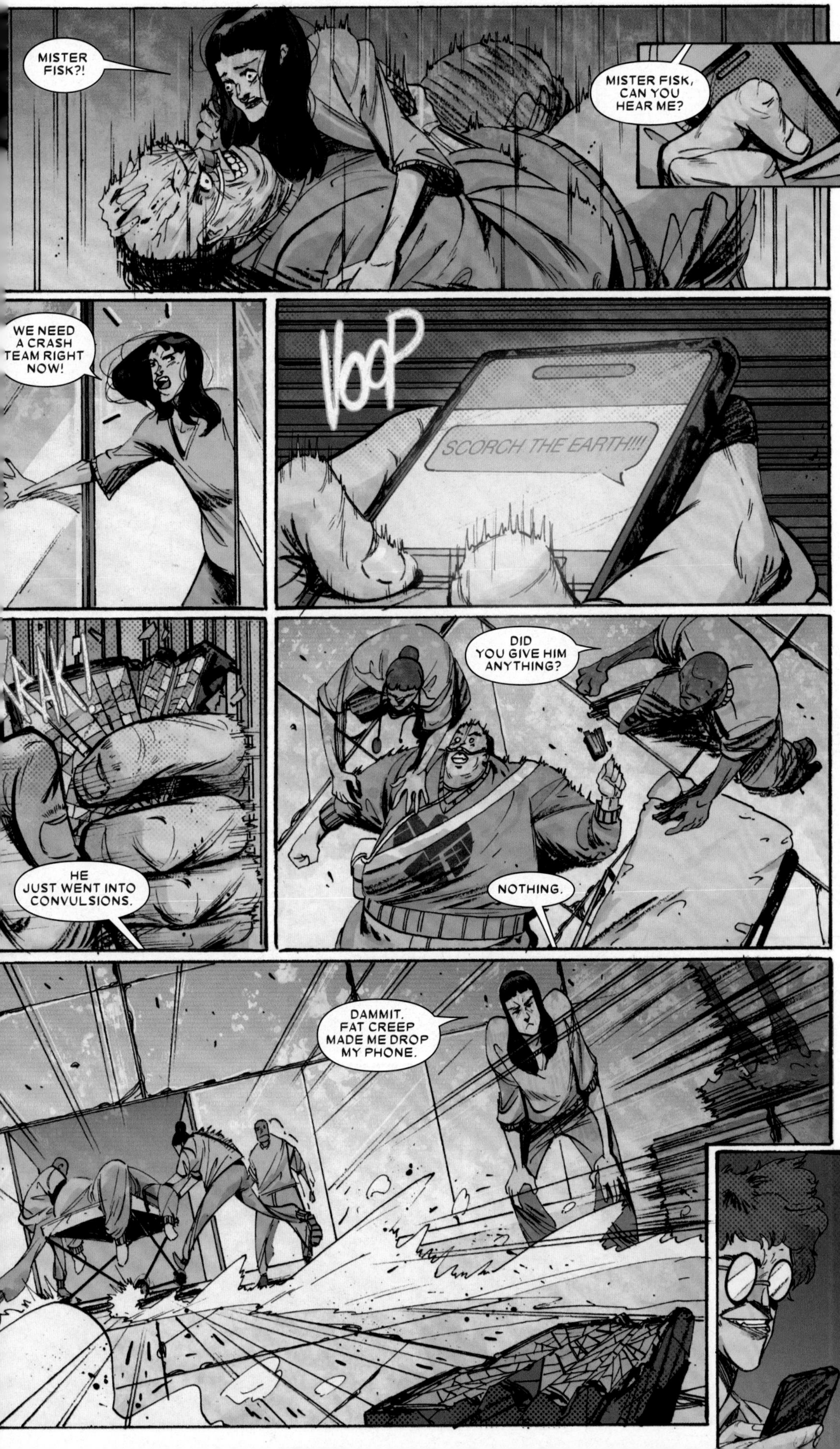

MISTER FISK?!
MISTER FISK, CAN YOU HEAR ME?
WE NEED A CRASH TEAM RIGHT NOW!
VOOP
SCORCH THE EARTH!!!
RAK!
HE JUST WENT INTO CONVULSIONS.
DID YOU GIVE HIM ANYTHING?
NOTHING.
DAMMIT. FAT CREEP MADE ME DROP MY PHONE.

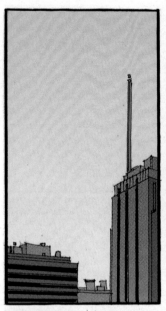

AND THE VULTURE SAYS, "THAT WAS HIS GRANDFATHER!"

TURK, YOU KNOW THE VULTURE WOULD TOTALLY DESTROY YOU IN A FIGHT, RIGHT?

THAT'S NOT THE POINT. I COULD--

HANG ON.

LOOK SHARP.

WAIT...

...I KNOW THIS GUY.

HEY! AGENT GUDMUNSDOTTIR, RIGHT?

YEAH. HEY. DAILEY SENT ME DOWN HERE TO TALK TO YOU ABOUT YOUR TRANSPORT DETAIL.

WHAT ABOUT IT? WE'RE ALREADY MOVING THE ASSET.

YEAH...I'M SORRY.

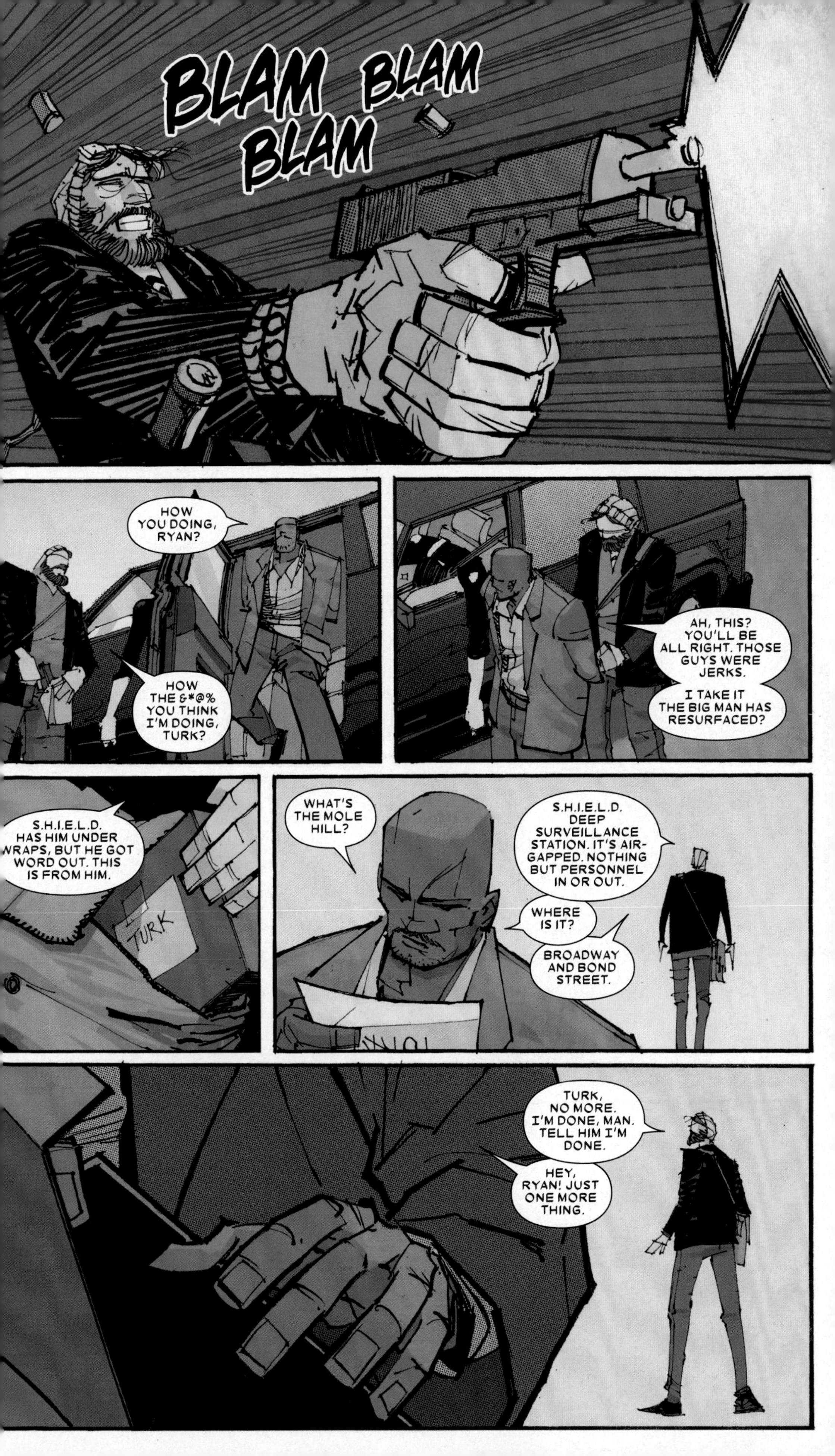
BLAM BLAM
BLAM
HOW YOU DOING, RYAN?
HOW THE &*@% YOU THINK I'M DOING, TURK?
AH, THIS? YOU'LL BE ALL RIGHT. THOSE GUYS WERE JERKS.
I TAKE IT THE BIG MAN HAS RESURFACED?
S.H.I.E.L.D. HAS HIM UNDER WRAPS, BUT HE GOT WORD OUT. THIS IS FROM HIM.
TURK
WHAT'S THE MOLE HILL?
S.H.I.E.L.D. DEEP SURVEILLANCE STATION. IT'S AIR-GAPPED. NOTHING BUT PERSONNEL IN OR OUT.
WHERE IS IT?
BROADWAY AND BOND STREET.
TURK, NO MORE. I'M DONE, MAN. TELL HIM I'M DONE.
HEY, RYAN! JUST ONE MORE THING.

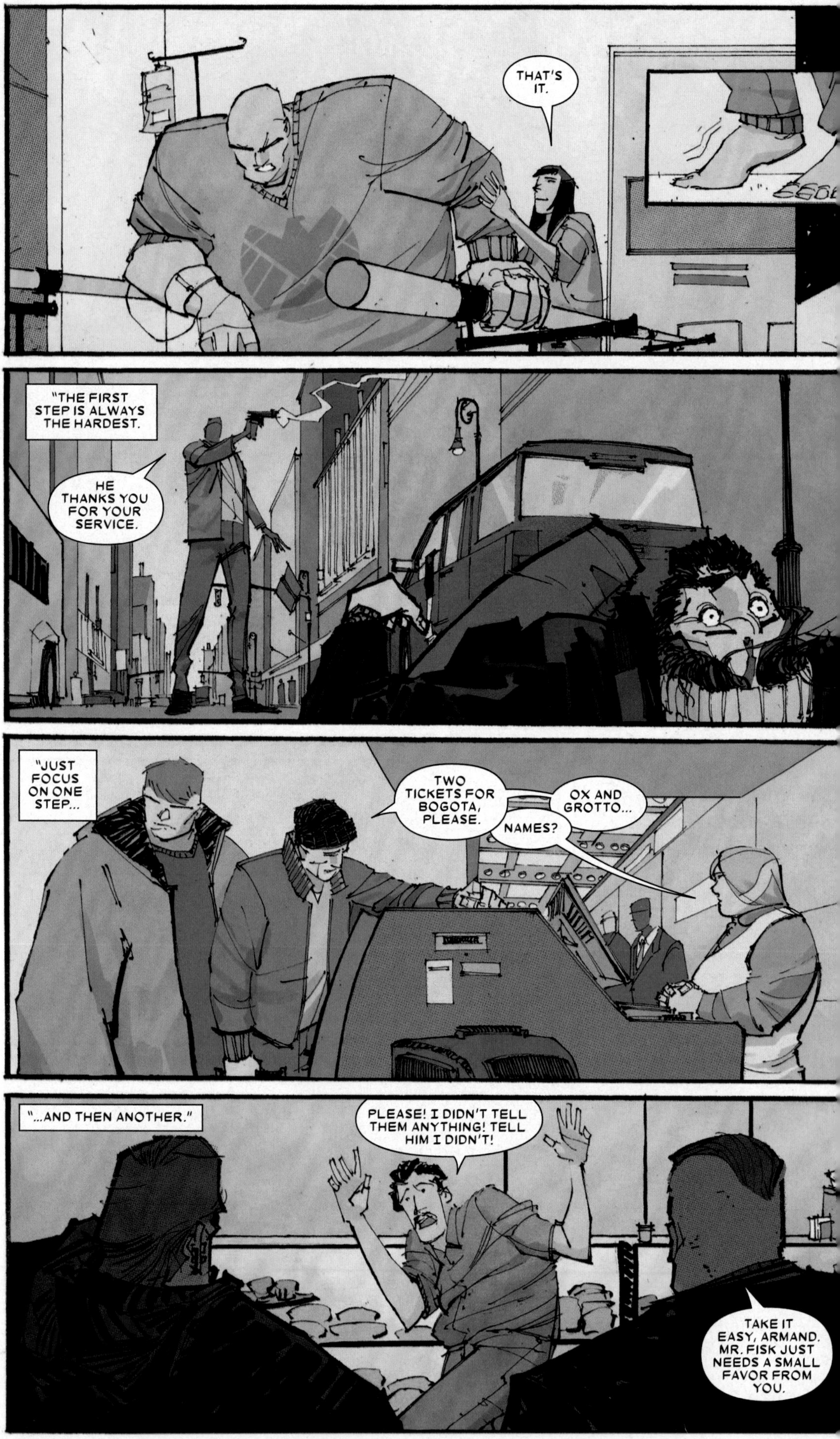
THAT'S IT.
"THE FIRST STEP IS ALWAYS THE HARDEST.
HE THANKS YOU FOR YOUR SERVICE.
"JUST FOCUS ON ONE STEP...
TWO TICKETS FOR BOGOTA, PLEASE.
NAMES?
OX AND GROTTO...
"...AND THEN ANOTHER."
PLEASE! I DIDN'T TELL THEM ANYTHING! TELL HIM I DIDN'T!
TAKE IT EASY, ARMAND. MR. FISK JUST NEEDS A SMALL FAVOR FROM YOU.

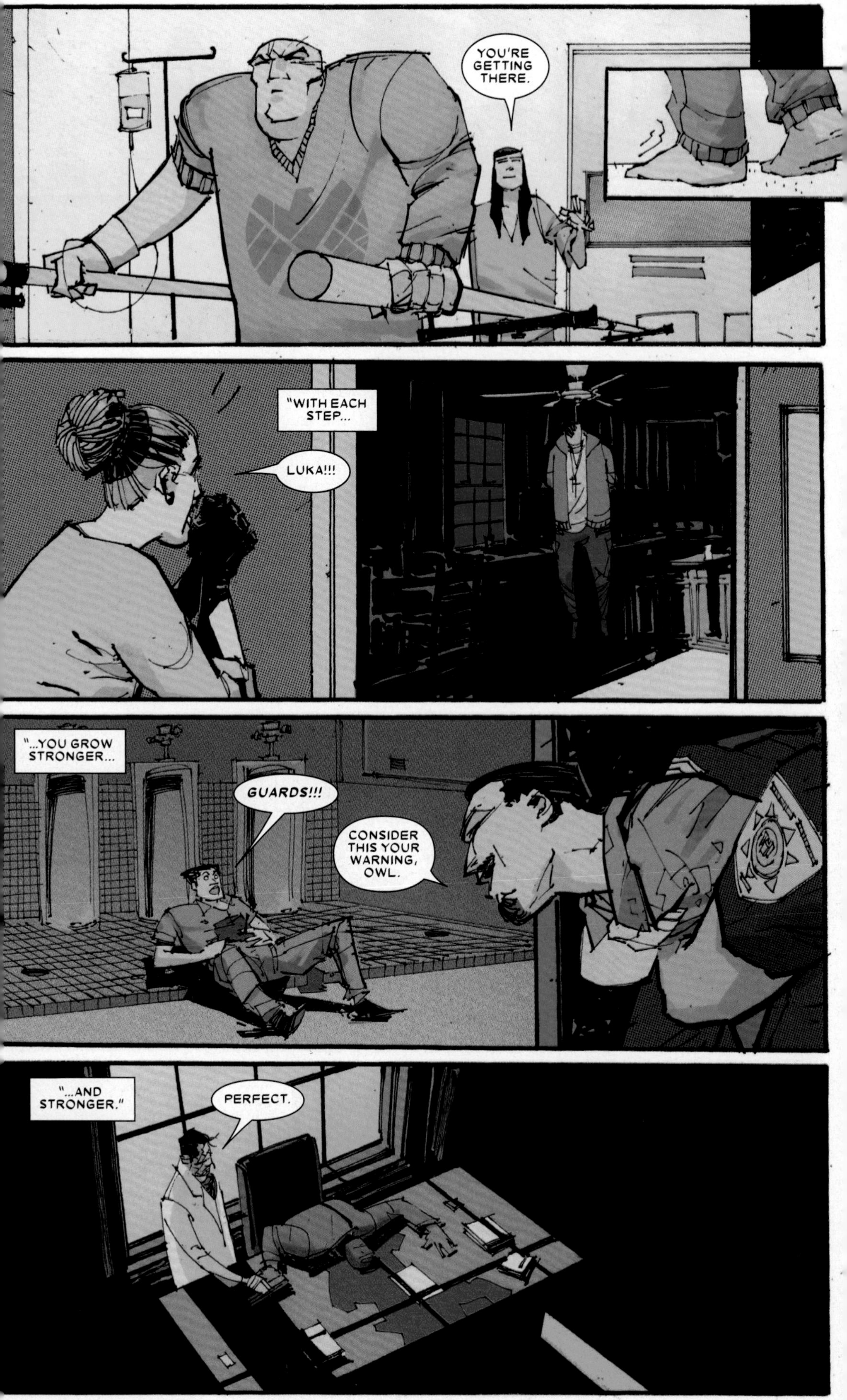
YOU'RE GETTING THERE.
"WITH EACH STEP...
LUKA!!!
"...YOU GROW STRONGER...
GUARDS!!!
CONSIDER THIS YOUR WARNING, OWL.
"...AND STRONGER."
PERFECT.

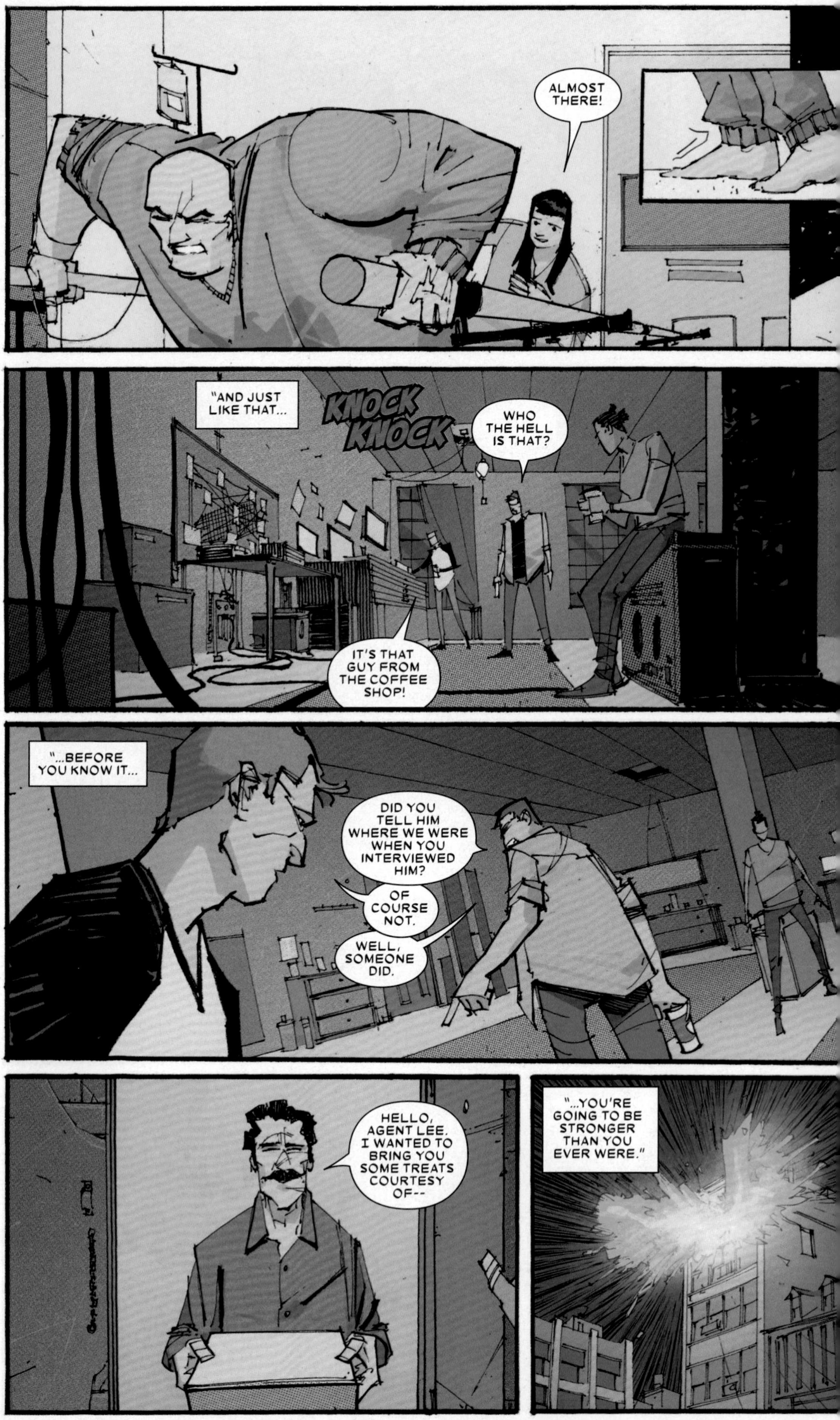
ALMOST THERE!
"AND JUST LIKE THAT...
KNOCK KNOCK
WHO THE HELL IS THAT?
IT'S THAT GUY FROM THE COFFEE SHOP!
"...BEFORE YOU KNOW IT...
DID YOU TELL HIM WHERE WE WERE WHEN YOU INTERVIEWED HIM?
OF COURSE NOT.
WELL, SOMEONE DID.
HELLO, AGENT LEE. I WANTED TO BRING YOU SOME TREATS COURTESY OF--
"...YOU'RE GOING TO BE STRONGER THAN YOU EVER WERE."

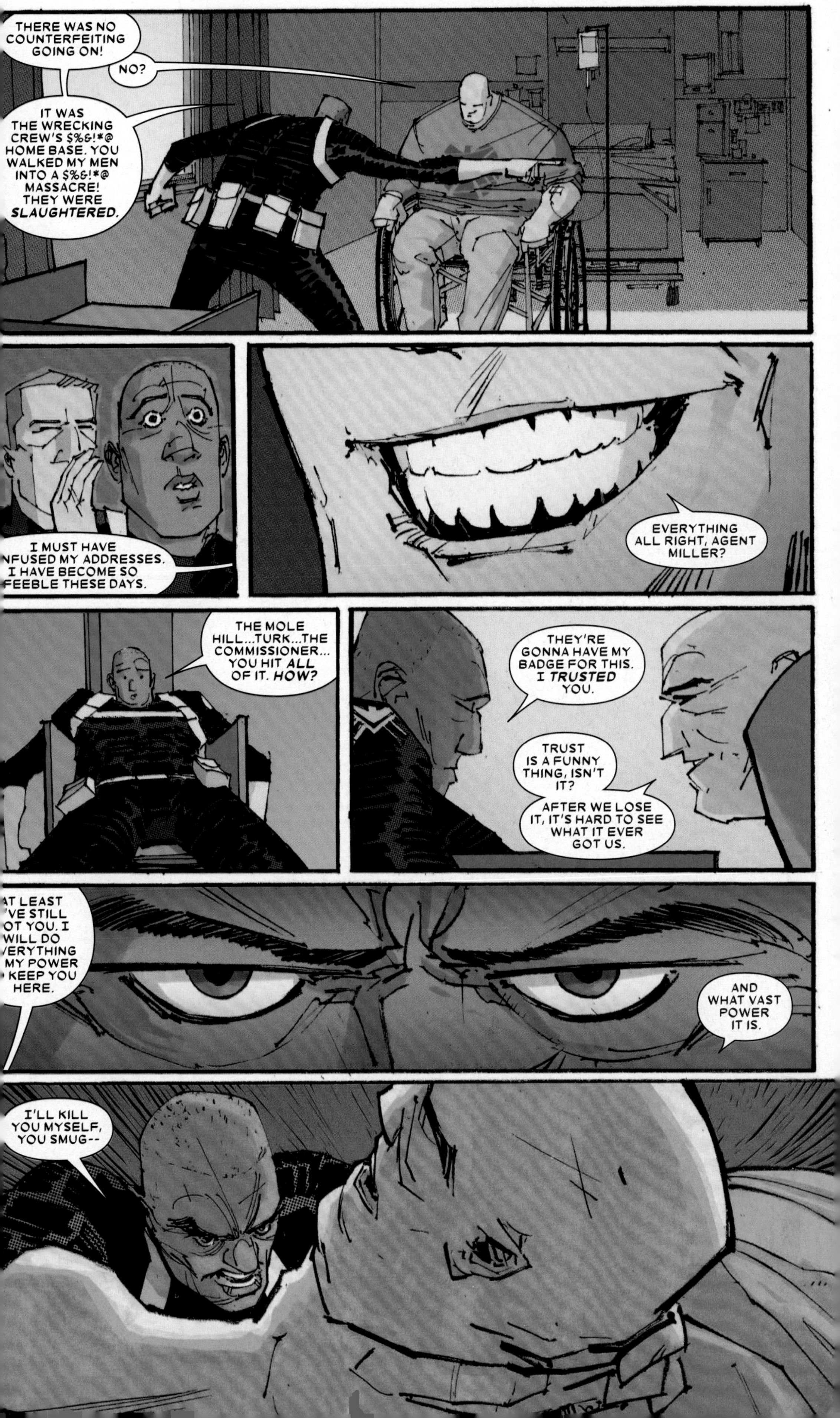
THERE WAS NO COUNTERFEITING GOING ON!
NO?
IT WAS THE WRECKING CREW'S $%&!*@ HOME BASE. YOU WALKED MY MEN INTO A $%&!*@ MASSACRE! THEY WERE *SLAUGHTERED.*
I MUST HAVE NFUSED MY ADDRESSES. I HAVE BECOME SO FEEBLE THESE DAYS.
EVERYTHING ALL RIGHT, AGENT MILLER?
THE MOLE HILL...TURK...THE COMMISSIONER... YOU HIT *ALL* OF IT. *HOW?*
THEY'RE GONNA HAVE MY BADGE FOR THIS. I *TRUSTED* YOU.
TRUST IS A FUNNY THING, ISN'T IT?
AFTER WE LOSE IT, IT'S HARD TO SEE WHAT IT EVER GOT US.
AT LEAST 'VE STILL OT YOU. I WILL DO VERYTHING MY POWER KEEP YOU HERE.
AND WHAT VAST POWER IT IS.
I'LL KILL YOU MYSELF, YOU SMUG--

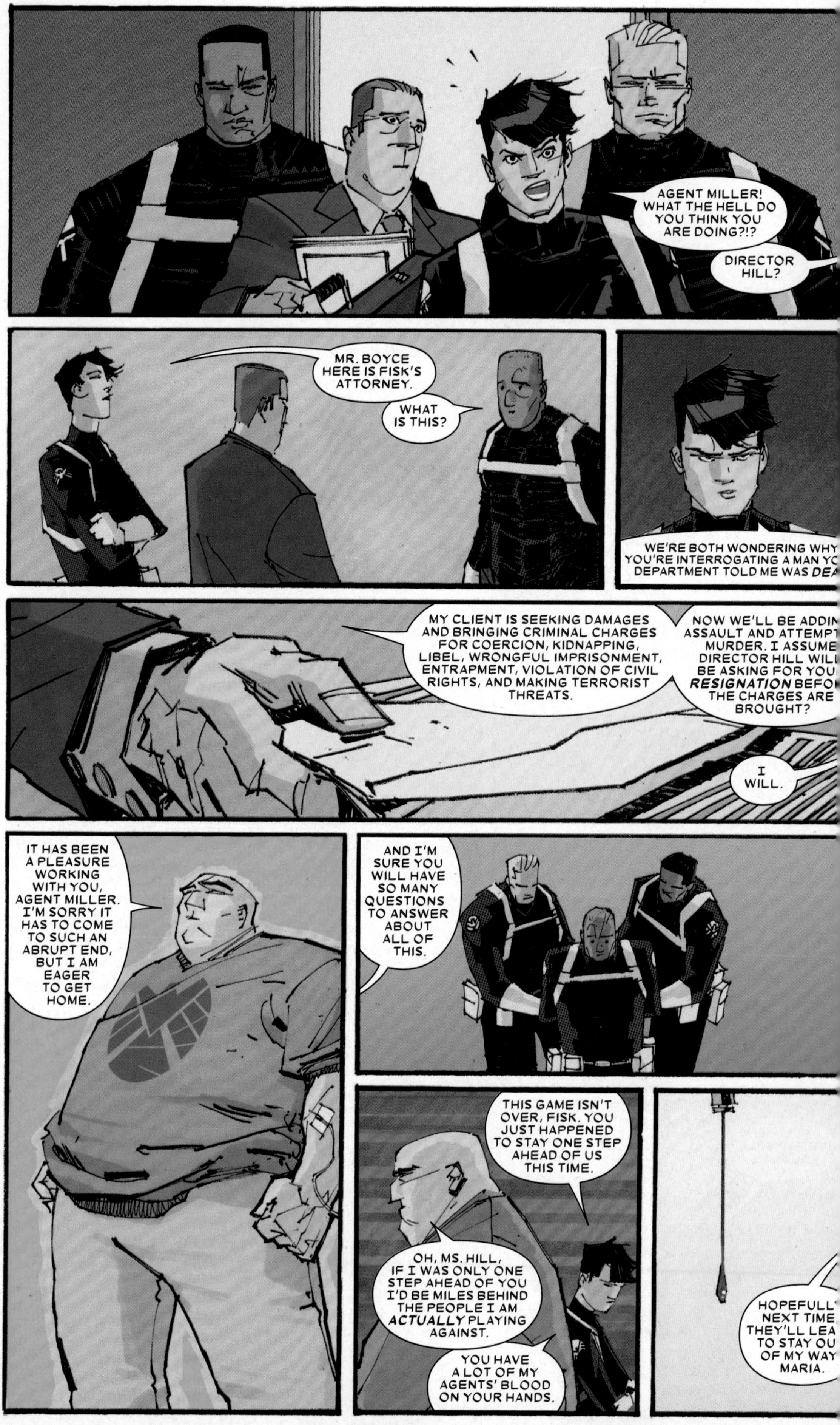

AGENT MILLER! WHAT THE HELL DO YOU THINK YOU ARE DOING?!?
DIRECTOR HILL?
MR. BOYCE HERE IS FISK'S ATTORNEY.
WHAT IS THIS?
WE'RE BOTH WONDERING WHY YOU'RE INTERROGATING A MAN YO DEPARTMENT TOLD ME WAS DEA
MY CLIENT IS SEEKING DAMAGES AND BRINGING CRIMINAL CHARGES FOR COERCION, KIDNAPPING, LIBEL, WRONGFUL IMPRISONMENT, ENTRAPMENT, VIOLATION OF CIVIL RIGHTS, AND MAKING TERRORIST THREATS.
NOW WE'LL BE ADDIN ASSAULT AND ATTEMPT MURDER. I ASSUME DIRECTOR HILL WIL BE ASKING FOR YOU *RESIGNATION* BEFO THE CHARGES ARE BROUGHT?
I WILL.
IT HAS BEEN A PLEASURE WORKING WITH YOU, AGENT MILLER. I'M SORRY IT HAS TO COME TO SUCH AN ABRUPT END, BUT I AM EAGER TO GET HOME.
AND I'M SURE YOU WILL HAVE SO MANY QUESTIONS TO ANSWER ABOUT ALL OF THIS.
THIS GAME ISN'T OVER, FISK. YOU JUST HAPPENED TO STAY ONE STEP AHEAD OF US THIS TIME.
OH, MS. HILL, IF I WAS ONLY ONE STEP AHEAD OF YOU I'D BE MILES BEHIND THE PEOPLE I AM *ACTUALLY* PLAYING AGAINST.
YOU HAVE A LOT OF MY AGENTS' BLOOD ON YOUR HANDS.
HOPEFULL NEXT TIME THEY'LL LEA TO STAY OU OF MY WAY MARIA.

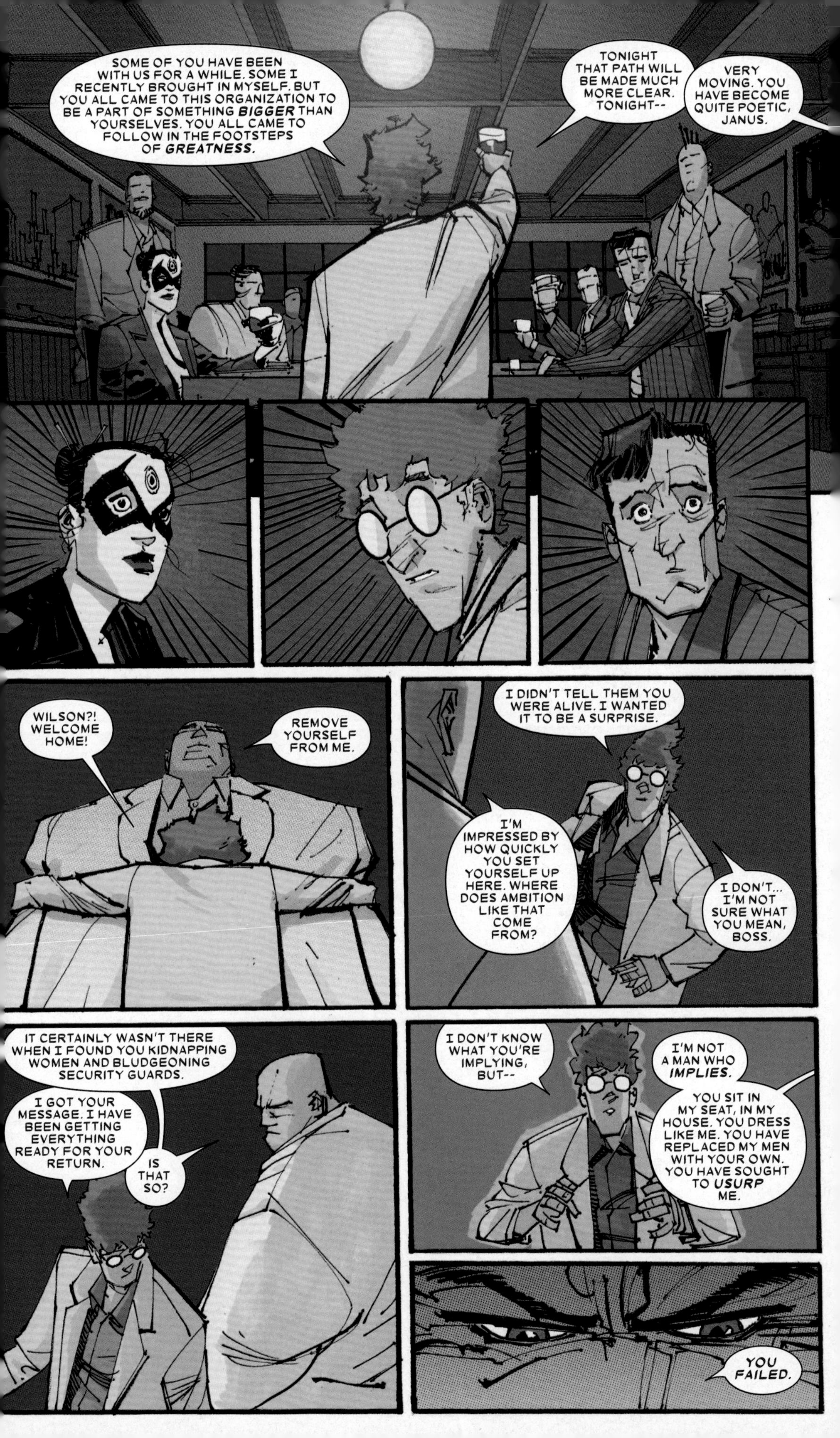
SOME OF YOU HAVE BEEN WITH US FOR A WHILE. SOME I RECENTLY BROUGHT IN MYSELF. BUT YOU ALL CAME TO THIS ORGANIZATION TO BE A PART OF SOMETHING BIGGER THAN YOURSELVES. YOU ALL CAME TO FOLLOW IN THE FOOTSTEPS OF GREATNESS.
TONIGHT THAT PATH WILL BE MADE MUCH MORE CLEAR. TONIGHT--
VERY MOVING. YOU HAVE BECOME QUITE POETIC, JANUS.
WILSON?! WELCOME HOME!
REMOVE YOURSELF FROM ME.
I DIDN'T TELL THEM YOU WERE ALIVE. I WANTED IT TO BE A SURPRISE.
I'M IMPRESSED BY HOW QUICKLY YOU SET YOURSELF UP HERE. WHERE DOES AMBITION LIKE THAT COME FROM?
I DON'T... I'M NOT SURE WHAT YOU MEAN, BOSS.
I GOT YOUR MESSAGE. I HAVE BEEN GETTING EVERYTHING READY FOR YOUR RETURN.
IS THAT SO?
IT CERTAINLY WASN'T THERE WHEN I FOUND YOU KIDNAPPING WOMEN AND BLUDGEONING SECURITY GUARDS.
I DON'T KNOW WHAT YOU'RE IMPLYING, BUT--
I'M NOT A MAN WHO IMPLIES.
YOU SIT IN MY SEAT, IN MY HOUSE. YOU DRESS LIKE ME. YOU HAVE REPLACED MY MEN WITH YOUR OWN. YOU HAVE SOUGHT TO USURP ME.
YOU FAILED.

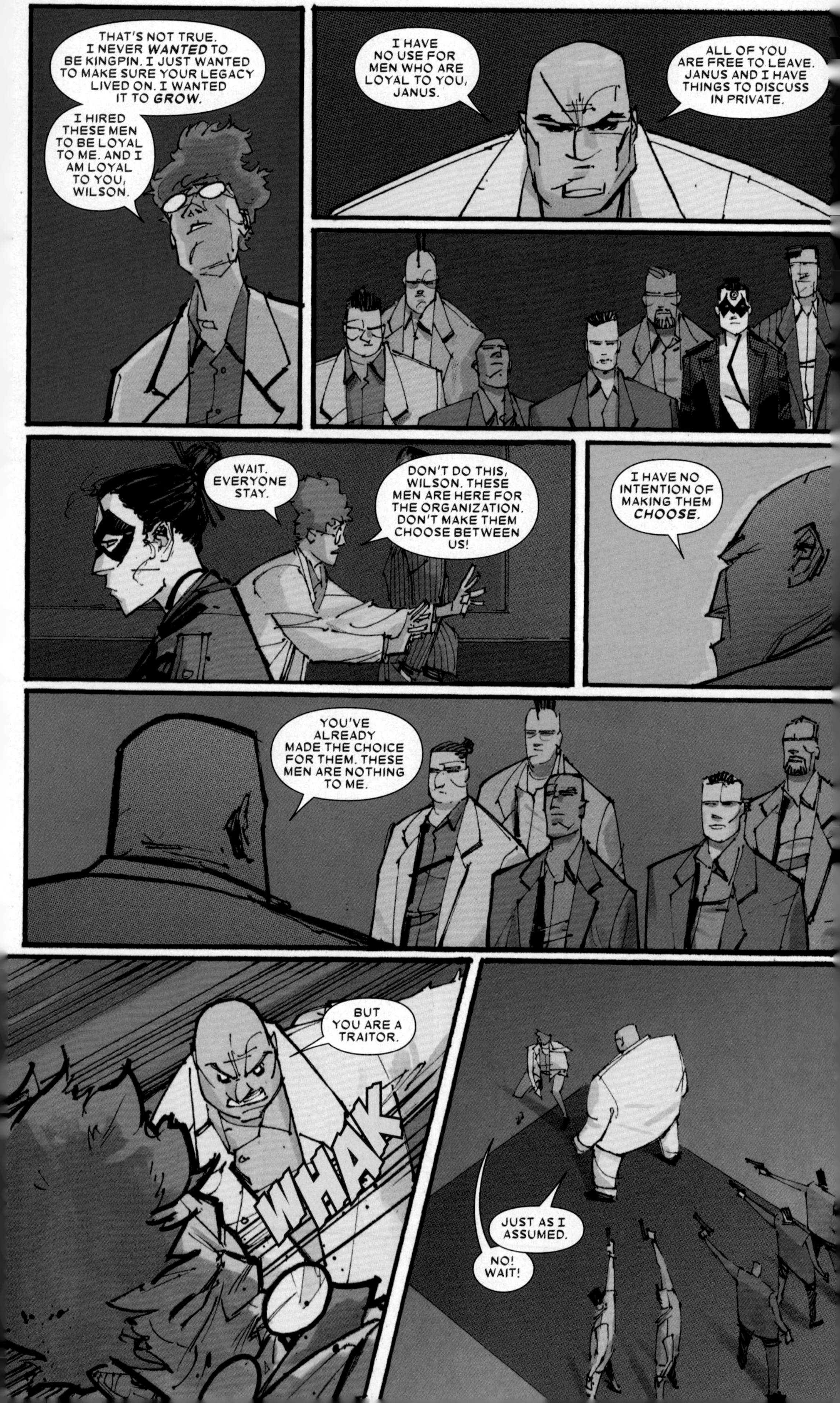

THAT'S NOT TRUE. I NEVER WANTED TO BE KINGPIN. I JUST WANTED TO MAKE SURE YOUR LEGACY LIVED ON. I WANTED IT TO GROW.
I HIRED THESE MEN TO BE LOYAL TO ME. AND I AM LOYAL TO YOU, WILSON.
I HAVE NO USE FOR MEN WHO ARE LOYAL TO YOU, JANUS.
ALL OF YOU ARE FREE TO LEAVE. JANUS AND I HAVE THINGS TO DISCUSS IN PRIVATE.
WAIT. EVERYONE STAY.
DON'T DO THIS, WILSON. THESE MEN ARE HERE FOR THE ORGANIZATION. DON'T MAKE THEM CHOOSE BETWEEN US!
I HAVE NO INTENTION OF MAKING THEM CHOOSE.
YOU'VE ALREADY MADE THE CHOICE FOR THEM. THESE MEN ARE NOTHING TO ME.
BUT YOU ARE A TRAITOR.
WHAK
JUST AS I ASSUMED.
NO! WAIT!

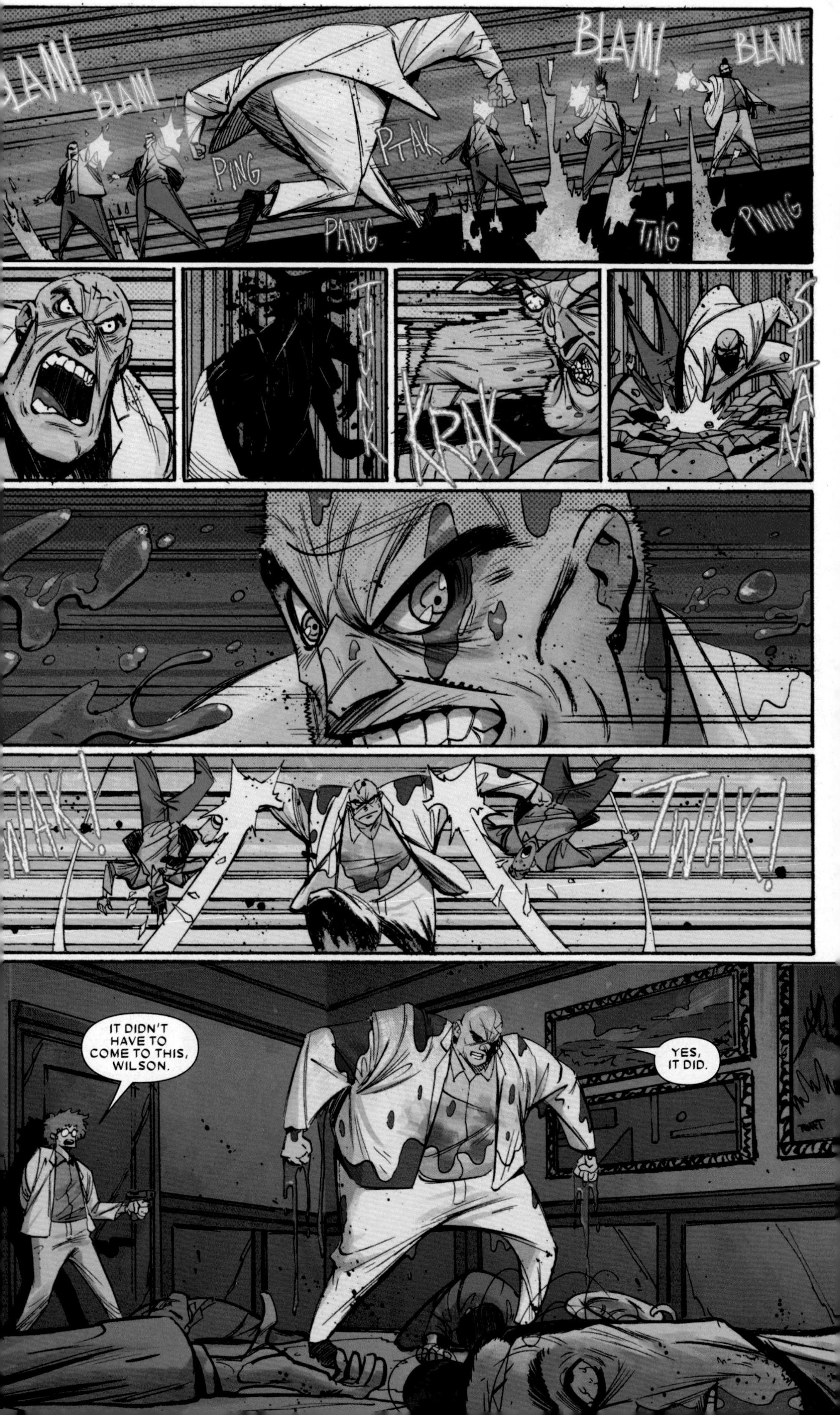
BLAM!
BLAM
BLAM!
BLAM!
PING
PTAK
PANG
TING
PWING
THUNK
KRAK
SLAM
TWAK!
TWAK!
IT DIDN'T HAVE TO COME TO THIS, WILSON.
YES, IT DID.

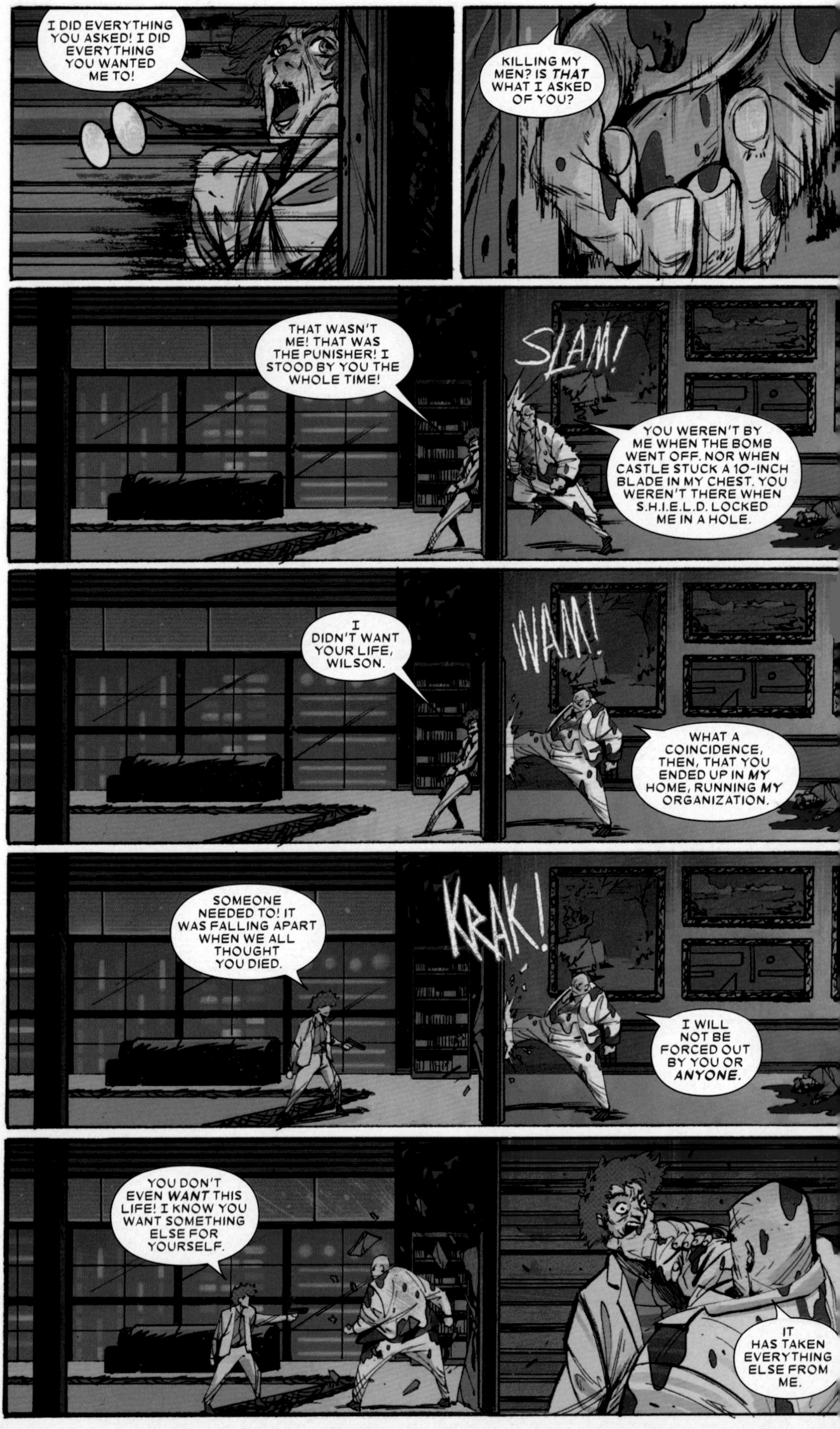
I DID EVERYTHING YOU ASKED! I DID EVERYTHING YOU WANTED ME TO!
KILLING MY MEN? IS *THAT* WHAT I ASKED OF YOU?
THAT WASN'T ME! THAT WAS THE PUNISHER! I STOOD BY YOU THE WHOLE TIME!
SLAM!
YOU WEREN'T BY ME WHEN THE BOMB WENT OFF. NOR WHEN CASTLE STUCK A 10-INCH BLADE IN MY CHEST. YOU WEREN'T THERE WHEN S.H.I.E.L.D. LOCKED ME IN A HOLE.
I DIDN'T WANT YOUR LIFE, WILSON.
WAM!
WHAT A COINCIDENCE, THEN, THAT YOU ENDED UP IN *MY* HOME, RUNNING *MY* ORGANIZATION.
SOMEONE NEEDED TO! IT WAS FALLING APART WHEN WE ALL THOUGHT YOU DIED.
KRAK!
I WILL NOT BE FORCED OUT BY YOU OR *ANYONE.*
YOU DON'T EVEN *WANT* THIS LIFE! I KNOW YOU WANT SOMETHING ELSE FOR YOURSELF.
IT HAS TAKEN EVERYTHING ELSE FROM ME.

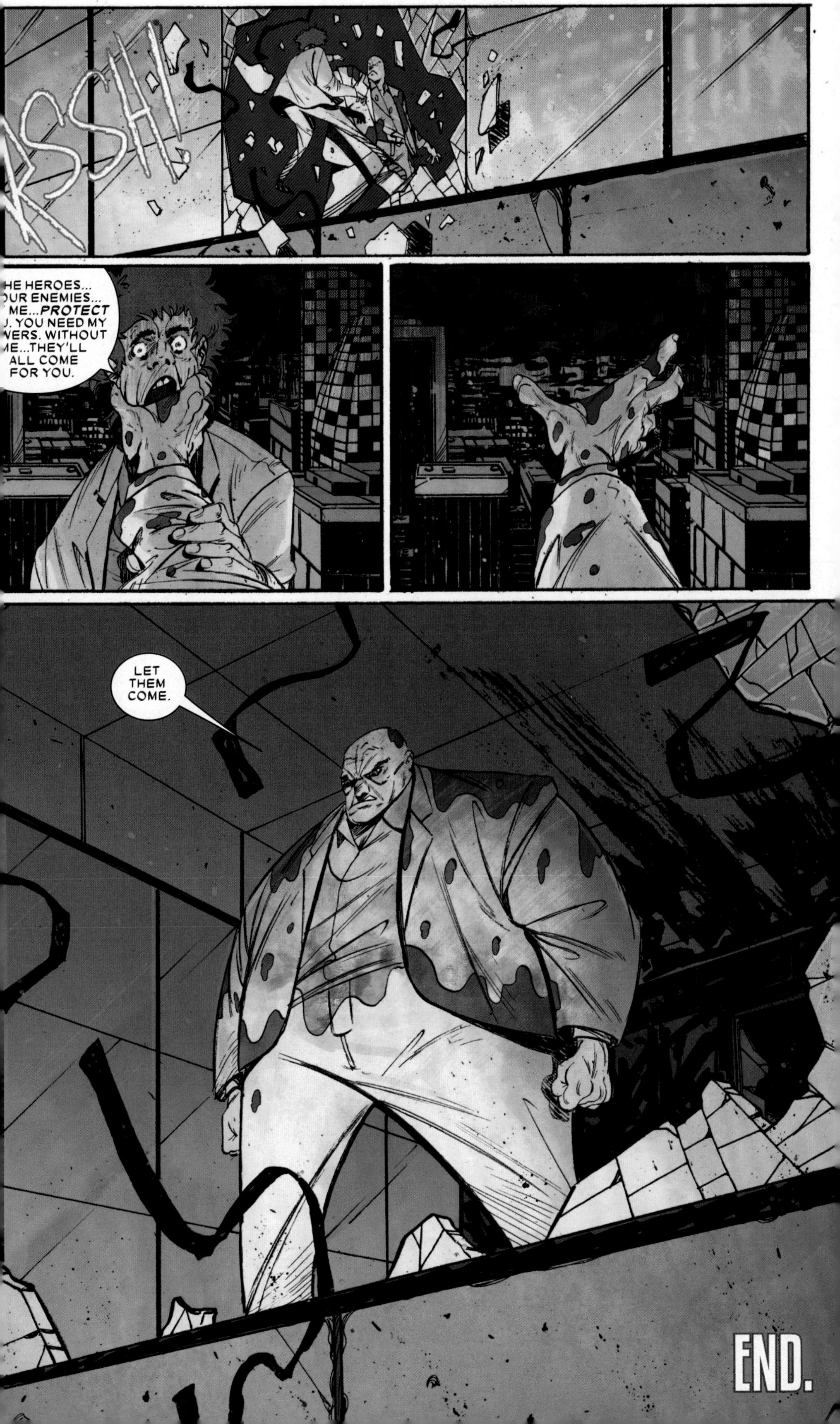
ASSH!
HE HEROES... OUR ENEMIES... ME...PROTECT U. YOU NEED MY WERS. WITHOUT ME...THEY'LL ALL COME FOR YOU.
LET THEM COME.
END.

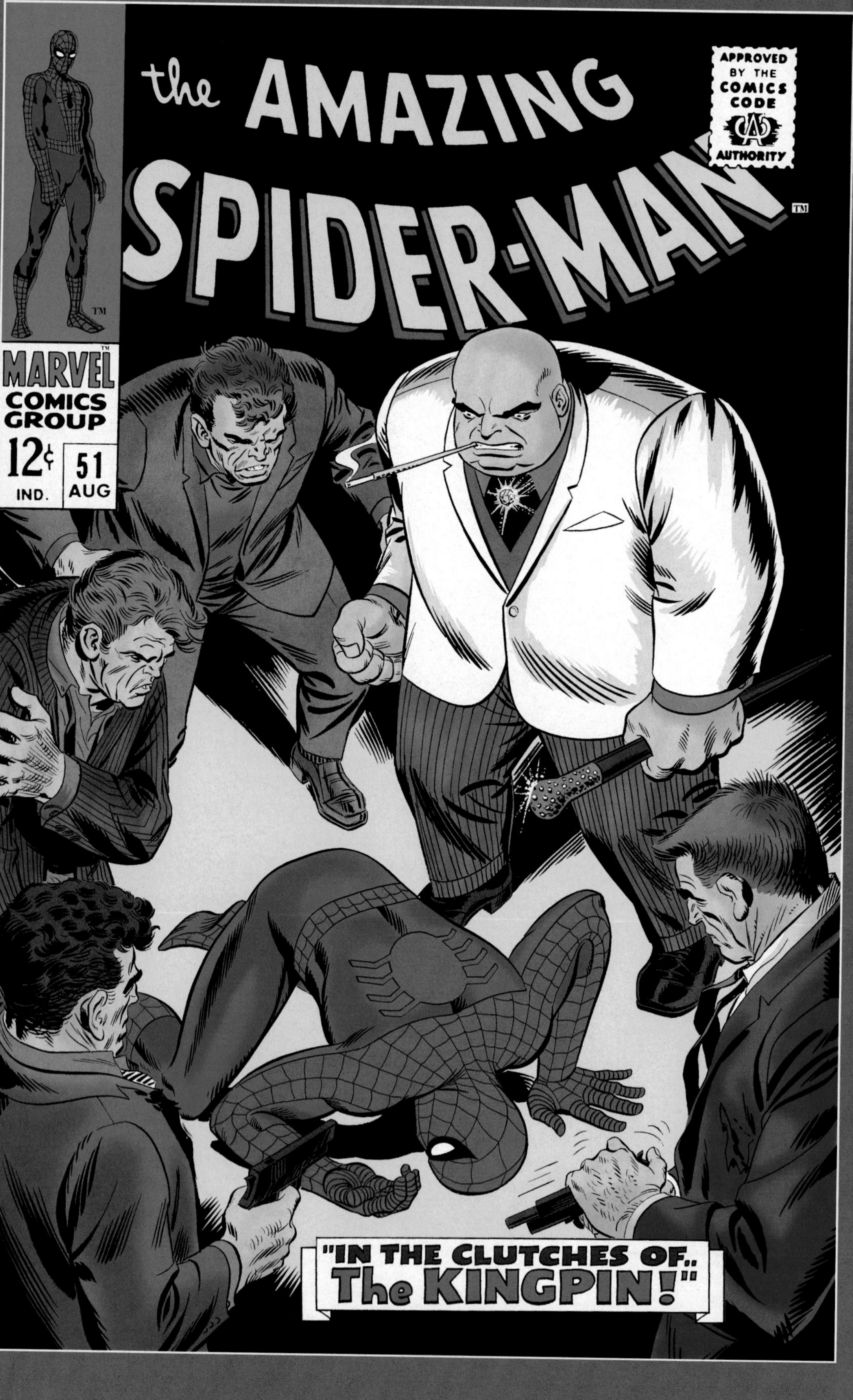

the AMAZING
SPIDER-MAN
APPROVED BY THE COMICS CODE AUTHORITY
MARVEL COMICS GROUP
12¢
IND.
51
AUG
"IN THE CLUTCHES OF.. The KINGPIN!"

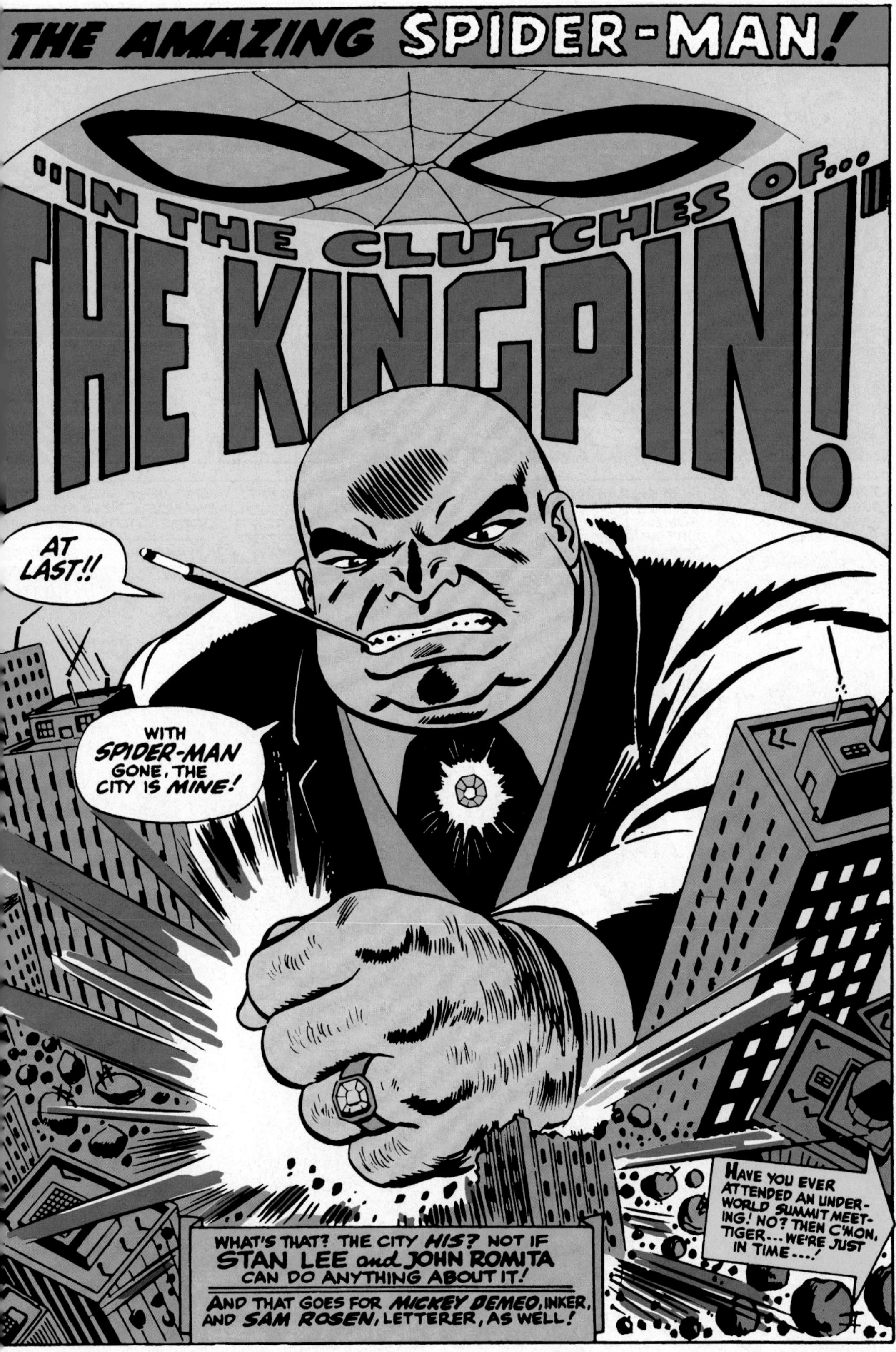
THE AMAZING SPIDER-MAN!
"IN THE CLUTCHES OF..."
THE KINGPIN!
AT LAST!!
WITH SPIDER-MAN GONE, THE CITY IS MINE!
WHAT'S THAT? THE CITY HIS? NOT IF STAN LEE and JOHN ROMITA CAN DO ANYTHING ABOUT IT!
AND THAT GOES FOR MICKEY DEMEO, INKER, AND SAM ROSEN, LETTERER, AS WELL!
HAVE YOU EVER ATTENDED AN UNDERWORLD SUMMIT MEETING! NO? THEN C'MON, TIGER... WE'RE JUST IN TIME...!

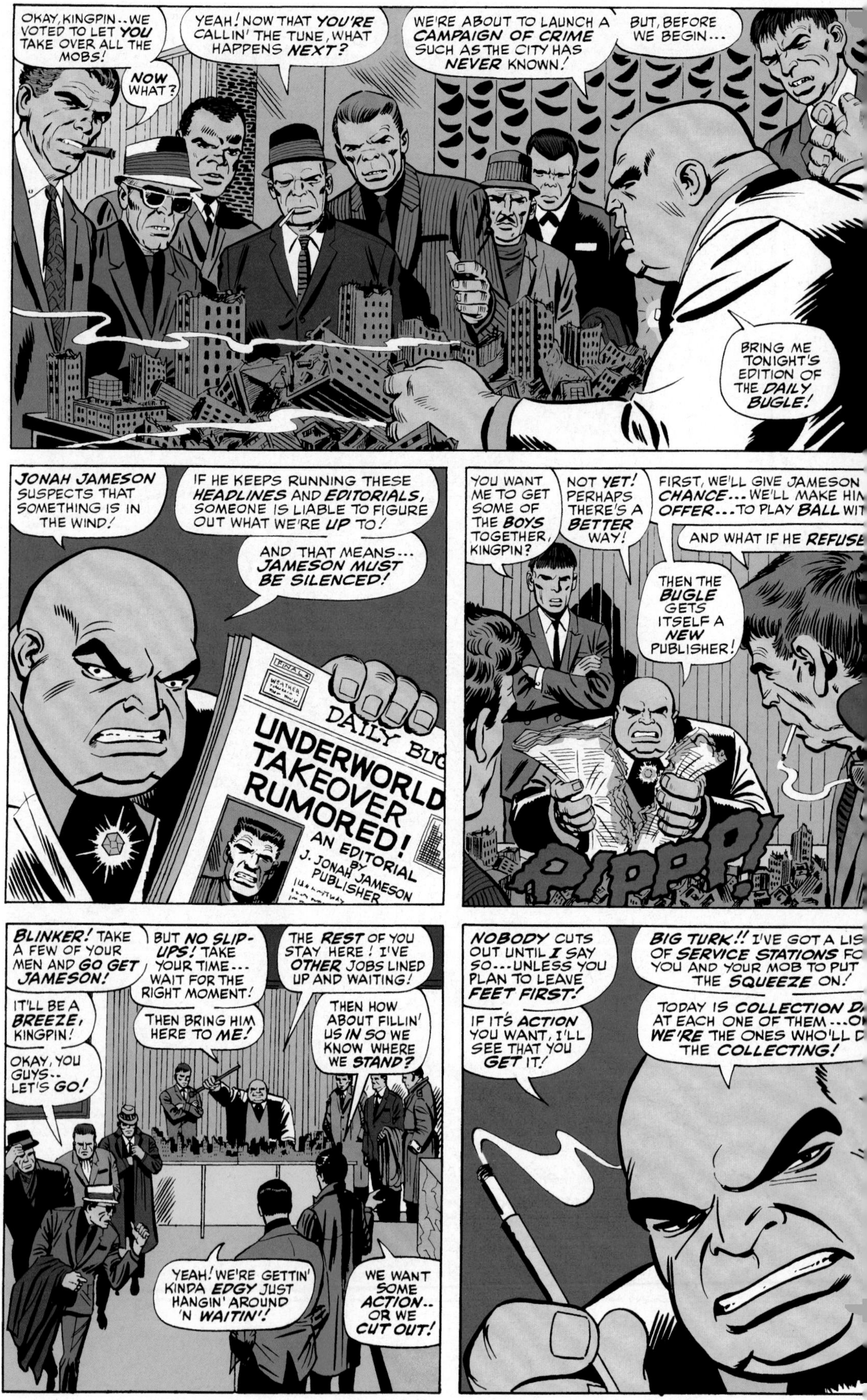
OKAY, KINGPIN.. WE VOTED TO LET YOU TAKE OVER ALL THE MOBS!
NOW WHAT?
YEAH! NOW THAT YOU'RE CALLIN' THE TUNE, WHAT HAPPENS NEXT?
WE'RE ABOUT TO LAUNCH A CAMPAIGN OF CRIME SUCH AS THE CITY HAS NEVER KNOWN!
BUT, BEFORE WE BEGIN...
BRING ME TONIGHT'S EDITION OF THE DAILY BUGLE!
JONAH JAMESON SUSPECTS THAT SOMETHING IS IN THE WIND!
IF HE KEEPS RUNNING THESE HEADLINES AND EDITORIALS, SOMEONE IS LIABLE TO FIGURE OUT WHAT WE'RE UP TO!
AND THAT MEANS... JAMESON MUST BE SILENCED!
DAILY BUG
UNDERWORLD TAKEOVER RUMORED!
AN EDITORIAL BY J. JONAH JAMESON PUBLISHER
YOU WANT ME TO GET SOME OF THE BOYS TOGETHER, KINGPIN?
NOT YET! PERHAPS THERE'S A BETTER WAY!
FIRST, WE'LL GIVE JAMESON CHANCE... WE'LL MAKE HI OFFER... TO PLAY BALL WIT
AND WHAT IF HE REFUSE
THEN THE BUGLE GETS ITSELF A NEW PUBLISHER!
RIPPP!
BLINKER! TAKE A FEW OF YOUR MEN AND GO GET JAMESON!
BUT NO SLIP-UPS! TAKE YOUR TIME... WAIT FOR THE RIGHT MOMENT!
THE REST OF YOU STAY HERE! I'VE OTHER JOBS LINED UP AND WAITING!
IT'LL BE A BREEZE, KINGPIN!
THEN BRING HIM HERE TO ME!
THEN HOW ABOUT FILLIN' US IN SO WE KNOW WHERE WE STAND?
OKAY, YOU GUYS.. LET'S GO!
YEAH! WE'RE GETTIN' KINDA EDGY JUST HANGIN' AROUND 'N WAITIN'!
WE WANT SOME ACTION.. OR WE CUT OUT!
NOBODY CUTS OUT UNTIL I SAY SO... UNLESS YOU PLAN TO LEAVE FEET FIRST!
IF IT'S ACTION YOU WANT, I'LL SEE THAT YOU GET IT!
BIG TURK!! I'VE GOT A LIS OF SERVICE STATIONS FO YOU AND YOUR MOB TO PUT THE SQUEEZE ON!
TODAY IS COLLECTION D AT EACH ONE OF THEM... O WE'RE THE ONES WHO'LL D THE COLLECTING!

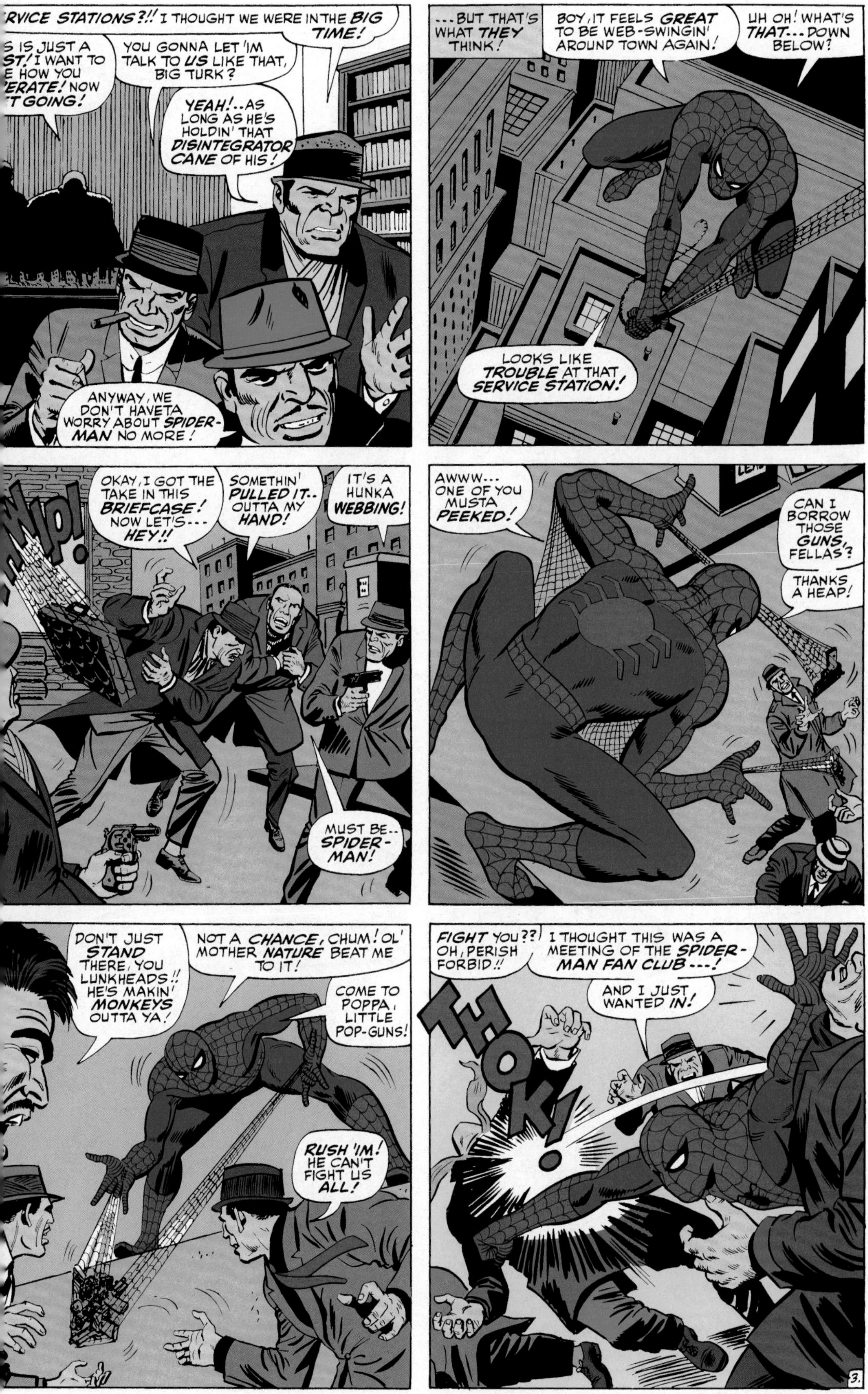

RVICE STATIONS?!! I THOUGHT WE WERE IN THE BIG TIME!
S IS JUST A ST! I WANT TO E HOW YOU ERATE! NOW T GOING!
YOU GONNA LET 'IM TALK TO US LIKE THAT, BIG TURK?
YEAH!..AS LONG AS HE'S HOLDIN' THAT DISINTEGRATOR CANE OF HIS!
ANYWAY, WE DON'T HAVETA WORRY ABOUT SPIDER-MAN NO MORE!
...BUT THAT'S WHAT THEY THINK!
BOY, IT FEELS GREAT TO BE WEB-SWINGIN' AROUND TOWN AGAIN!
UH OH! WHAT'S THAT...DOWN BELOW?
LOOKS LIKE TROUBLE AT THAT SERVICE STATION!
OKAY, I GOT THE TAKE IN THIS BRIEFCASE! NOW LET'S--- HEY!!
SOMETHIN' PULLED IT.. OUTTA MY HAND!
IT'S A HUNKA WEBBING!
MUST BE.. SPIDER-MAN!
AWWW... ONE OF YOU MUSTA PEEKED!
CAN I BORROW THOSE GUNS, FELLAS?
THANKS A HEAP!
DON'T JUST STAND THERE, YOU LUNKHEADS!! HE'S MAKIN' MONKEYS OUTTA YA!
NOT A CHANCE, CHUM! OL' MOTHER NATURE BEAT ME TO IT!
COME TO POPPA, LITTLE POP-GUNS!
RUSH 'IM! HE CAN'T FIGHT US ALL!
FIGHT YOU?? OH, PERISH FORBID!!
I THOUGHT THIS WAS A MEETING OF THE SPIDER-MAN FAN CLUB---!
AND I JUST WANTED IN!
THOK!
3.

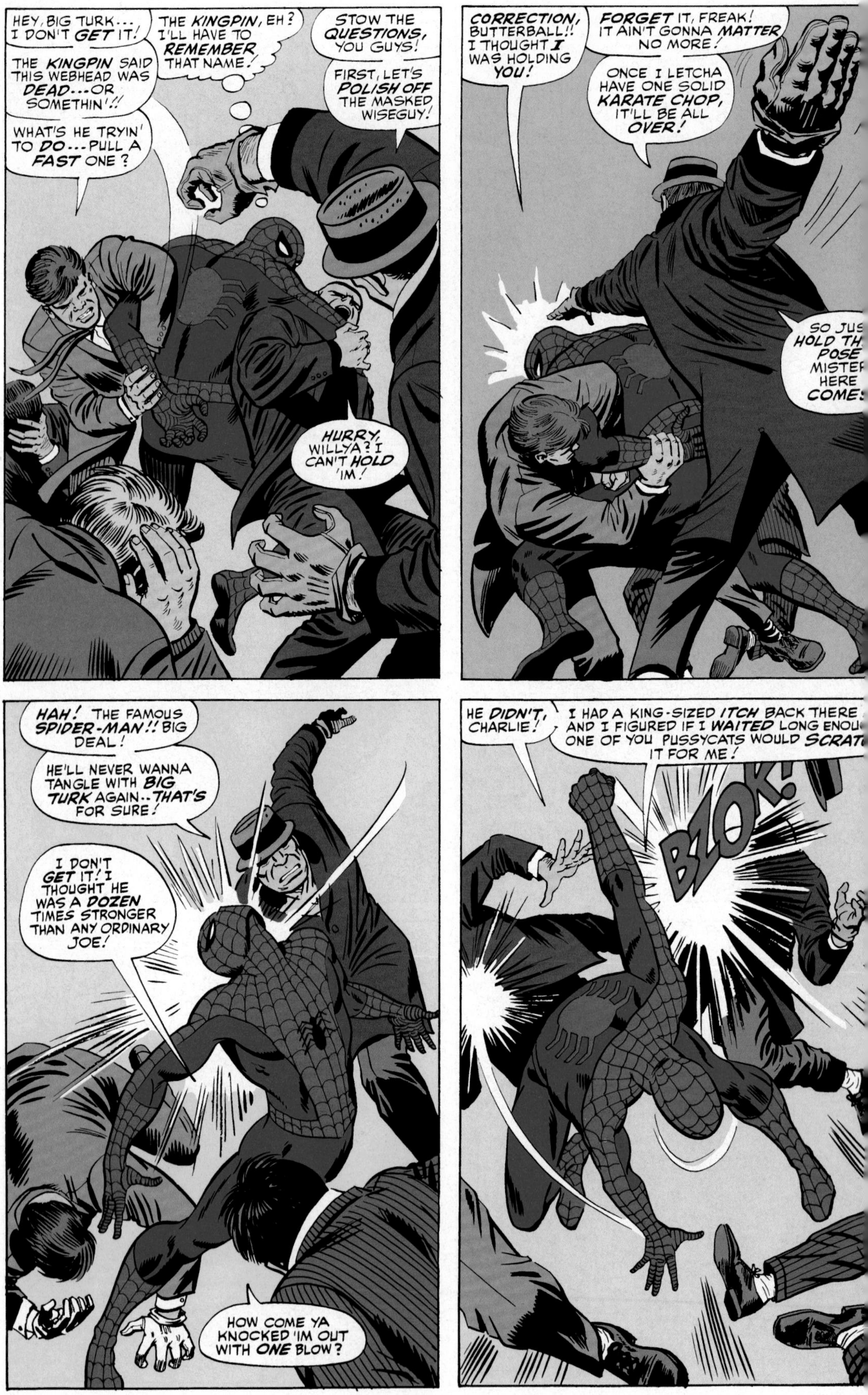
HEY, BIG TURK... I DON'T GET IT!
THE KINGPIN, EH? I'LL HAVE TO REMEMBER THAT NAME!
THE KINGPIN SAID THIS WEBHEAD WAS DEAD... OR SOMETHIN'!!
WHAT'S HE TRYIN' TO DO... PULL A FAST ONE?
STOW THE QUESTIONS, YOU GUYS!
FIRST, LET'S POLISH OFF THE MASKED WISEGUY!
HURRY, WILLYA? I CAN'T HOLD 'IM!
CORRECTION, BUTTERBALL!! I THOUGHT I WAS HOLDING YOU!
FORGET IT, FREAK! IT AIN'T GONNA MATTER NO MORE!
ONCE I LETCHA HAVE ONE SOLID KARATE CHOP, IT'LL BE ALL OVER!
HAH! THE FAMOUS SPIDER-MAN!! BIG DEAL!
HE'LL NEVER WANNA TANGLE WITH BIG TURK AGAIN.. THAT'S FOR SURE!
I DON'T GET IT! I THOUGHT HE WAS A DOZEN TIMES STRONGER THAN ANY ORDINARY JOE!
HOW COME YA KNOCKED 'IM OUT WITH ONE BLOW?
HE DIDN'T, CHARLIE!
BZOK!

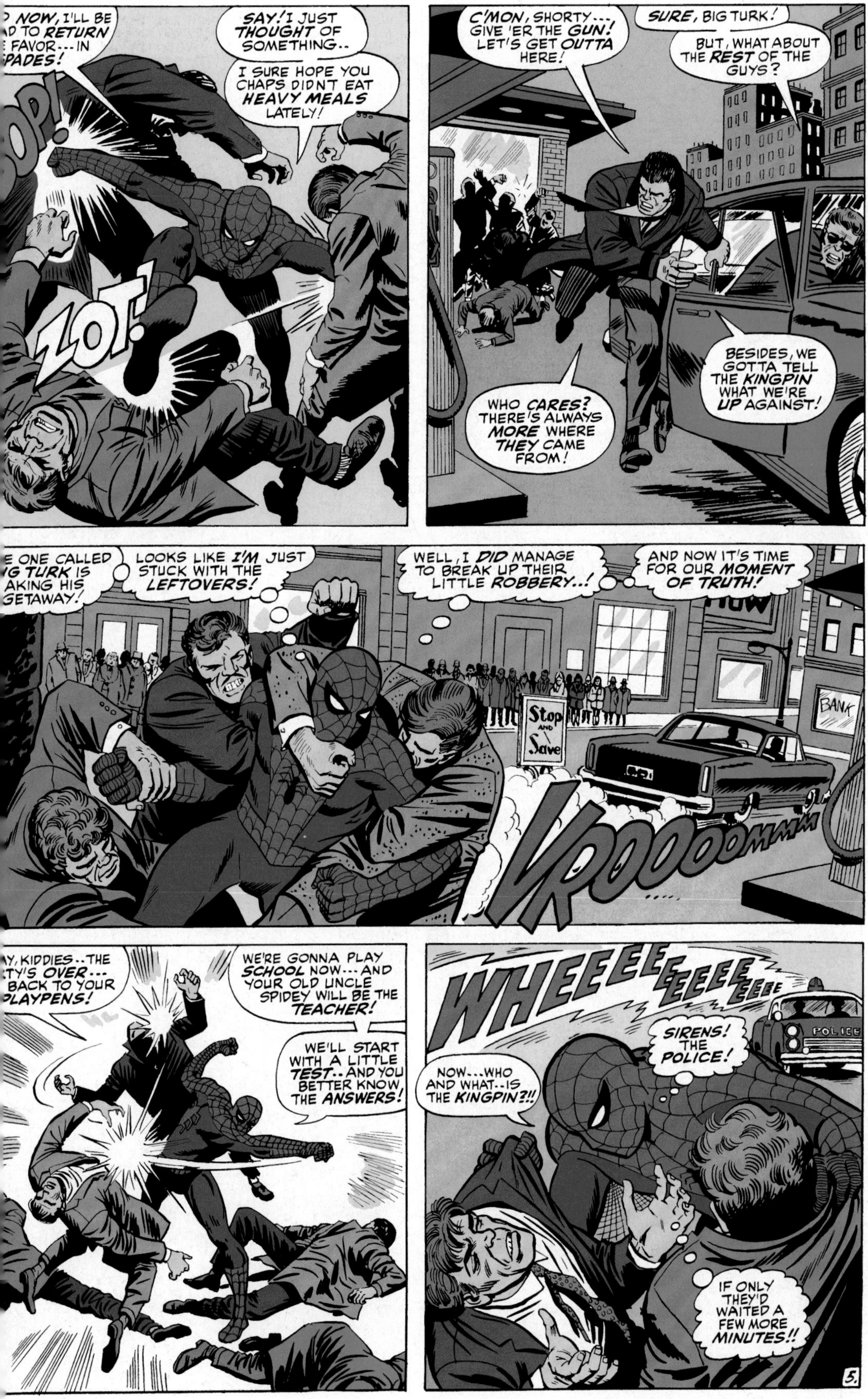
NOW, I'LL BE
TO RETURN
FAVOR... IN
PADES!
SAY! I JUST THOUGHT OF SOMETHING..
I SURE HOPE YOU CHAPS DIDN'T EAT HEAVY MEALS LATELY!
ZOT!
C'MON, SHORTY... GIVE 'ER THE GUN! LET'S GET OUTTA HERE!
SURE, BIG TURK!
BUT, WHAT ABOUT THE REST OF THE GUYS?
WHO CARES? THERE'S ALWAYS MORE WHERE THEY CAME FROM!
BESIDES, WE GOTTA TELL THE KINGPIN WHAT WE'RE UP AGAINST!
E ONE CALLED
G TURK IS
AKING HIS
GETAWAY!
LOOKS LIKE I'M JUST STUCK WITH THE LEFTOVERS!
WELL, I DID MANAGE TO BREAK UP THEIR LITTLE ROBBERY..!
AND NOW IT'S TIME FOR OUR MOMENT OF TRUTH!
Stop AND Save
BANK
VROOOOOMMM
Y, KIDDIES.. THE
TY'S OVER...
BACK TO YOUR
PLAYPENS!
WE'RE GONNA PLAY SCHOOL NOW... AND YOUR OLD UNCLE SPIDEY WILL BE THE TEACHER!
WE'LL START WITH A LITTLE TEST.. AND YOU BETTER KNOW THE ANSWERS!
WHEEEEEEEEEEEE
POLICE
SIRENS! THE POLICE!
NOW... WHO AND WHAT.. IS THE KINGPIN?!!
IF ONLY THEY'D WAITED A FEW MORE MINUTES!!
5.

WELL, THAT'S MY CUE TO DO A LITTLE WALL-CRAWLING!

THE POLICE WILL BE ABLE TO TAKE UP WHERE I LEFT OFF!

AS FOR ME, I'LL JUST COLLECT MY AUTOMATIC CAMERA AND SELL THE SPIDEY PIX TO JOLLY JONAH!

UH OH! I JUST REMEMBERED--!

WHEN I THOUGHT I WAS FINISHED WITH THE SPIDER-MAN BIT, I TOLD JAMESON WHERE TO GET OFF!

NOW I'VE GOTTA SWALLOW PRIDE, AND CONVINCE HIM WAS--ULP--ONLY KIDDIN'

BUT, THERE IS ONE MAN WHO ALMOST NEVER KIDS! SUPPOSE WE VISIT HIM AGAIN NOW--

I'LL SLIDE THE DRAPES BACK AND OBSERVE OUR CAPTIVE THROUGH THE HIDDEN ONE-WAY MIRROR!

SO, FREDRICK FOSWELL THOUGHT I WOULD LET HIM TAKE OVER OUR OPERATION, SIMPLY BECAUSE HE HAD ONCE BEEN THE BIG MAN BEFORE HE SUPPOSEDLY WENT STRAIGHT!

WHY DON'TCHA JUST POLISH HIM OFF NOW, KINGPIN?

HE AIN'T DOIN' ANYBODY ANY GOOD IN THERE!

NO! I HAVE OTHER PLANS FOR MR. FOSWELL!

CLICK!

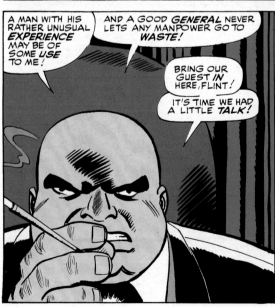

A MAN WITH HIS RATHER UNUSUAL EXPERIENCE MAY BE OF SOME USE TO ME!

AND A GOOD GENERAL NEVER LETS ANY MANPOWER GO TO WASTE!

BRING OUR GUEST IN HERE, FLINT!

IT'S TIME WE HAD A LITTLE TALK!

AND SO...

I THOUGHT YOU'D REALIZE YOU NEEDED ME, KINGPIN!

INDEED? WHAT MADE SO SURE

BECAUSE NOBODY'S EVER BEEN ABLE TO TAKE OVER ALL THE MOBS BEFORE--- EXCEPT ME!

I KNOW HOW HARD IT IS TO KEEP THEM ALL IN LINE!

YOU'D BE A FOOL TO PASS UP ANY HELP YOU CAN GET!

AND THERE IS ONE THING WE BOTH KNOW...

THE KINGPIN IS NOT A FOOL!

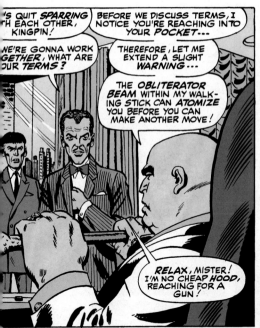

'S QUIT *SPARRING* 'TH EACH OTHER, KINGPIN! WE'RE GONNA WORK 'GETHER, WHAT ARE 'OUR *TERMS*?

BEFORE WE DISCUSS TERMS, I NOTICE YOU'RE REACHING INTO YOUR *POCKET*...

THEREFORE, LET ME EXTEND A SLIGHT *WARNING*...

THE *OBLITERATOR BEAM* WITHIN MY WALKING STICK CAN *ATOMIZE* YOU BEFORE YOU CAN MAKE ANOTHER MOVE!

RELAX, MISTER! I'M NO CHEAP *HOOD*, REACHING FOR A GUN!

I DO MY FIGHTING WITH MY *BRAINS*!

FLINT! GIVE ME A *LIGHT*!

WHO DO YOU THINK YOU'RE *TALKIN'* TO LITTLE MAN?

YOU *HEARD* THE MAN, FLINT! GIVE HIM A LIGHT!

KLIK!

OKAY! HERE..!

WE'LL GET ALONG JUST *FINE*, FOSWELL!

I LIKE YOUR *STYLE*!

AM!

SO! *SPIDER-MAN'S OUT OF ACTION*, HUH?

WHAT WERE YA TRYIN' TO *PULL*, YA FINK!

THUMP!

BIG TURK!!

WE JUST GOT AWAY BY THE SKIN OF OUR *TEETH*!

THEY SAW.. *SPIDER-MAN*??

YOU DARE BREAK IN *HERE*.. ON THE *KINGPIN*.. LIKE THIS?!!

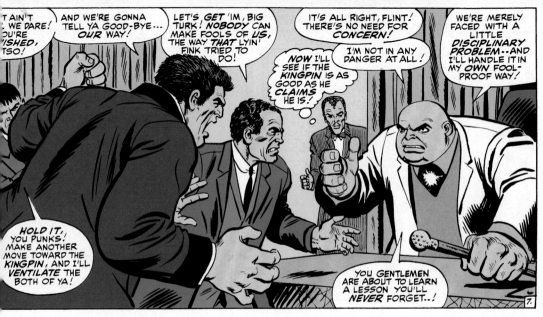

T AIN'T WE DARE! 'OU'RE 'ISHED, 'TSO!

AND WE'RE GONNA TELL YA GOOD-BYE... *OUR* WAY!

LET'S *GET* 'IM, BIG TURK! *NOBODY* CAN MAKE FOOLS OF *US*, THE WAY *THAT* LYIN' FINK TRIED TO DO!

IT'S ALL RIGHT, FLINT! THERE'S NO NEED FOR *CONCERN*!

I'M NOT IN ANY *DANGER* AT ALL!

NOW I'LL SEE IF THE *KINGPIN* IS AS GOOD AS HE *CLAIMS* HE IS!

WE'RE MERELY FACED WITH A LITTLE *DISCIPLINARY PROBLEM*--AND I'LL HANDLE IT IN MY *OWN* FOOL-PROOF WAY!

HOLD IT, YOU PUNKS! MAKE ANOTHER MOVE TOWARD THE *KINGPIN*, AND I'LL *VENTILATE* THE BOTH OF YA!

YOU GENTLEMEN ARE ABOUT TO LEARN A LESSON YOU'LL *NEVER* FORGET..!

7.

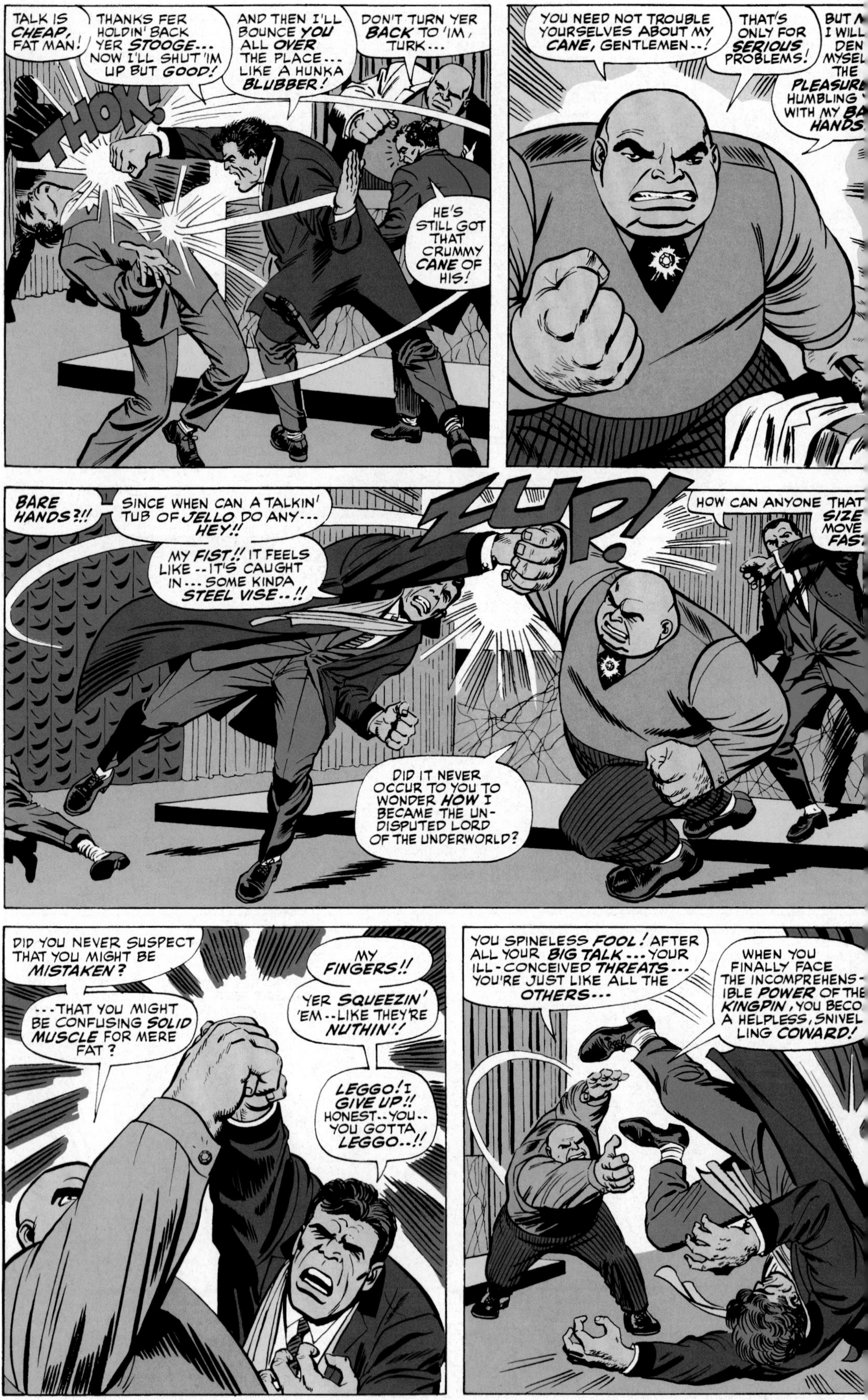
TALK IS CHEAP, FAT MAN!
THANKS FER HOLDIN' BACK YER STOOGE... NOW I'LL SHUT 'IM UP BUT GOOD!
AND THEN I'LL BOUNCE YOU ALL OVER THE PLACE... LIKE A HUNKA BLUBBER!
DON'T TURN YER BACK TO 'IM, TURK...
THOK!
HE'S STILL GOT THAT CRUMMY CANE OF HIS!
YOU NEED NOT TROUBLE YOURSELVES ABOUT MY CANE, GENTLEMEN..!
THAT'S ONLY FOR SERIOUS PROBLEMS!
BUT I WILL DEN MYSEL THE PLEASURE HUMBLING WITH MY BA HANDS
BARE HANDS?!!
SINCE WHEN CAN A TALKIN' TUB OF JELLO DO ANY--- HEY!!
ZUP!
HOW CAN ANYONE THAT SIZE MOVE FAS
MY FIST!! IT FEELS LIKE--IT'S CAUGHT IN... SOME KINDA STEEL VISE..!!
DID IT NEVER OCCUR TO YOU TO WONDER HOW I BECAME THE UNDISPUTED LORD OF THE UNDERWORLD?
DID YOU NEVER SUSPECT THAT YOU MIGHT BE MISTAKEN?
---THAT YOU MIGHT BE CONFUSING SOLID MUSCLE FOR MERE FAT?
MY FINGERS!!
YER SQUEEZIN' 'EM--LIKE THEY'RE NUTHIN'!
LEGGO! I GIVE UP!! HONEST..YOU.. YOU GOTTA LEGGO..!!
YOU SPINELESS FOOL! AFTER ALL YOUR BIG TALK... YOUR ILL-CONCEIVED THREATS... YOU'RE JUST LIKE ALL THE OTHERS...
WHEN YOU FINALLY FACE THE INCOMPREHENSIBLE POWER OF THE KINGPIN, YOU BECO A HELPLESS, SNIVELLING COWARD!

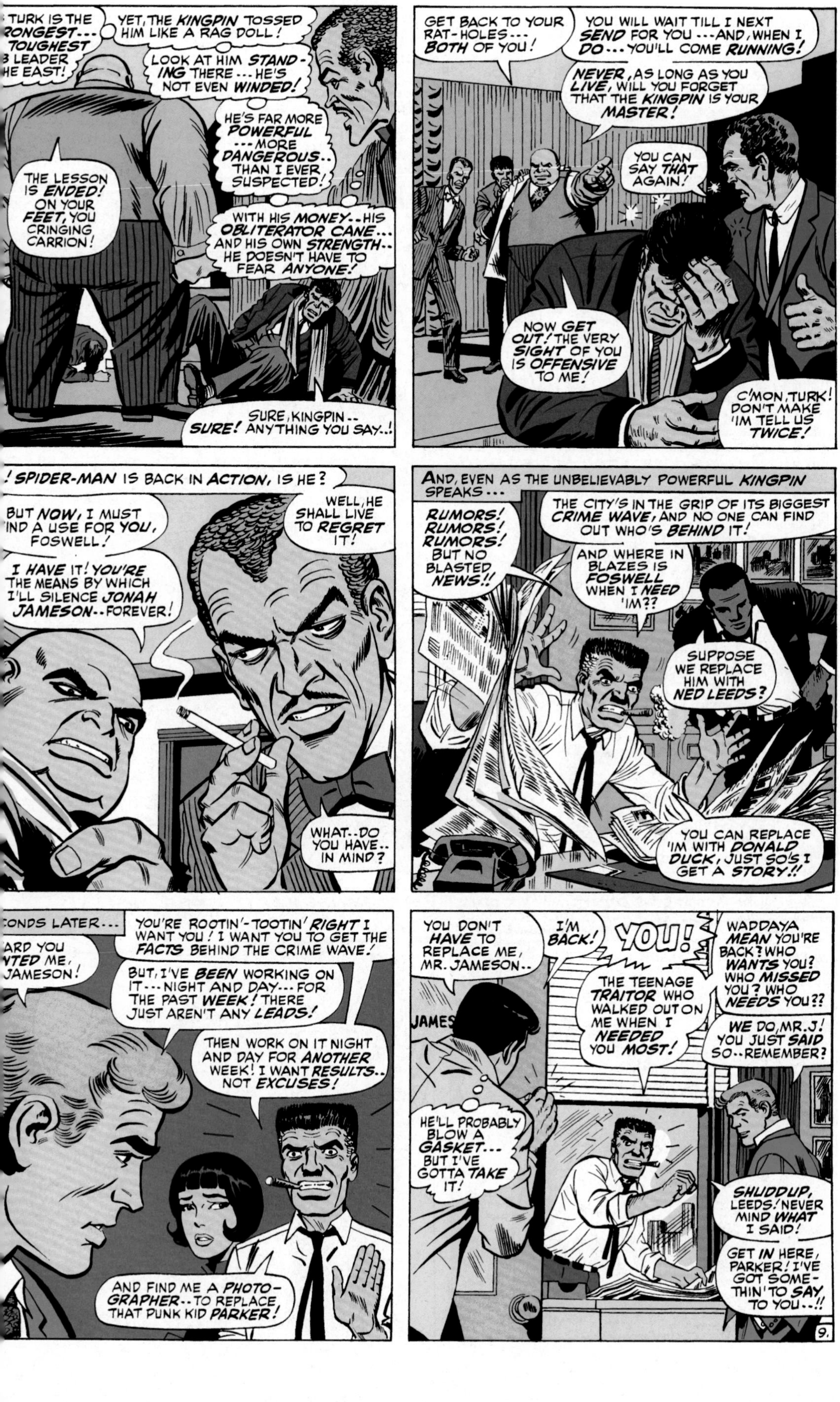
TURK IS THE RONGEST--- TOUGHEST B LEADER HE EAST!
YET, THE KINGPIN TOSSED HIM LIKE A RAG DOLL!
LOOK AT HIM STANDING THERE --- HE'S NOT EVEN WINDED!
HE'S FAR MORE POWERFUL --- MORE DANGEROUS.. THAN I EVER SUSPECTED!
THE LESSON IS ENDED! ON YOUR FEET, YOU CRINGING CARRION!
WITH HIS MONEY--HIS OBLITERATOR CANE... AND HIS OWN STRENGTH-- HE DOESN'T HAVE TO FEAR ANYONE!
SURE, KINGPIN-- SURE! ANYTHING YOU SAY..!
GET BACK TO YOUR RAT-HOLES--- BOTH OF YOU!
YOU WILL WAIT TILL I NEXT SEND FOR YOU --- AND, WHEN I DO--- YOU'LL COME RUNNING!
NEVER, AS LONG AS YOU LIVE, WILL YOU FORGET THAT THE KINGPIN IS YOUR MASTER!
YOU CAN SAY THAT AGAIN!
NOW GET OUT! THE VERY SIGHT OF YOU IS OFFENSIVE TO ME!
C'MON, TURK! DON'T MAKE 'IM TELL US TWICE!
! SPIDER-MAN IS BACK IN ACTION, IS HE?
WELL, HE SHALL LIVE TO REGRET IT!
BUT NOW, I MUST IND A USE FOR YOU, FOSWELL!
I HAVE IT! YOU'RE THE MEANS BY WHICH I'LL SILENCE JONAH JAMESON--FOREVER!
WHAT--DO YOU HAVE.. IN MIND?
AND, EVEN AS THE UNBELIEVABLY POWERFUL KINGPIN SPEAKS...
RUMORS! RUMORS! RUMORS! BUT NO BLASTED NEWS!!
THE CITY'S IN THE GRIP OF ITS BIGGEST CRIME WAVE, AND NO ONE CAN FIND OUT WHO'S BEHIND IT!
AND WHERE IN BLAZES IS FOSWELL WHEN I NEED 'IM??
SUPPOSE WE REPLACE HIM WITH NED LEEDS?
YOU CAN REPLACE 'IM WITH DONALD DUCK, JUST SO'S I GET A STORY!!
CONDS LATER...
ARD YOU NTED ME, JAMESON!
YOU'RE ROOTIN'-TOOTIN' RIGHT I WANT YOU! I WANT YOU TO GET THE FACTS BEHIND THE CRIME WAVE!
BUT, I'VE BEEN WORKING ON IT--- NIGHT AND DAY--- FOR THE PAST WEEK! THERE JUST AREN'T ANY LEADS!
THEN WORK ON IT NIGHT AND DAY FOR ANOTHER WEEK! I WANT RESULTS.. NOT EXCUSES!
AND FIND ME A PHOTOGRAPHER--TO REPLACE THAT PUNK KID PARKER!
YOU DON'T HAVE TO REPLACE ME, MR. JAMESON..
I'M BACK!
YOU!
JAMES
THE TEENAGE TRAITOR WHO WALKED OUT ON ME WHEN I NEEDED YOU MOST!
WADDAYA MEAN YOU'RE BACK? WHO WANTS YOU? WHO MISSED YOU? WHO NEEDS YOU??
WE DO, MR. J! YOU JUST SAID SO--REMEMBER?
HE'LL PROBABLY BLOW A GASKET--- BUT I'VE GOTTA TAKE IT!
SHUDDUP, LEEDS! NEVER MIND WHAT I SAID!
GET IN HERE, PARKER! I'VE GOT SOMETHIN' TO SAY TO YOU--!!
9.

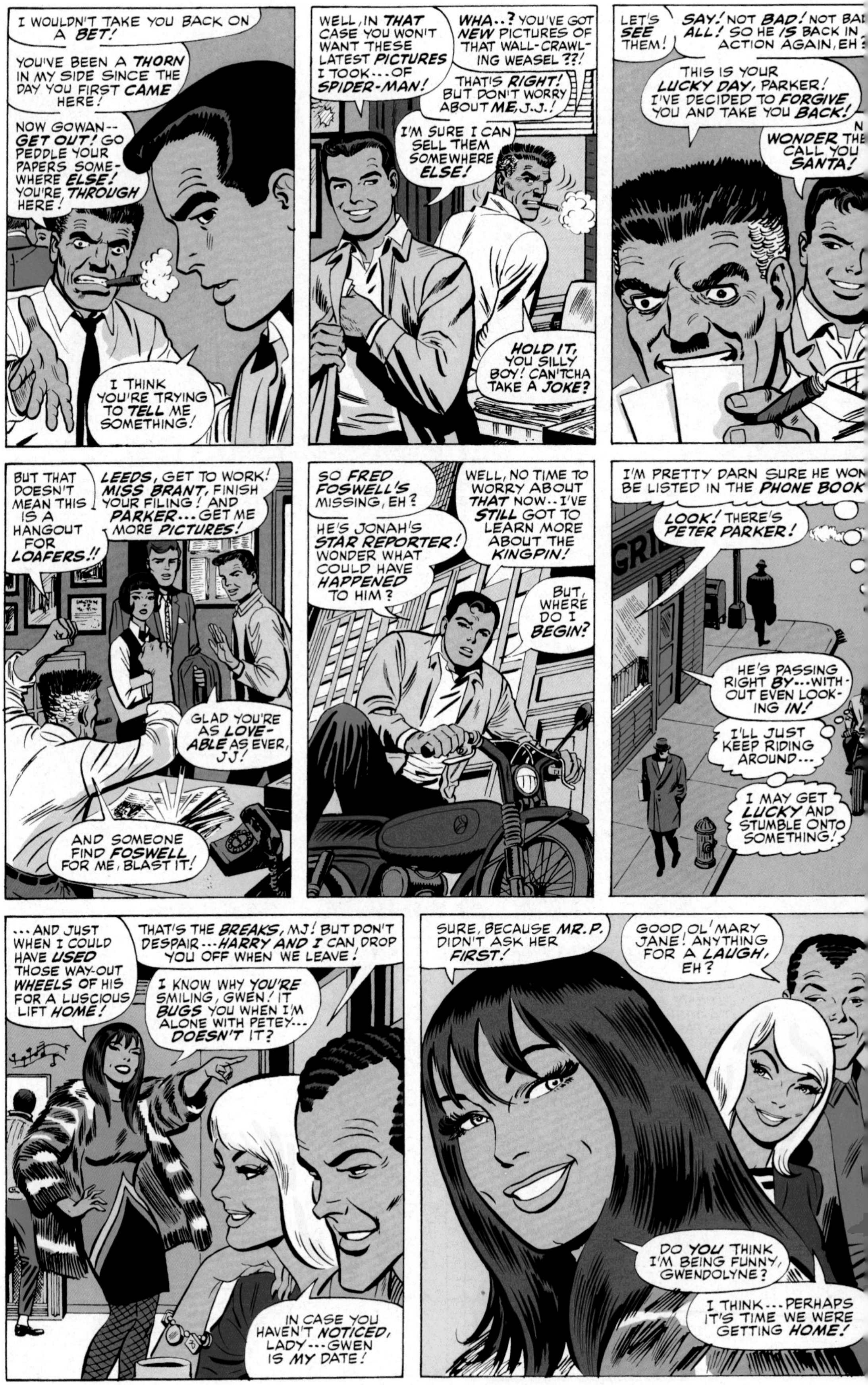

I WOULDN'T TAKE YOU BACK ON A BET!
YOU'VE BEEN A THORN IN MY SIDE SINCE THE DAY YOU FIRST CAME HERE!
NOW GOWAN-- GET OUT! GO PEDDLE YOUR PAPERS SOMEWHERE ELSE! YOU'RE THROUGH HERE!
I THINK YOU'RE TRYING TO TELL ME SOMETHING!
WELL, IN THAT CASE YOU WON'T WANT THESE LATEST PICTURES I TOOK--- OF SPIDER-MAN!
WHA..? YOU'VE GOT NEW PICTURES OF THAT WALL-CRAWLING WEASEL ??!
THAT'S RIGHT! BUT DON'T WORRY ABOUT ME, J.J.!
I'M SURE I CAN SELL THEM SOMEWHERE ELSE!
HOLD IT, YOU SILLY BOY! CAN'TCHA TAKE A JOKE?
LET'S SEE THEM!
SAY! NOT BAD! NOT BA ALL! SO HE IS BACK IN ACTION AGAIN, EH?
THIS IS YOUR LUCKY DAY, PARKER! I'VE DECIDED TO FORGIVE YOU AND TAKE YOU BACK!
WONDER THE CALL YOU SANTA!
BUT THAT DOESN'T MEAN THIS IS A HANGOUT FOR LOAFERS!!
LEEDS, GET TO WORK! MISS BRANT, FINISH YOUR FILING! AND PARKER... GET ME MORE PICTURES!
GLAD YOU'RE AS LOVE-ABLE AS EVER, JJ!
AND SOMEONE FIND FOSWELL FOR ME, BLAST IT!
SO FRED FOSWELL'S MISSING, EH?
HE'S JONAH'S STAR REPORTER! WONDER WHAT COULD HAVE HAPPENED TO HIM?
WELL, NO TIME TO WORRY ABOUT THAT NOW..I'VE STILL GOT TO LEARN MORE ABOUT THE KINGPIN!
BUT, WHERE DO I BEGIN?
I'M PRETTY DARN SURE HE WON BE LISTED IN THE PHONE BOOK
LOOK! THERE'S PETER PARKER!
HE'S PASSING RIGHT BY...WITHOUT EVEN LOOKING IN!
I'LL JUST KEEP RIDING AROUND...
I MAY GET LUCKY AND STUMBLE ONTO SOMETHING!
...AND JUST WHEN I COULD HAVE USED THOSE WAY-OUT WHEELS OF HIS FOR A LUSCIOUS LIFT HOME!
THAT'S THE BREAKS, MJ! BUT DON'T DESPAIR...HARRY AND I CAN DROP YOU OFF WHEN WE LEAVE!
I KNOW WHY YOU'RE SMILING, GWEN! IT BUGS YOU WHEN I'M ALONE WITH PETEY... DOESN'T IT?
IN CASE YOU HAVEN'T NOTICED, LADY---GWEN IS MY DATE!
SURE, BECAUSE MR. P. DIDN'T ASK HER FIRST!
GOOD OL' MARY JANE! ANYTHING FOR A LAUGH, EH?
DO YOU THINK I'M BEING FUNNY, GWENDOLYNE?
I THINK... PERHAPS IT'S TIME WE WERE GETTING HOME!

...P, IT'S TIME *WE* WERE BRACING ...R NEW *ACTION*--!

...W IS MY ...DY ...SE ...GLING? ...I SEE ...R ...V, ENTER-- ...THAT ...NKY ...ATE ...B--!

BUT, I BETTER PARK MY BIKE AND GET INTO *COSTUME*... JUST IN CASE!

NOTHING SEEMS TO BE *WRONG!* AND YET...

I CAN'T AFFORD TO TAKE ANY *CHANCES!* MY LITTLE BUILT-IN *BUZZER* HASN'T EVER FAILED ME *YET!*

UH OH! I WAS *RIGHT!*

WHILE NOBODY ELSE IS *NOTICING*, THOSE FOUR GOONS HAVE THE *MANAGER* OFF IN A CORNER...

AND I CAN TELL... EVEN FROM *HERE*... THAT THEY'RE ABOUT TO *LEAN* ON HIM!

ONE OF 'EM IS PULLING A *GUN!*

NO TIME TO FIND AN OPEN WINDOW-- I'VE GOTTA *MOVE*..!!

...KINGPIN ...'T LIKE ...'S WHO ...E US ANY ...UBLE, ...EE ??

THEN THE *KINGPIN* IS GONNA BE REAL *ANNOYED* AT YOUR FRIENDLY NEIGHBORHOOD *SPIDER-MAN*, GENTS!

HEADS UP, YOU GUYS! IT'S THE *WALL-CRAWLER* AGAIN!!

RASH!

YOU OUGHTTA BE *ASHAMED* OF YOURSELVES!

NOT ONLY DO YOU TRY TO *HIJACK* ONE OF THE *CLASSIEST* PLACES IN TOWN...

-- BUT YOU DIDN'T EVEN PHONE AHEAD TO MAKE A *RESERVATION!*

UHH!

OOOFF!

TSK TSK! HOW *GAUCHE* CAN YOU BE?

LOOK OUT!!

11.

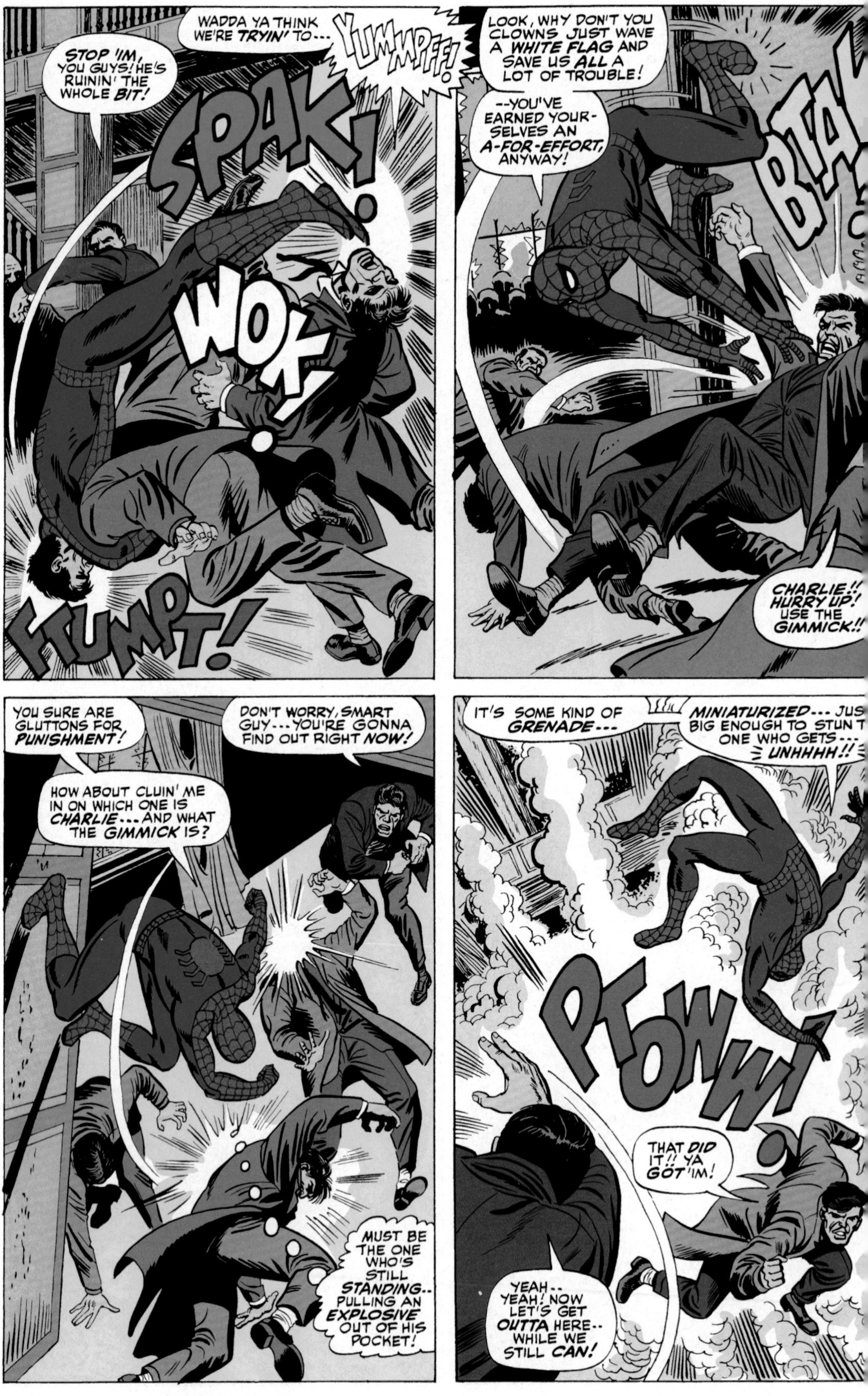
STOP 'IM, YOU GUYS! HE'S RUININ' THE WHOLE BIT!
WADDA YA THINK WE'RE TRYIN' TO---
YUMMPFF!
SPAK!
WOK
FTUMPT!
LOOK, WHY DON'T YOU CLOWNS JUST WAVE A WHITE FLAG AND SAVE US ALL A LOT OF TROUBLE!
--YOU'VE EARNED YOURSELVES AN A-FOR-EFFORT, ANYWAY!
CHARLIE!! HURRY UP! USE THE GIMMICK!!
YOU SURE ARE GLUTTONS FOR PUNISHMENT!
DON'T WORRY, SMART GUY--- YOU'RE GONNA FIND OUT RIGHT NOW!
HOW ABOUT CLUIN' ME IN ON WHICH ONE IS CHARLIE--- AND WHAT THE GIMMICK IS?
MUST BE THE ONE WHO'S STILL STANDING.. PULLING AN EXPLOSIVE OUT OF HIS POCKET!
IT'S SOME KIND OF GRENADE---
MINIATURIZED--- JUS
BIG ENOUGH TO STUN T
ONE WHO GETS---
UNHHHH!!
PTOWW!
THAT DID IT!! YA GOT 'IM!
YEAH.. YEAH! NOW LET'S GET OUTTA HERE.. WHILE WE STILL CAN!

...FOR...MY SPIDER STRENGTH...I'D BE...A GONER BY NOW!

...GRENADE...MORE POWERFUL...THAN I THOUGHT...!

LOOK! THAT EXPLOSION WEAKENED THE BEAMS!!

THE WHOLE CEILING IS ABOUT TO FALL! WE'LL ALL BE CRUSHED!

MOVE IT, YOU GUYS! THIS PLACE AIN'T GONNA LAST MUCH LONGER!

SPIDER-MAN!! THIS IS ALL YOUR DOING!!

LOOKS LIKE I'LL END UP GETTING THE BLAME...AS USUAL!

BUT, I CAN'T LET THAT WORRY ME NOW...!

I'M GONNA BE A MIGHTY BUSY LITTLE WEB-SLINGER FOR THE NEXT FEW SECONDS!

FIRST THING TO DO IS SLAP MY STICKY SPIDEY TRACER ON ONE OF THOSE HOODS!

THEN, I'VE GOTTA GET UNDER THE MAIN BEAM--!

DON'T JUST STAND THERE, BRIGHT EYES! GET THIS PLACE CLEARED OUT!

I DON'T FIGURE TO MAKE A LIFE'S WORK OUT OF HOLDING UP SAGGIN' CEILINGS!

HE'S ROOTED TO THE SPOT...ALMOST NUMB WITH SHOCK AND FEAR!

I...I CAN'T HOLD OUT MUCH LONGER!!

...THEN...

HE FINALLY SNAPPED OUT OF IT!

IF I CAN HANG ON...ANOTHER FEW SECONDS...EVERYONE WILL BE SAFE!

AND THEN..

...IF I CAN MAKE IT THROUGH THE WINDOW FAST ENOUGH...

I'LL LIVE TO CRAWL ANOTHER WALL!

13.

THERE SHE GOES! ...I GUESS THEY JUST DON'T BUILD 'EM LIKE THEY USED TO!

WELL, IT COULDA BEEN WORSE! AT LEAST NO ONE WAS HURT!

NOW, ALL I'VE GOT TO DO IS PICK UP MY LITTLE TRACER'S TRAIL!

AND, UNLESS I'M WAY OFF BASE, IT'LL LEAD ME RIGHT TO COUSIN KINGPIN!

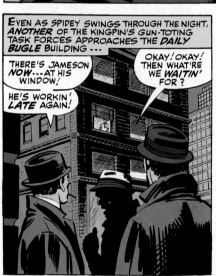

EVEN AS SPIDEY SWINGS THROUGH THE NIGHT, ANOTHER OF THE KINGPIN'S GUN-TOTING TASK FORCES APPROACHES THE DAILY BUGLE BUILDING ...

THERE'S JAMESON NOW ...AT HIS WINDOW!

HE'S WORKIN' LATE AGAIN!

OKAY! OKAY! THEN WHAT'RE WE WAITIN' FOR?

ON YOUR FEET, MISTER! YOU BEEN WORKIN' TOO HARD... SO WE'RE GIVIN' YOU A VACATION!

YEAH! WE'RE TAKIN' YA FOR A NICE LITTLE RIDE ...TO VISIT THE KINGPIN!

THE KINGPIN! THEN WAS RIGHT! THERE SOMEONE BEHIND T CRIME WAVE!

BUT... WHAT DOES HE WANT WITH ME??

BRIEF MINUTES LATER ...

ARE YOU NICE AND COMFY, JAMESON?

THIS IS INSANE! NOBODY GETS TAKEN FOR RIDES ANY MORE...

WHEN THE KINGPIN SAYS RIDE, BROTHER.. YOU RIDE!

WHO IN BLAZES IS THE KINGPIN??

··EXCEPT ON THE UNTOUCHABLES!

HE'S OUR SCOUTMASTER! NOW SHUDDUP!

FINALLY...

WELL, WELL! IF IT ISN'T JONAH JAMESON! HOW NICE OF YOU TO DROP IN!

COME, COME, GENTLEMEN... DON'T KEEP OUR GUEST STANDING OUT IN THE HALL!

YOU HEARD THE KINGPIN!

WALK!!

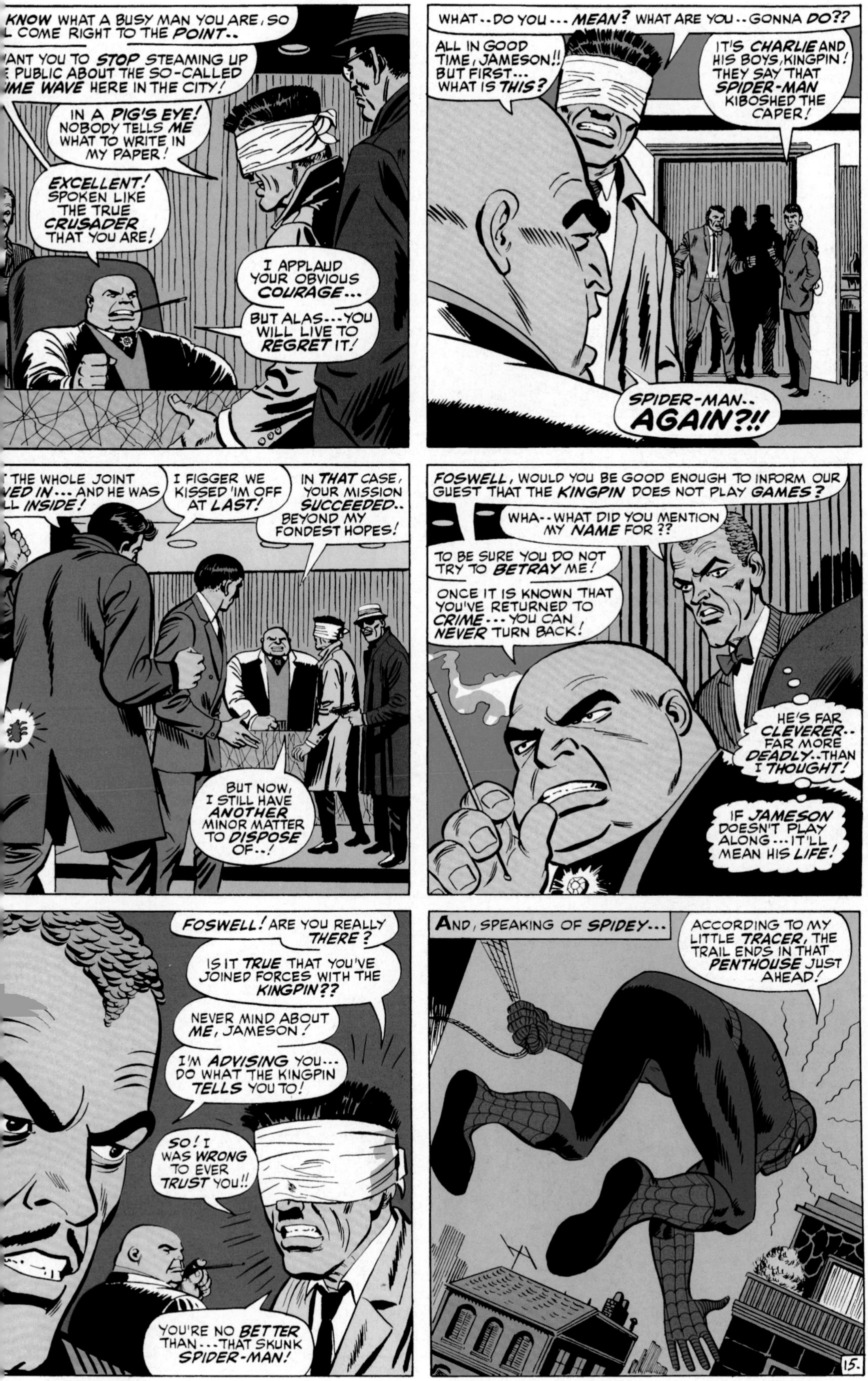
KNOW WHAT A BUSY MAN YOU ARE, SO
L COME RIGHT TO THE POINT..
ANT YOU TO STOP STEAMING UP
E PUBLIC ABOUT THE SO-CALLED
IME WAVE HERE IN THE CITY!
IN A PIG'S EYE! NOBODY TELLS ME WHAT TO WRITE IN MY PAPER!
EXCELLENT! SPOKEN LIKE THE TRUE CRUSADER THAT YOU ARE!
I APPLAUD YOUR OBVIOUS COURAGE...
BUT ALAS...YOU WILL LIVE TO REGRET IT!
WHAT..DO YOU...MEAN? WHAT ARE YOU..GONNA DO??
ALL IN GOOD TIME, JAMESON!! BUT FIRST... WHAT IS THIS?
IT'S CHARLIE AND HIS BOYS, KINGPIN! THEY SAY THAT SPIDER-MAN KIBOSHED THE CAPER!
SPIDER-MAN.. AGAIN?!!
THE WHOLE JOINT
ED IN...AND HE WAS
L INSIDE!
I FIGGER WE KISSED 'IM OFF AT LAST!
IN THAT CASE, YOUR MISSION SUCCEEDED.. BEYOND MY FONDEST HOPES!
BUT NOW, I STILL HAVE ANOTHER MINOR MATTER TO DISPOSE OF..!
FOSWELL, WOULD YOU BE GOOD ENOUGH TO INFORM OUR GUEST THAT THE KINGPIN DOES NOT PLAY GAMES?
WHA--WHAT DID YOU MENTION MY NAME FOR??
TO BE SURE YOU DO NOT TRY TO BETRAY ME!
ONCE IT IS KNOWN THAT YOU'VE RETURNED TO CRIME...YOU CAN NEVER TURN BACK!
HE'S FAR CLEVERER.. FAR MORE DEADLY..THAN I THOUGHT!
IF JAMESON DOESN'T PLAY ALONG...IT'LL MEAN HIS LIFE!
FOSWELL! ARE YOU REALLY THERE?
IS IT TRUE THAT YOU'VE JOINED FORCES WITH THE KINGPIN??
NEVER MIND ABOUT ME, JAMESON!
I'M ADVISING YOU... DO WHAT THE KINGPIN TELLS YOU TO!
SO! I WAS WRONG TO EVER TRUST YOU!!
YOU'RE NO BETTER THAN...THAT SKUNK SPIDER-MAN!
AND, SPEAKING OF SPIDEY...
ACCORDING TO MY LITTLE TRACER, THE TRAIL ENDS IN THAT PENTHOUSE JUST AHEAD!
15.

That MAN MOUNTAIN... BEHIND THE MARBLE DESK...

AND...IT LOOKS LIKE I'VE REALLY STUMBLED ONTO SOMETHING!

IT MUST BE HIM...THE KING-PIN!

THEY'VE GOT JOLLY JONAH THERE...BLINDFOLDED!! HE MUST BE A PRISONER!

BUT, THAT'S NOT WHAT GRABS ME! BEHIND THE KINGPIN--IT'S FOSWELL!

HE'S TURNE CROOK AGAIN! HE ONE OF T MOB!

HEY... LOOK! WHAT'S THAT?!!

IT'S THE SPIDER-MAN SIGNAL! ...COMIN' FROM THE WINDOW!

THE WALL-CRAWLER'S STILL ALIVE! HE FOUND US...HE'S ON THE TERRACE!

AFTER HIM!! QUICK!

LET'S GO! I'D RATHER FACE SPIDER-MAN THAN GET THE KINGPIN MAD AT US!

BUT...WHERE IS HE?

LOOK ALIVE, YOU FOOLS! HE MUSTN'T GET AWAY!

FAN OUT! HE'S GOTTA BE HERE SOMEWHERE!

THERE AIN'T A SIGN OF HIM!

THANKS, BOYS! NICE OF YOU TO MA A FELLA FEEL WANTED!

THERE HE IS!

NOW YOU TELL US

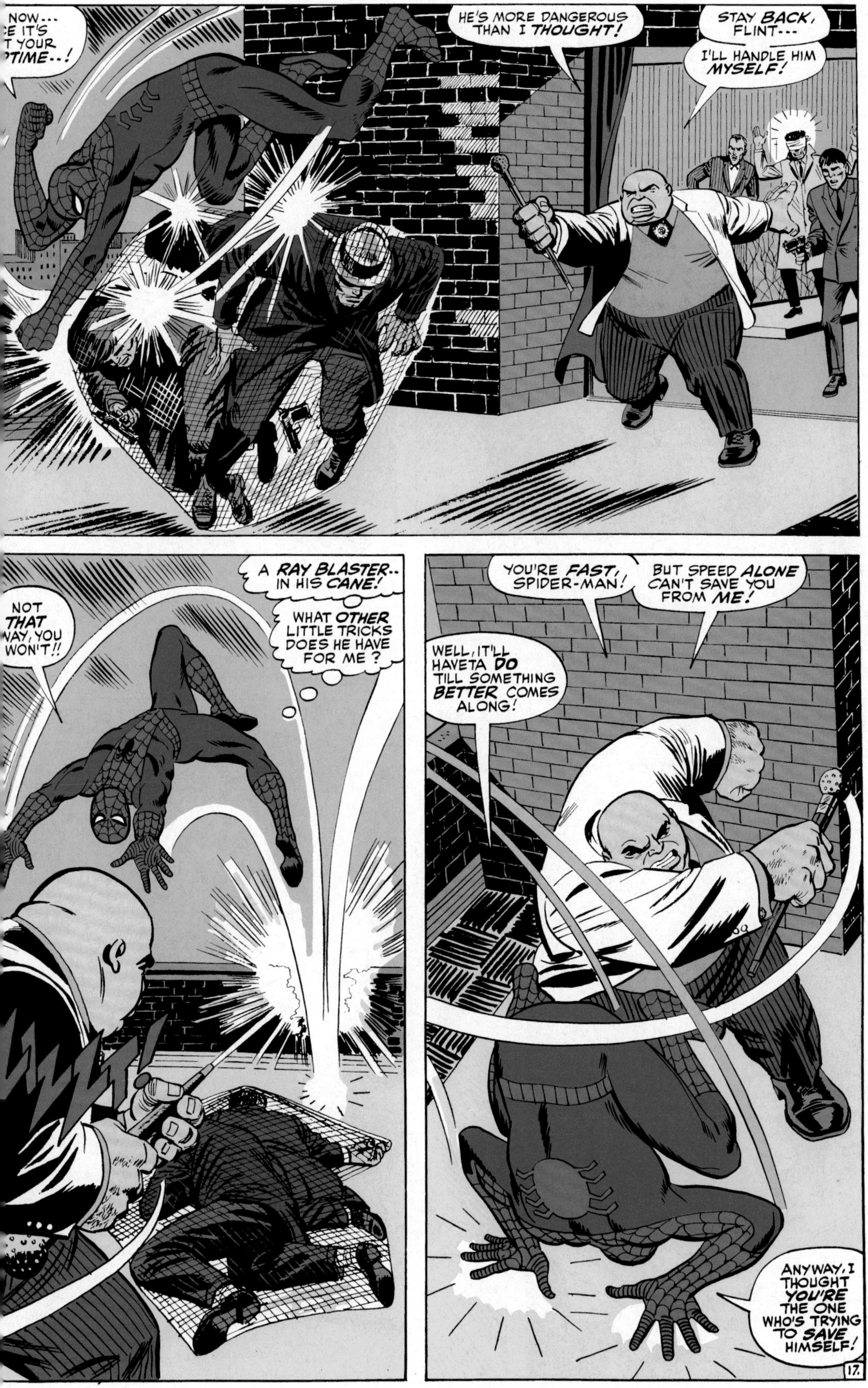

NOW...
'E IT'S
T YOUR
'TIME..!
HE'S MORE DANGEROUS THAN I THOUGHT!
STAY BACK, FLINT---
I'LL HANDLE HIM MYSELF!
NOT THAT WAY, YOU WON'T!!
A RAY BLASTER.. IN HIS CANE!
WHAT OTHER LITTLE TRICKS DOES HE HAVE FOR ME ?
YOU'RE FAST, SPIDER-MAN!
BUT SPEED ALONE CAN'T SAVE YOU FROM ME!
WELL, IT'LL HAVETA DO TILL SOMETHING BETTER COMES ALONG!
ANYWAY, I THOUGHT YOU'RE THE ONE WHO'S TRYING TO SAVE HIMSELF!
17

YEOWWF!

COUNT YOUR BLESSINGS, PUDGY...

YOU'RE LUCKY I'M NOT WEARING BASEBALL SHOES!

THWIPP!

SAY! W DOES IT TO SEND BEDDY.

OH NO YOU DON'T!

THAT CANE OF YOURS IS OFF-LIMITS NOW!

SORRY ABOUT THAT, SWEETIE!

SPAK!

UNHHH..!

NOT AS SORRY AS YOU'RE GOING TO

YOU MADE THE SA FATAL MISTAK AS EVERYONE ELSE WHO FACE THE KINGPIN--

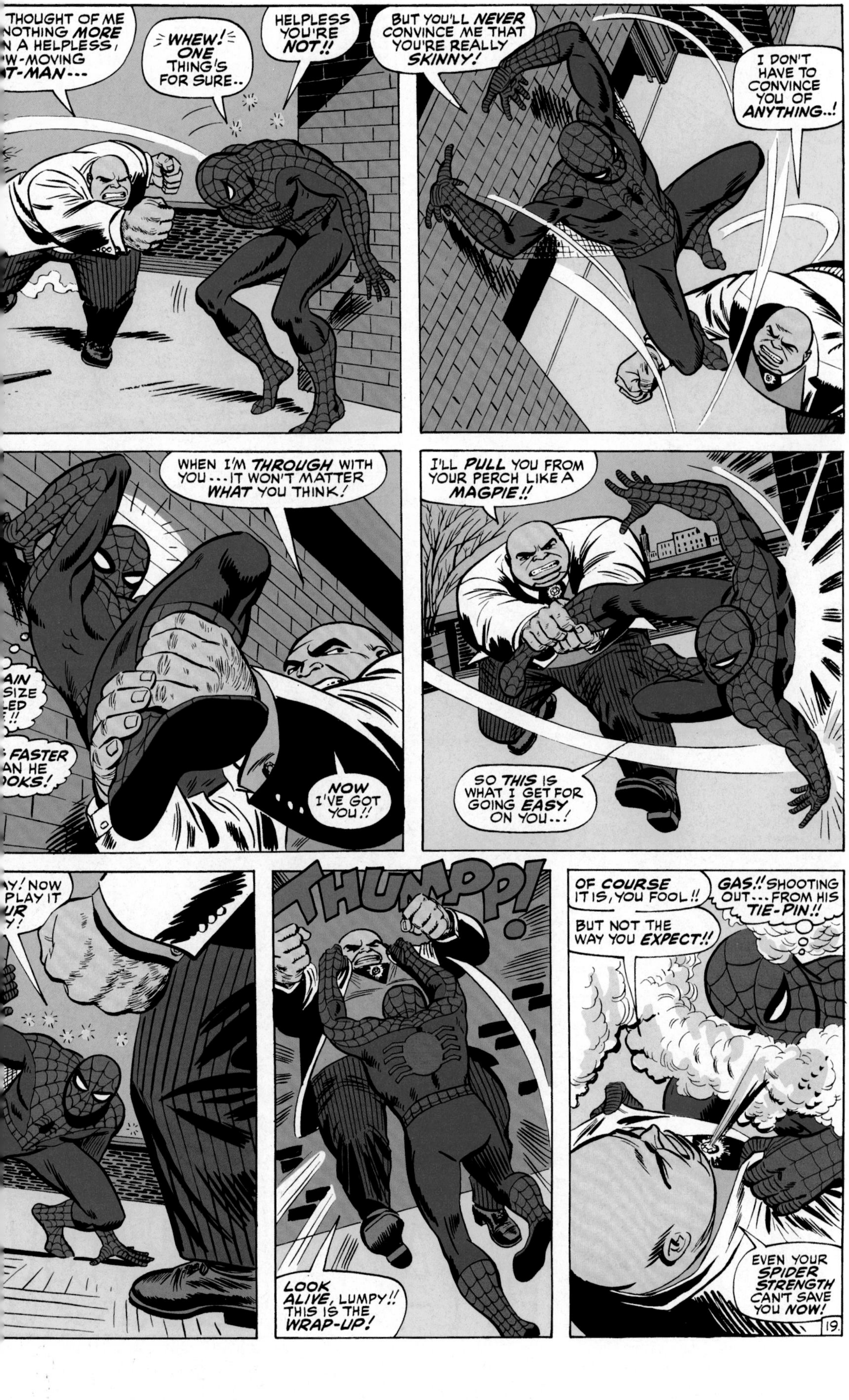
THOUGHT OF ME NOTHING MORE N A HELPLESS, W-MOVING T-MAN---
WHEW! ONE THING'S FOR SURE..
HELPLESS YOU'RE NOT!!
BUT YOU'LL NEVER CONVINCE ME THAT YOU'RE REALLY SKINNY!
I DON'T HAVE TO CONVINCE YOU OF ANYTHING..!
WHEN I'M THROUGH WITH YOU...IT WON'T MATTER WHAT YOU THINK!
AIN SIZE LED !!
FASTER AN HE OKS!
NOW I'VE GOT YOU!!
I'LL PULL YOU FROM YOUR PERCH LIKE A MAGPIE!!
SO THIS IS WHAT I GET FOR GOING EASY ON YOU..!
Y! NOW PLAY IT UR Y!
THUMPP!
LOOK ALIVE, LUMPY!! THIS IS THE WRAP-UP!
OF COURSE IT IS, YOU FOOL!!
BUT NOT THE WAY YOU EXPECT!!
GAS!! SHOOTING OUT...FROM HIS TIE-PIN!!
EVEN YOUR SPIDER STRENGTH CAN'T SAVE YOU NOW!
19.

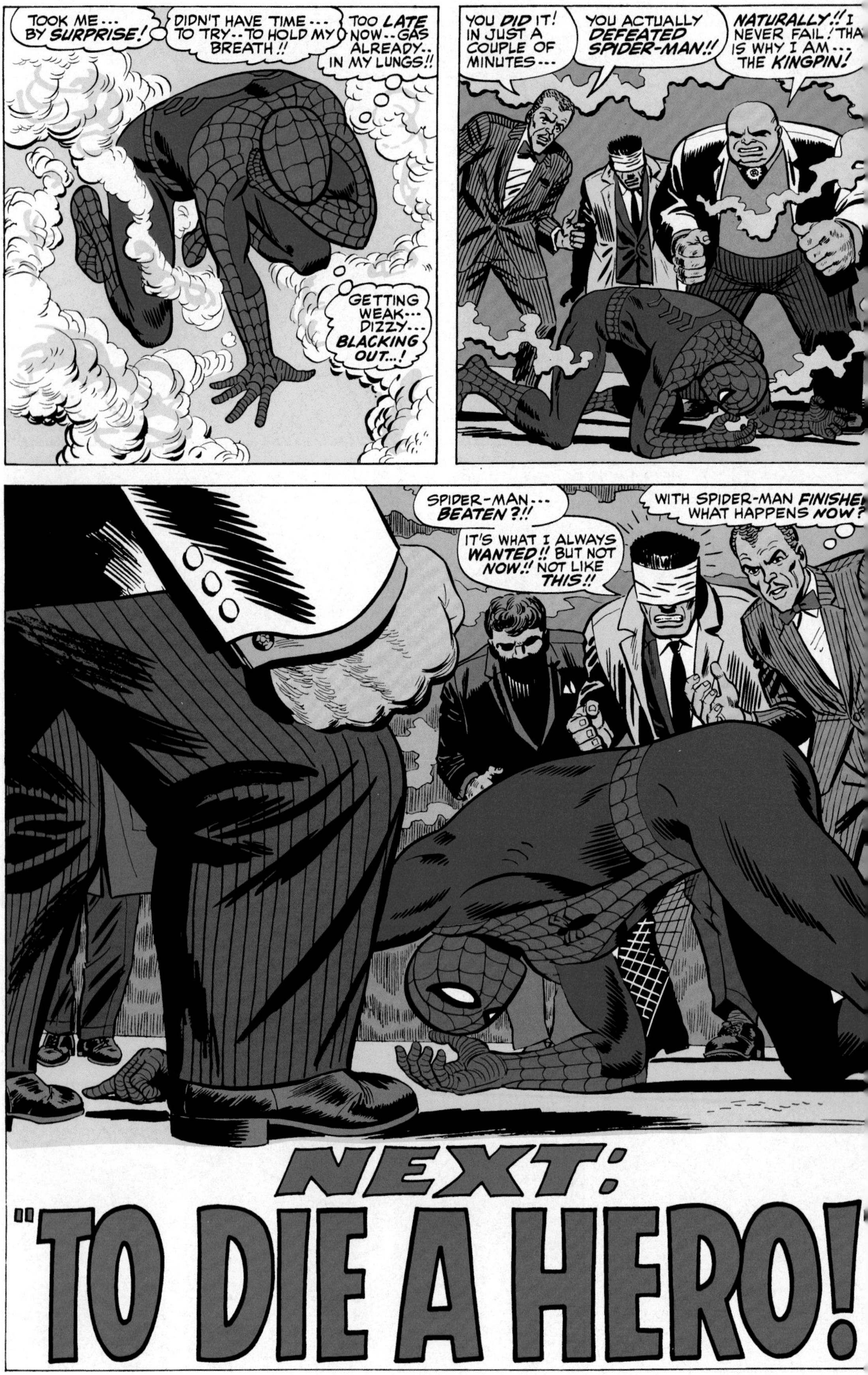
TOOK ME... BY SURPRISE!
DIDN'T HAVE TIME... TO TRY.. TO HOLD MY BREATH!!
TOO LATE NOW.. GAS ALREADY.. IN MY LUNGS!!
GETTING WEAK... DIZZY... BLACKING OUT...!
YOU DID IT! IN JUST A COUPLE OF MINUTES...
YOU ACTUALLY DEFEATED SPIDER-MAN!!
NATURALLY!! I NEVER FAIL! THA IS WHY I AM... THE KINGPIN!
SPIDER-MAN... BEATEN?!!
IT'S WHAT I ALWAYS WANTED!! BUT NOT NOW!! NOT LIKE THIS!!
WITH SPIDER-MAN FINISHE WHAT HAPPENS NOW?
NEXT:
"TO DIE A HERO!"

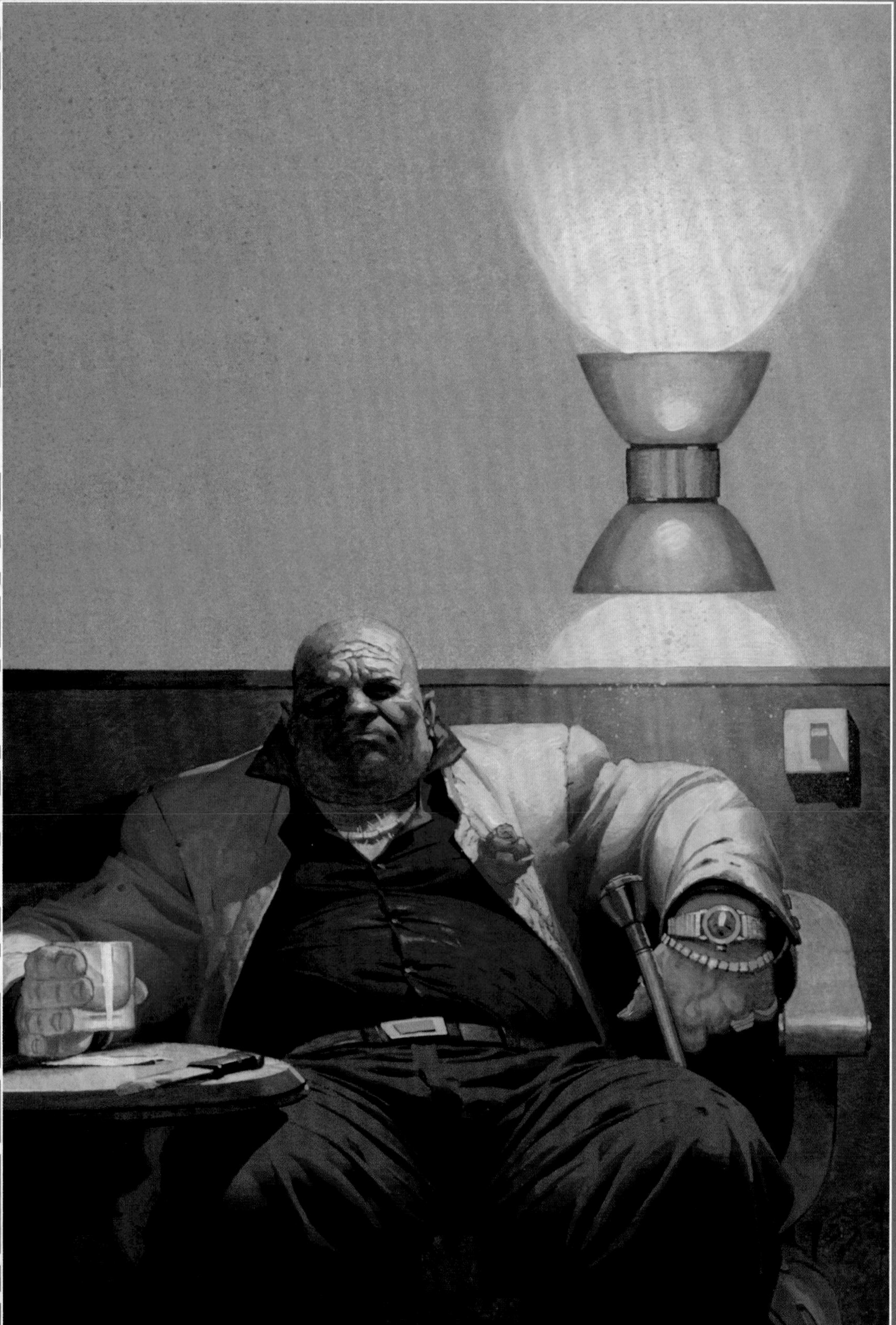

#1 VARIANT BY ESAD RIBIC

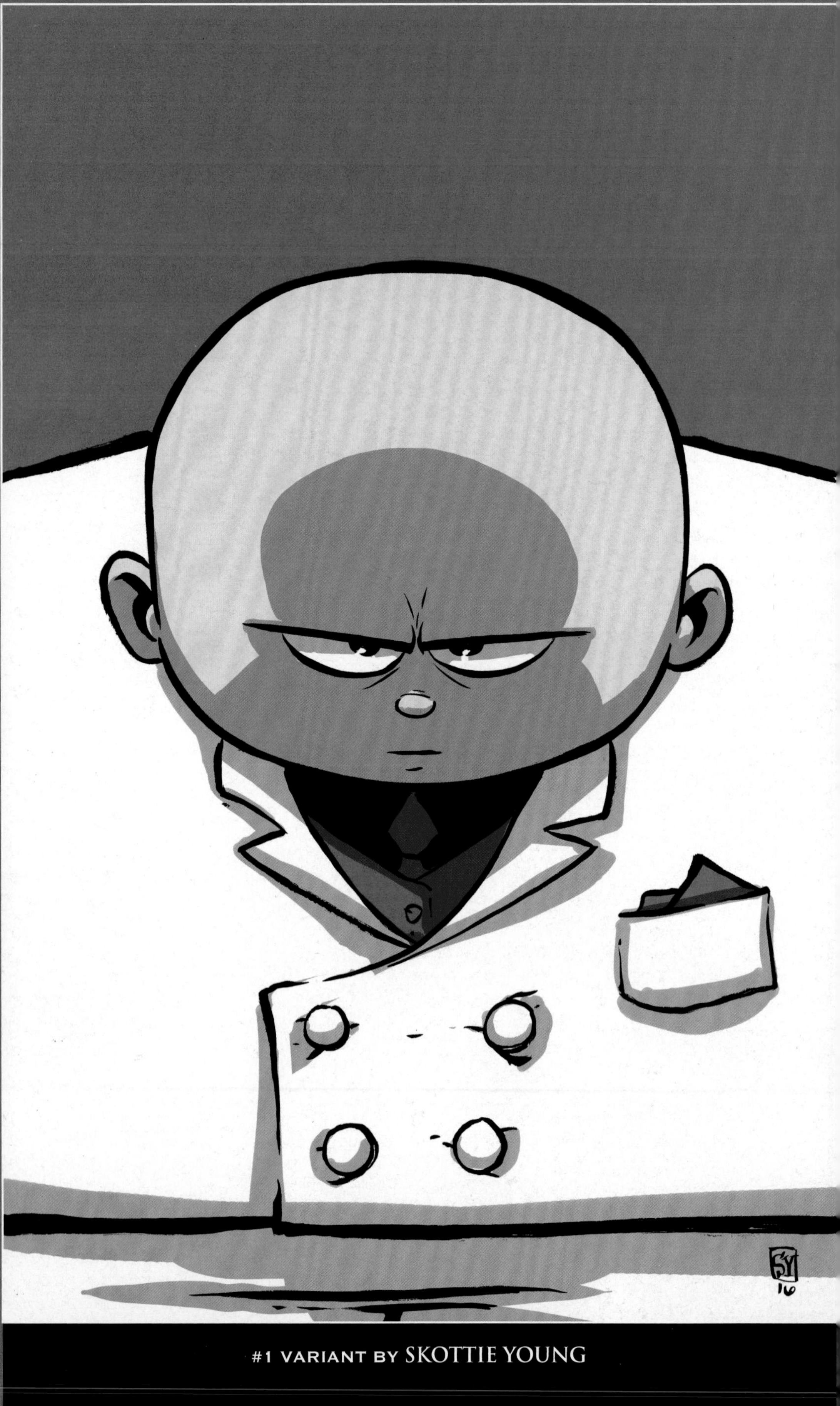

#1 VARIANT BY SKOTTIE YOUNG

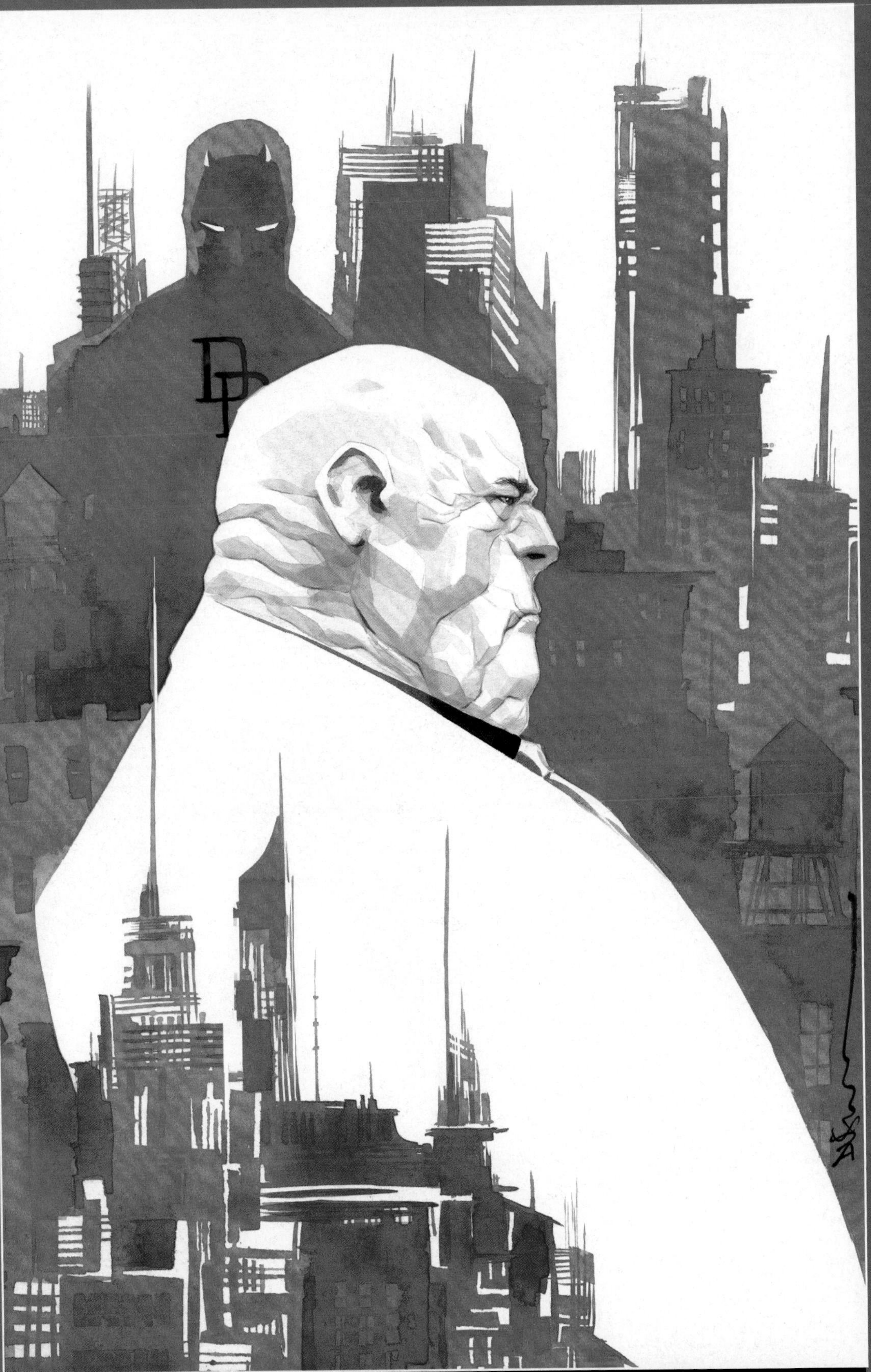

#2 VARIANT BY DUSTIN NGUYEN

#3 VARIANT BY
STEVE EPTING

#4 VARIANT BY
KYLE BAKER

Collected Editions

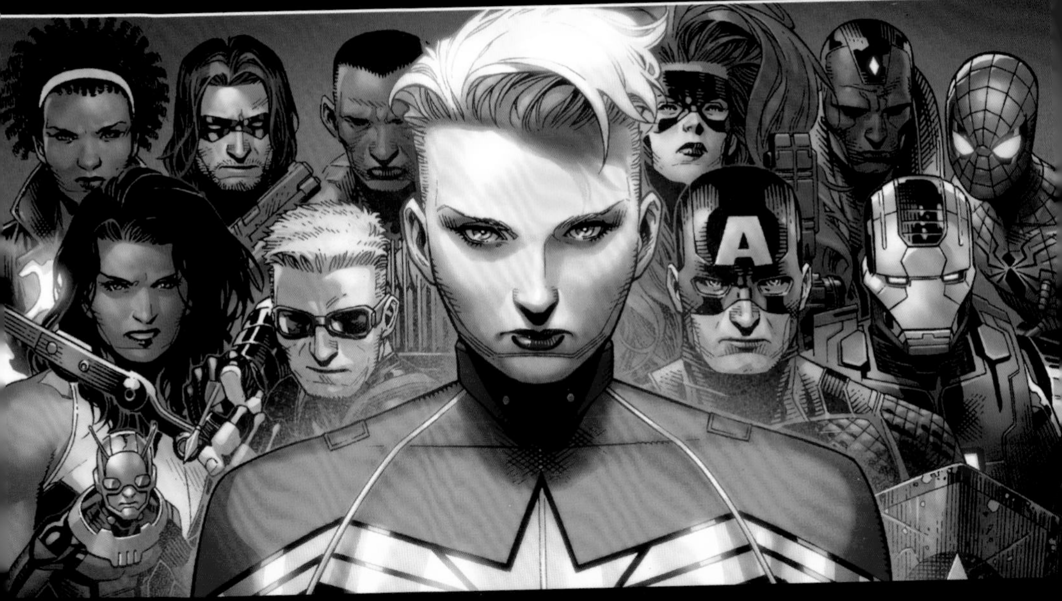

CIVIL WAR II

MARVEL

CHOOSING SIDES

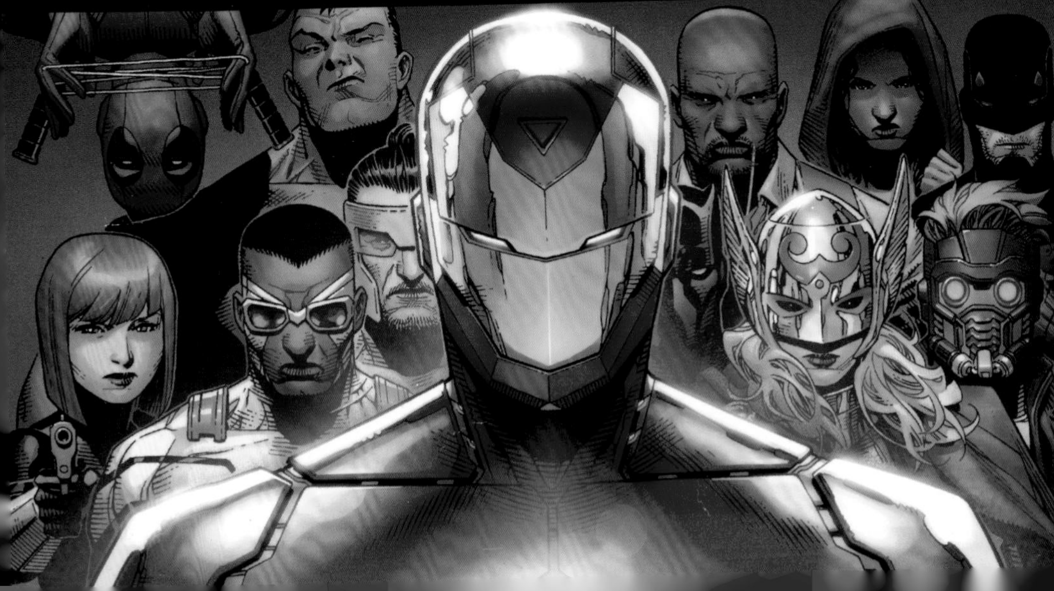

CIVIL WAR ██ OPPORTUNITY — AND BUSINESS IS BOOMING FOR THE KINGPIN!

WHEN EARTH'S HEROES GO TO WAR, THE VILLAINS GO TO WORK! AND FEW HAVE THE KNOW-HOW TO TAKE ADVANTAGE LIKE THE KINGPIN. WHILE AN INHUMAN WITH THE ABILITY TO PREDICT THE FUTURE HAS INSPIRED A CLAMPDOWN ON CRIME BEFORE IT CAN EVEN HAPPEN, WILSON FISK HAS MANAGED TO STAY ONE STEP AHEAD OF THE GOOD GUYS. BUT WHAT'S HIS SECRET? ONE THING'S FOR SURE — HIS COMPETITORS ARE JEALOUS, AND THAT'S BAD NEWS FOR FISK'S MEN. WORSE STILL, FISK HAS REASON TO BELIEVE THAT ONE OF HIS OWN IS PLOTTING AGAINST HIM. BUT ENEMIES INSIDE AND OUT ARE NOTHING COMPARED TO THE ULTIMATE THREAT TO HIS EMPIRE — THE PUNISHER! AS CONFLICT RAGES ALL AROUND HIM, CAN WILSON FISK STAY THE KINGPIN OF A WORLD WITHOUT CRIME?

"Dynamic art combined with inventive storytelling."

OLLECTING *CIVIL WAR II: KINGPIN* #1-4
Y MATTHEW ROSENBERG, RICARDO LÓPEZ ORTIZ AND
AT LOPES — PLUS ONE OF WILSON FISK'S EARLIEST
PPEARANCES FROM *AMAZING SPIDER-MAN (1963)* #51

ISBN 978-1-302-90253-7

5 159

$15.99 US $20.99 CAN
MARVEL.COM

9 781302 902537